W9-BDD-223

GREAT
CHEFS
OF FRANCE

GREAT CHEFS
OF FRANCE

The masters of haute cuisine and their secrets

ANTHONY BLAKE   QUENTIN CREWE

Harry N. Abrams, Inc.
Publishers · New York

**Great Chefs of France, an idea conceived by Anthony Blake,
was edited and designed by Marshall Editions Limited,
71 Eccleston Square, London SW1V 1PJ**

Library of Congress Catalogue Card Number: 78-56042
International Standard Book Number: 0-8109-0969-3
Published in 1978 by Harry N. Abrams, Incorporated, New York

Printed and bound in Spain.

My grandfather, Georges Auguste Escoffier, would have welcomed this book. It is a fitting tribute to the calling to which he devoted his life.

While the last 400 years have seen many great practitioners of the culinary art, it is true that 100 years ago, as he noted in his diaries, 'Society had little regard for the culinary profession. This should not have been so, since cuisine is a science and an art and he who devotes his talent to its service deserves full respect and consideration.'

In his lifetime, my grandfather succeeded in profoundly changing the status of the chef. By the 1920s, his own reputation was such that no important gastronomic event in Europe or the United States was contemplated without his advice. He was promoted to *Officier de la Légion d'Honneur* and at the inauguration of the Hotel Pierre in New York, there was a special celebration for his Eighty-fifth birthday.

But, needless to say, it was not for himself, but for his profession and all those within it who strove to achieve excellence, that Escoffier sought public recognition and esteem. Today, his disciples at the *Fondation Auguste Escoffier* and the *Institut Joseph Donon* are continuing his work as, indeed, are the present great chefs.

So it would have particularly pleased my grandfather to see such a book as this dedicated not just to one outstanding individual, but to a whole generation of eminent *chefs-patron*.

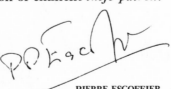

PIERRE ESCOFFIER

It is 6.00am

At Talloires, the sun has just come over the mountain's rim to brighten the waters of Lake Annecy. At L'Auberge du Père Bise, by the lake's edge, François Bise is already in his kitchen, making *croissants* for the breakfasts of his overnight guests.

7.30am

For Paul Bocuse, at Collonges-au-Mont-d'Or on the outskirts of Lyon, the market is the first business of the day. As Bise's *croissants* come out of the oven, Bocuse drives his Peugeot to the great markets of Lyon, which have flourished since Roman times. He will spend at least two hours there, watching supplies arrive from all over France, gossiping with friends, wandering among the stalls, chatting with the prettiest girls and all the while choosing the best produce to be had in the best market in the world. At Colmar in Alsace, just west of the Rhine, Marc Haeberlin is buying the day's supplies for L'Auberge de l'Ill, where his father, Paul, is *chef-patron*. The market, in a warehouse, is smaller than at Lyon, but Haeberlin, like Bocuse, buys only the best. The best available produce varies with the season and even from day to day. So only when the day's produce is in the kitchens do the chefs begin to plan the day's menu around it.

8.00am

At Valence, on the Rhône, one hundred kilometres south of Lyon, there is no important market, so Jacques Pic, of the restaurant Pic, is on the phone to suppliers in Lyon and Paris or to local growers, ordering the best, never counting the cost. In the wildness of Provence, at Les Baux, Raymond Thuilier is checking his various enterprises—two restaurants, a hotel, stables and gardens—to make sure all is running smoothly. In his eighties, Thuilier is the doyen of the three-star *chefs-patron*.

8.30am

The staff have arrived in the twelve most notable kitchens of provincial France; they put on the white tunics which, since the edict of Escoffier, chefs have never worn outside their kitchens. A junior lights the ovens below the 'piano', the cooking surface which provides a 'scale' of temperatures, and the *plongeurs*, who will spend much of the day washing up, give the floor the first of many daily moppings.

8.45am

Pic is off the telephone. He briefs his *brigade* with scrupulous attention to detail, distributing the work among the *chefs-de-partie*—the individual specialists who make up the full complement. At about this time a similar briefing is in progress in all the other three-star kitchens. According to what the market has yielded, the set menu is decided and posted up, sometimes with the weights of prime ingredients to be used in each serving.

9.00am

At the Restaurant de la Pyramide, farther up the Rhône at Vienne, a daily ritual is enacted as Madame Point, widow of the illustrious Fernand Point, descends to the wine-cellars to greet the *sommelier*, Louis Thomasi. He is damping the sandy floor to maintain the correct humidity. Back at Pic, a junior fills a stockpot with veal knuckles and trotters, whole birds and fresh vegetables. Two *gardes-manger* and their assistants are preparing the day's produce—trussing birds, trimming meat, mixing *terrines* and *pâtés* and apportioning the necessary supplies for the service. The *sauciers* are beginning the *demi-glace*. The *poissonnier* and his assistant are simmering their *fumets* and pounding shellfish debris for a *bisque*. The *pâtissier* and his assistant are whisking up a snow of egg-white, filling flans and baking *gâteaux*. The *rôtisseur* is getting ready his poultry and game. All the while the *chef-de-cuisine* and *sous-chef* are supervising and checking that these jobs, and many others, are being done exactly right. With variations, this is the pattern for all France's three-star restaurants as the day's work gets under way.

10.30am

Pic takes some time to attend to paperwork, using a spare hotplate as a desk top. After a while he finds·it dull and turns to slice some turbot with his *couteau d'office*. At Le Moulin de Mougins, in the hills above Cannes, Roger Vergé takes a break from his kitchen. He wanders out to tell a visiting journalist a favourite story—how he cooked a dinner for Princess Margaret in Uganda, using oildrums as a kitchen range. At Les Baux, Thuilier's morning dispositions are complete and he goes off to attend to his duties as Mayor of the village. In Tours, capital of the châteaux country along the Loire Valley, Charles Barrier checks a delivery of lamb on the weighing-machine at the back door of his restaurant. Michel Guérard, at Eugénie-les-Bains in the remote countryside of the Landes, has done his telephone orders and dealt with the morning mail. While his wife checks the proofs of his latest book, Guérard is instructing a new recruit to the hotel kitchen. At La Pyramide, Madame Point writes out the menu of the day in her firm, clear script.

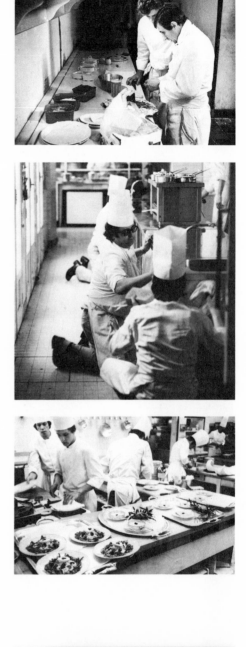

11.00am

Lunch for the staffs and *chefs-patron*. At Les Frères Troisgros in Roanne, not so far from Lyon, the Troisgros family sit at table in a niche in their new kitchen. Pic lunches upstairs in his flat with his wife and daughter, Thuilier in his restaurant with friends, Bocuse in a private room next to his collection of steam organs. The meal might be *choucroute* at the Haeberlins, pickled pigeons at Troisgros, *oeuf en cocotte* at Barrier— simple dishes usually not on the menu and, sometimes, experiments which may find their way onto it.

11.30am

The jokes stop, *vin de table* is recorked and the *plongeurs* clean the kitchens again. Alain Chapel checks the dining-room place-settings in his restaurant at Mionnay, near Lyon. Thuilier, back from his mayoral stint, is tasting sauces, while his *pâtissier's* handiwork is being arranged on the dessert trolley. At his restaurant in La Napoule, near Cannes, Louis Outhier is garnishing his *foie gras* specialities with *gelée* and toasted almonds.

12.15pm

The first customers arrive for lunch. At Chapel, a junior immediately turns up his gas ring to deep-fry the little fish (gudgeon from Lake Annecy) for the *amuse-gueule* which is served to the customers before their orders are taken. The waiters hand the orders to the *chef-de-cuisine*, who calls them out to the *chefs-de-partie*: 'Brioche de foie gras . . . saumon . . . caneton. . . .' Each chef responds with a brief '*oui*' and sets about his particular task. A *garde-manger* reaches for the long loaf of *foie gras* he has prepared and cuts a generous slice. Another *garde-manger* fetches a duck he has trussed that morning, while the *rôtisseur* chooses a pan and adjusts the heat of the oven. The *poissonnier* selects a fillet of salmon while his assistant starts to complete the appropriate sauce. The *chef-de-cuisine* hangs the orders on numbered pegs on a board.

12.45pm

The pace quickens. Orders come faster and faster. Each man must remember which of the many dishes he is cooking will be needed next. The *entremetier* chops, trims and slices his vegetables, to be ready exactly at the same time as the *rôtisseur's* duck.

1.15pm

The heat mounts in the kitchens. Outhier opens the door to the street; passers-by gaze in as if at a fairground show. Running to his tank of live *écrevisses*, Guérard picks one out to drop into a bubbling pot of vegetable stock before hanging it on the side of a bowl of *soupe aux écrevisses de rivière*. Bocuse takes out his folding Opinel knife and cuts wafer-thin slices of truffle over a salad. Pierre Troisgros chases after a dish which a waiter is carrying, to wipe a drop of sauce from the rim of the plate. Bise rejects a piece of toast which he judges to be slightly burnt.

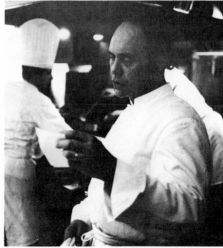

2.15pm

The pace begins to slacken as the desserts are served. Outhier adjusts the position of a *marron glacé* on one of his chocolate desserts; the end of a meal at La Napoule must be as memorable as the beginning. Thuilier wanders into the dining-room to speak to each of his customers. Jean-Pierre Haeberlin is explaining the exact method by which a pear is grown in a bottle for *eau-de-vie de poire*. Barrier, the philosopher-chef, is quoting Jean-Paul Sartre to a bemused couple who have never doubted the existence of anything.

3.00pm

The *chefs-patron* are saying goodbye to their customers as if the day were over.

5.00pm

It isn't. The whole cycle, with its excitement and *crescendo*, must start again as if it had never happened before. The chefs will have used their short afternoon break in different ways. Thuilier may have outlined a landscape painting; Vergé has quite possibly been for a rapid drive on the twisting roads of the Riviera, using speed to stimulate his imagination; Pic may have watched some football on television; Bise may have been diving with his aqualung. It is equally likely that all of them have been doing accounts, sorting out supplies, searching for a new *pâtissier*, discussing a new boutique, tasting wine, planning a dinner in Chicago or telephoning each other for advice. Perhaps one of them has been visiting a girl-friend. Now the waiters are setting out china and glass again. The *plongeurs* are scrubbing the floor. The *chefs-de-partie* are at their posts, preparing, stirring, mixing, tasting.

6.45pm

Supper for the staffs is over. The kitchens get another clean from the *plongeurs*. The chefs set their dishes going.

7.00pm

Service. The customers arrive. Orders start to come thick and fast, the chorus of '*oui*' mounts from the *chefs-de-partie* and the tension is as great as before.

11.00pm

The *chefs-patron* are saying goodbye again. The ovens are being cleaned, the floors scrubbed.

11.30pm

Nothing is left in the kitchens. Every day is a fresh start. 'Every morning,' said Fernand Point, 'one begins again from zero, with nothing on the stoves. That is cuisine.'

12.00

François Bise is asleep at Talloires. He will be up before six to bake the next day's *croissants*. But Roger Vergé and Louis Outhier may still be offering that hospitality which is the hallmark of every great chef, as if they had all the time in the world.

The chefs who live through such a day as this are not slaves nor are they driven by financial greed. They are artists dedicated to the pursuit of excellence. They could come only from one country—France. In no other society would a man sacrifice so much time, suffer so much discomfort for so little reward, merely (as some would say) for the sake of food.

They come from a long tradition of similar men whose lives were even harder. For in the past, even France has seldom seen fit to accord to its culinary artists a standing equal to that of its painters, writers and musicians. A handful of chefs, such as Carême, Soyer and Escoffier, were recognized as eminent in their day. But the vast majority of men whose labours raised French cuisine to an art went unacclaimed. It is only today that France's greatest chefs, not just one or two, but a dozen or more, have achieved recognition as supreme artists in their field. It is this agreeable fact that our book sets out to celebrate.

The relative indifference shown to its chefs in the past only compounds the mystery of why France is the only Western country to have made cooking into an art and raised its appreciation to the level of connoisseurship. The solution to this puzzle is not easy to find, but the search for it is an intriguing quest.

There are a number of broad reasons why eating should have become so large a branch of the tree of French culture. Geography and climate have favoured France to the extent that virtually anything that grows or is bred in Europe will thrive somewhere within its borders. It is warmer than Germany, Scandinavia or Britain; not so hot as Italy or Spain. The Atlantic and English Channel in the west and north and the Mediterranean in the south ensure a rich supply of fish, crustaceans and shellfish, augmented by freshwater species from France's plentiful rivers and lakes. The unity of France embraces a regional diversity, both physical and cultural, so that each historic province contributes its particular produce and style of cooking to the national table.

Geography and climate are necessary, but not sufficient, conditions for France's culinary pre-eminence. For both already applied during the Middle Ages, when eating habits in France were not yet substantially different from elsewhere in Europe, including England. To a remarkable extent the pattern of medieval eating was derived from the legacy left by occupying Roman legions. The Romans had been fond of oysters which they used to import from Britain and northern France. In order to get them to Rome in an even half-edible condition, they put them in pitch-lined barrels, pickling them in vinegar. They arrived in a poor state and the Romans would further disguise their sour taste with *garum* (a kind of spicy brine squeezed from fish), honey and other spices, or a mixture of pounded almonds, ginger and cloves.

Unbelievably, although they could have eaten perfectly fresh oysters, the British were still ruining their shellfish with almost identical concoctions 500 years after the Romans had left. Quite possibly the present-day custom of proffering tabasco and vinegar with oysters, when anything but the merest squeeze of lemon is a folly, is a relic of this habit.

If this could be true of oysters, it is not hard to believe that more ordinary eating and cooking habits of the Romans also survived. The Roman way of cutting up and mixing meats in stews and pies was still the normal way of preparing meat in the Middle Ages. It was not to change until the general introduction of the fork in the late sixteenth century. Heavy seasonings of *garum*, cinnamon, mustard, nutmeg, garlic, cloves, ginger and mace and the use in sauces of fermented wheat-flour porridge or frumenty and honey were typical of both Roman and medieval cuisine.

Like the Romans, medieval Europeans were also fond of extravagant-looking food—not only when cooked, but before it was killed. For instance they preferred peacocks, swans, herons and decorative ducks to plainer but undoubtedly more tender birds. The Middle Ages could go to bizarre and cruel lengths in pursuit of a good flavour. In fifteenth-century Avignon, for instance, the townspeople ate geese which had been plucked and roasted alive. The cooks kept the birds going while surrounded by fire, by sponging their heads and giving them dishes of water and maize. The hope was that the final collapse of the goose would coincide with its being done to a turn—so that it could be served while still trembling with the last vital spark.

It is interesting to compare two of the earliest cookery books of northern Europe. In 1390, Richard II of England's cooks compiled *The Forme of Cury* (i.e. the art of cookery) with advice about 'hacking' meat and other rough treatment of food, such as 'ramming' chickens together and 'hewing' hares to gobbets. Fifteen years earlier, Guillaume Tirel, otherwise known as Taillevent, had produced in France a rather more delicately phrased book, *Le Viandier*. In both books, many recipes were roughly the same and used similar terms, such as 'galantine' (French) and 'galyntyne' (English) for fish or meat in aspic; 'veel' (English and French) for veal; and 'darioll' (French) and 'daryols' (English) for custard tarts. They stressed equally the importance of heavy seasoning and extolled the virtues of almond milk, used with almost anything.

It is not surprising that this should have been so, for no major new culinary influence had spread over Europe since the Romans. The incursions of the Norsemen had brought little in the cooking line. This is not to say that the nobles and princes of the feudal age did not care about food. When Henry V of England married Catherine of France in 1420, the wedding lunch on a fasting day included twenty-nine different fish dishes, out of forty, as well as a 'subtlety' which was a huge tableau made of marchpane (marzipan), the ancestor of the great *pièces montées* of the nineteenth century. One hundred years later, in May 1522, when the Emperor Charles V came to England to visit Henry VIII, he brought with him 'ung maystre keux, ung pâtissier, ung potegier, ung saucier'.

From the early sixteenth century, French culture began to be transformed by Renaissance influences through France's involvement in the Italian wars. The Frenchmen who fought and travelled in Italy came home with Renaissance ideas on everything from architecture to gardening. Cookery was no exception. It was not surprising that the Italian cities, with their wealth accumulated through cosmopolitan trade over several centuries, should have developed a refined cuisine while the rest of Europe was still eating in the medieval fashion. Possibly, too, the more refined tradition of Roman eating had survived in Italy, in contrast to the cruder version exported by the Roman legions.

It was in Italy that the first printed cookery book was published, in Venice in 1475. Written in Latin, this was *De Honesta Voluptate*, compiled by the Vatican librarian Bartolomeo de Sacchi, or, as he was better known, Platina. It was a compendium of advice about health and food and wise, enjoyable living, encompassing the digestion, bad temper and even the amorous habits of mating bears. The first French translation appeared in 1505 and introduced the French to many new possibilities, especially in the way of pastries, the use of aspic and unfamiliar combinations of food.

In 1533, the Italian influence on French eating and manners received a fresh boost with the marriage of an Italian princess, Catherine de Medici, to the Duc d'Orléans, later Henri II of France. To his court she brought with her fifty chefs, waiters and household comptrollers.

Her Italians introduced a measure of simplicity and elegance, producing dishes which were far less heavily spiced and which involved quite new ingredients. Catherine was immensely greedy, eating so much at Mademoiselle Martigue's wedding that even she thought she might burst, although her favourite dishes of cockerels' crests and kidneys and artichokes are not so filling. Catherine also raised the tone of mealtimes in two ways which must have had their effect on the refinement of cuisine. In courts, women had hitherto eaten separately from men, but Catherine brought the sexes together. She also regarded the traditional entertainments by acrobats, jugglers and fools as coarse and introduced ballet dancers instead.

The process by which the French absorbed Italian influences, and combined them with their own traditions and produce to develop a distinctive cuisine, was a gradual one. People did not suddenly change the eating habits of centuries overnight, for there is no area in which human nature is so conservative as in food. The development was spread over many decades. First, the nobles were anxious to outdo each other in copying the royal court. Some unexpected people joined in. The shady astrologer, Nostradamus, in among his predictions, gave useful and precise advice as to how to make soft preserves of fruit, rather than the dried versions then customary. Even natural disasters played a part. The near famines of the 1560s produced an edict that no-one might eat more than three courses at one meal. To circumvent this, chefs invented dishes which combined many different ingredients. Similarly, fast days prompted chefs to enhance fish dishes by adding vegetables and interesting sauces. The end of the sixteenth century saw a period of comparative peace and prosperity. In Paris, even the labouring classes could afford to buy game such as venison and partridge, as well as good mutton, salmon and herrings.

Today, Lyon is considered the gastronomic capital of the world and many of France's greatest chefs work or have been trained there. It was in the sixteenth century that the city's gastronomic reputation, which it had enjoyed in Roman times, was revived. Lyon became a diplomatic and commercial crossroads in France's relations with Italy. Many Florentine merchants settled there, bringing their chefs with them. It was

CATHERINE DE MEDICIS.
Reine de France

The Florentine chefs imported by Catherine de Medici are popularly supposed to have begun the refinement of French cuisine in the Renaissance—an idea that can be traced back to Montaigne's glowing description of an Italian chef at the French court. In fact, the Italian influence on French cookery began well before Catherine's arrival. However, her favourite dish, cockerels' crest and kidneys, has remained in the French repertoire until today, and appears on the menus of such chefs as Alain Chapel and Michel Guérard.

there that Rabelais lived while he wrote *Pantagruel* and *Gargantua*, with their emphasis on the joys of feasting and elaborate eating.

The Italian connection gave Lyon a fresh shot of culinary expertise as copies of another influential Italian cookery book found their way there: the *Cuoco Secreto di Papa Pio Quinto*, published in 1570 by Bartolomeo Scappi. Compared with *De Honesta Voluptate*, published nearly a century earlier, Scappi speaks of a more organized, politer cuisine. His book contained the first printed picture of a fork and showed what we would call a place-setting, with three eating utensils. He discussed service by waiters, carvers working at a sideboard and the need to change plates several times during a meal. Most important, there are among his recipes dishes which one would be pleased to see today, not for their curiosity value but for themselves – *prosciutto* cooked in wine and served with capers, quails roasted on the spit and covered with slices of aubergine, puff pastries filled with sweetbreads and *prosciutto* (in other words *vol-au-vent*), rabbit with crushed pinenuts and pigeons stewed with mortadella sausages and onions.

In 1651, François Pierre de La Varenne published *Le Cuisinier François*. From this one can see the transformation which had come over cuisine in France since the Middle Ages. Gone was the ubiquitous almond milk, gone were the thick glutinous sauces, reeking of spices. Now there were mushrooms and truffles to give more delicate tastes. Butter was used for making pastries instead of oil, and also in sauces. The sauces, however, were infinitely light, often not much more than vinegar or lemon added to the pan juices.

La Varenne was the first great chef of modern times. He had started by working for the Duchesse de Bar, the sister of Henri IV. Henri was married to a much younger cousin of Catherine de Medici, Marie, who in her turn had brought from Italy a complement of Florentine chefs. It was from them that La Varenne learned much of his craft, although he was, as far as Henri was concerned, of more service in another capacity. He acted as go-between for Henri and one of his mistresses, carrying the king's *poulets* or love notes to the lady, thereby making himself a considerable fortune. 'You have done better,' the Duchess observed to him, 'by carrying my brother's *poulets* than you have by larding mine.'

Whether this wealth enabled him to leave the royal service is unclear, but little is known of where he worked except that he was an official in the household of the Marquis d'Uxelles. There he is believed to have created *duxelles*, a sauce of mushrooms and shallots. Certainly he published a recipe for exactly that sauce, though he called it *champignons à l'Olivier*. La Varenne was an inventive chef, producing amazing dishes for the battlefield such as his *poulet en ragoût dans une boteille*, actually cooked in a bottle, but his real importance lay in setting out a whole basis from which cuisine could develop. His books encompassed the complete field of cooking from utensils and ovens to his actual recipes, which were the first of any consequence to be written in France since *Le Viandier* some 300 years before. La Varenne was additionally a beautiful writer, so that his contribution to the cuisine of France has been matched only by Carême and Escoffier.

The pattern was set for the reign of Louis XIV, during which French cuisine was to emerge into the supreme art for which France is so famous. When La Varenne's first book appeared, Henri Vatel, perhaps the most honourable chef of any century, was finishing his apprenticeship as a *pâtissier*. Despite his humble origins—he was the son of a labourer—Vatel's talents had won him an education. He studied literature and mathematics and was regarded, even at the age of nineteen, as something of a genius. So it was that he was summoned by Nicholas Fouquet, the Treasurer of France and one of the most powerful, ambitious and dishonest men in the country.

Vatel was to be his chef, but after some years and having been put in charge of establishing the vast household of Fouquet's first country estate, he was made *maître d'hôtel*. He became as grand in his apparel and number of attendants as many grandees. When Fouquet built his enormous château at Vaux-le-Vicomte, Vatel was responsible for the whole project, which cost more than 300,000 livres. Fouquet said Vatel had 'the best organized head in the world' and used him to buy all the horses for the army, to deliver gold to Cardinal Mazarin at the battlefront, and naturally, to organize Fouquet's great

reception at Vaux for Louis XIV in 1661, for which he served a sumptuous feast on 6000 silver dishes, engaging Molière and his troupe of actors for entertainment and Lully for musical diversion. By his unparalleled skill on this occasion, Vatel did himself out of a job. Having enjoyed himself thoroughly, the King decided that any subject who could put on such a display was both corrupt and intolerable. He put Fouquet in jail and Vatel was dismissed.

He was worse than penniless because, unlike Fouquet, he had never appropriated one sou of the money he had handled and his incarcerated master had been good enough to borrow all Vatel's legitimate savings.

Vatel went to England and then Belgium, but was lured back by an egregious friend, Monsieur Gourville, to work for the impoverished Prince de Condé at Chantilly. At first it was gloomy—the servants rarely got their wages and everything was run down. Then, the mysterious Monsieur Gourville somehow restored the Prince's fortunes. The château came to life and Vatel was once more in his element. He was still only forty. Ten years had passed since the great evening at Vaux. Now the King was to come to Chantilly. Vatel was determined to put on a spectacular show.

The preparations had tired 'the best organized head in the world.' Vatel had had no sleep for twelve nights and somehow he became confused. When little things went wrong, he started to doubt himself. One table had no meat, the musicians had no chairs, a sauce had gone wrong, another dish had failed.

He went to his room to rest. But had he ordered the fish for the next day? He went down. A boy was delivering a small parcel of fish. He needed hundreds of fish. He must have forgotten. Now completely distraught, Vatel returned to his room, took up his sword and killed himself.

Meanwhile, the fish which he had ordered arrived after all and they wondered how to cook it. Where was Vatel? When they found him, they told the impassive Gourville. Nothing should disturb the party. They put Vatel's body on a cart and buried him in a field. No-one remembered where.

Vatel was the epitome of the organizational skills required of chefs and the romantic model of the perfectionism which drives them. He was also the victim of the social disregard for the profession which he served. His story, which is usually thought to typify the dedication of chefs, is quite as much the story of the disdain of princes for their employees.

Everywhere, but particularly in France, fine cuisine was the prerogative of royalty and nobles. The hunting of game, which would otherwise have been a cheap source of food for the poor, was the preserve of the nobility, poaching being from time to time, a capital offence. In England, where social mobility had always been greater and snobbery less calculated, there had been books published for the middle classes. In 1588, there was *The Good Hous-wives Treasurie* and in 1597, *A Booke of Cookerie*, otherwise known as *The Good Huswifes Handmaide for the Kitchin*. In France, the first acknowledgement that anyone other than aristocrats might be interested in food came in the title of François Massialot's book *Le Cuisinier Roial et Bourgeois*, published in 1691. However, none of the dishes described in this book differed from the grand menus of the court. It was followed in 1692 by Audiger's *La Maison Réglée*, which claimed to be 'useful and necessary for all sorts of persons of quality, Gentlemen of the Provinces, Foreigners, Bourgeois, Officers of Great Houses and Liqueur Merchants.'

Under Louis XIV, a certain order was introduced into meals. Instead of everything being hugger-mugger on the table, service became simpler and more methodical. In 1674, the author of *L'Art de Bien Traiter, ouvrage nouveau, curieux et fort galant* said, 'There is today no longer a prodigious overflowing of dishes, with an abundance of *ragoûts* and hotch-potches, no confused piling of diverse varieties, mountains of roasts, all bizarrely served. Instead there is an exquisite choice of meats, finesse in their seasoning, politeness and propriety in serving them, their quantity measured by the number of guests.'

The new simplicity coincided with the rise, economically at least, of the bourgeoisie of merchants, professional people and bureaucrats. This growth was already setting up the political strains which, within a century, were to rend apart the *Ancien Régime* in the Revolution. But in cuisine the rivalry of classes had more benign results. The middle-class desire to emulate aristocratic manners, but on more modest resources, had the effect of spreading aristocratic refinement while at the same time tempering its excesses. As it spread to the provincial towns, this refinement began to affect regional cooking, with results that were distinctively French—and which were to become the common property of all classes. The process was to continue through the eighteenth century and the Revolution, to reach a definitive stage in the early nineteenth century.

In 1739, two cookery books appeared: Menon's *Nouveau Traité de la Cuisine* and François Marin's *Les Dons de Comus*. Menon's first book was very much in the usual style of grandeur, although his later volumes, of which there were a great many, including *La Cuisinière Bourgeoise* (1746) and *Les Soupers de la Cour* (1755), were directed towards the growing middle classes. Both his books and Marin's reveal that cuisine was progressing rapidly towards something which we would find acceptable. Marin produced a section on sauces, listing at least one hundred. It is the first clue we get to chefs producing plain dishes which depend on the sauce for their interest, rather than sauces serving a purely moistening, binding or masking purpose.

While Menon eventually became the more important writer, Marin seems to have been the merrier fellow. He had not hesitated to address his book to the middle classes. He sounded a note of what he called 'pure caprice', devising menus made up of dishes which all came from one animal—tongue, eyes, cheeks, ears, ribs, innards, testicles, tail and feet. His beef menu comprised eighteen dishes. Marin also referred to the habit, first mentioned in print by Massialot, of naming dishes after famous people. Marin's first sauce was *béchamel*, called after the Marquis de Béchameil, Louis XIV's *maître d'hotel*, a person as stodgy as some chefs now think his eponymous sauce.

Naturally, it was not the Marquis who would have invented the sauce, but his chef. In the same way the Prince de Condé never made his soup, nor Madame de Pompadour her *filets de sole*. The list of grandees whose names are attached to a dish

'Louis the Grand, the love and delight of his people'—Louis XIV dines in state at the Hôtel de Ville, Paris, 1687. The service is *le grand couvert*, with all the dishes for a course placed on the table at the same time. The first definitive French cookery book, La Varenne's *Le Cuisinier François*, appeared in 1651, eight years after Louis XIV's accession. During the Sun King's long reign, French cuisine reached its first peak, having absorbed earlier influences.

is endless—*les cailles à la Talleyrand, les filets de sole Richelieu, le pigeonneau Villeroy, les côtelettes d'agneau Conti*. The names of the true creators, their chefs, are forgotten. No-one appears to know the first name of Menon and we only know his surname because of his books. Although food was of supreme importance in France throughout the seventeenth and eighteenth centuries, chefs were underprivileged people. They are remembered only if they wrote cookbooks and, with very few exceptions, for instance Briand's *Dictionnaire des Aliments* of 1750, after Menon there were no really original cookery books published until after the Revolution.

If chefs were despised or, at any rate, much ignored, women cooks were barely thought to exist. Louis XV refused to believe that their cookery in any way could be compared with that of men. Madame du Barry, in a gently feminist mood, secretly arranged for a woman cook to prepare a dinner for the King. For a Bourbon, he had a delicate palate (although he was just as greedy as the rest of them). The dinner was an unqualified success. The King, planning to steal such a paragon of a chef for the royal kitchens, asked to see him. 'Right, France, I have you,' said Madame du Barry, 'it wasn't a chef who cooked dinner, it was a woman. And I demand a reward which is worthy of both her and your Majesty. My negro, Zamon, is now Governor of Luciennes, by your royal bounty, so for my *cuisinière*, I cannot accept less than a *cordon bleu*.' The *cordon bleu* was the Royal Order of Saint Esprit. The term *cordon-bleu* cook should only be applied to women, a small recognition won for them by the wit of Madame du Barry.

While little is known of the lives of chefs in the reigns of Louis XV and XVI it is plain that the development of cuisine continued throughout this time. The Duc d'Orléans, Regent from 1715 to 1723, is said by some writers to have restored French cuisine, at least at court, where bad habits had crept in because Louis XIV's appetite was merely gluttonous. (When the Sun King's body was cut open to remove his heart for pickling and storing, he was found to have a stomach and bowel twice the size of any normal man.) An eminent theoretician, the Duc would also actually cook in his private flat, producing excellent dishes for his dissolute companions, using the solid silver utensils he kept for the purpose. Louis XV continued the good work and, at his court, many indigestible dishes were finally discarded, the last violent sauces were banned. Taste was treated as a superior sense, worthy of respect.

There was a receptive and outward-looking spirit among those interested in cuisine. There was a wave of Anglophilia, partly originating from French interest in England's agricultural revolution (the complement of the coming Industrial Revolution), which resulted in a considerable exchange of ideas across the Channel. Although in culinary matters it might have been presumed to be a one-way traffic, this was far from the case. Many French chefs went to the great houses of England and brought back various techniques which were added to the French repertoire. The words *à l'anglais* became quite common and respected on menus. The English skill in roasting meat was one example: the French were much impressed with what they called *rosbif* and they took to referring even to *rosbif d'agneau*.

In 1758 was born the first of that uniquely French series of legendary figures, the gourmet writer and critic. In no other country could a man put on his visiting-card as his profession the word 'gourmet'. The first, while perhaps not the most famous, was without question the most representative of this curious collection of men who are known for their knowledge of food. Grimod de la Reynière was the son of a *fermier-général*, or superior tax-collector, and the grandson of a *charcutier*. He trained as a lawyer, but his principal concern was always with food. He was not an attractive man to look at and his unprepossessing appearance was accentuated, in his own eyes, by the fact that his hands were deformed, so that he needed false fingers to enable him to write. He became a misogynist, diverting his sensual appetites into gastronomy. His role was to promote produce, introduce the general public to good food and to be the originator of gastronomic publicity.

As with so many turning points in history, it is tempting to imagine that daily life in France changed overnight with the Revolution, whereas, in reality, everyday affairs, particularly outside Paris, went on in much the same way as they had done in the past decades. There were still great houses in which grand food was served, by Talleyrand, d'Aligre, Murat, d'Orsay, de Portalis, Madame Tallien—the cast may have changed slightly, but the style had not. When Napoleon became Emperor in 1804, the Imperial kitchens, under his chef, Dunant, became quite as spectacular as those of the decapitated King and Queen.

The long-term effects of the Revolution were, however, profound. Although grand life was by no means extinguished, a far larger proportion of the population was gradually able to indulge in the pleasures of the table. Between 1789 and 1815, the number of small peasant-owners of land increased by a million. The age of the *petit-bourgeois*, the small property owner, was dawning. The seigneurial dues had been abolished, so that wealth was gradually more widely distributed. The hunting laws had been changed, so that different produce was available to more people. Naturally the French spent their newfound riches on food.

Two institutions, peasant proprietorship on the land and an efficient bureaucracy—both results of the Revolution and Napoleon—combined to give nineteenth-century France an underlying placidity which was never seriously threatened by the revolutionary spasms which continued throughout the period. On this secure basis the bourgeoisie flourished and cuisine reached its classic state. Above all, the close liaison between cuisine and the produce of the land—perhaps the most distinctive feature of present-day French cooking—was guaranteed by the fact that France, in contrast to Britain and Germany, remained a predominantly agricultural nation until well into the nineteenth century. Even today, when France is a leading industrial nation, its soul is rural—and the roots of good cooking are always in the soil.

It was a remarkable curiosity of the anarchic outbursts of the French Revolution that they were never directed against anything to do with food. While *aristos* might be accused of any other excess, gluttony was rarely included. Although the shortage of food in Paris grew to proportions of famine in 1794, no-one apparently resented or envied those who were fortunate enough to have something, or even a lot, to eat. Their complaint was only that *they* lacked enough to eat.

One account of the days of Revolution refers to the butchers and bakers furnishing 'sumptuous feasts, feasts which take place side by side with sessions of committees which decide the life or death of a man. The most important post, after the executioner himself, is the one of pantry-boy.'

This dispensation applied even to the loathed *aristos*, waiting in gaol for the guillotine. As Honoré Blanc described it: 'The victims in the prisons worshipped their stomachs. The most exquisite victuals were to be seen going through the narrow gate, going to men who were about to eat their last meal on earth and were quite conscious of the fact. From the depths of a dungeon, arrangements were made with a restaurant and a contract signed by both parties, with specific clauses dealing with the matter of early vegetables in season and the freshness of the fruit.'

It was a pattern that was to be repeated in the siege of Paris in 1870. The Goncourts in their *Journal* in 1871 wrote: 'Truly, the Parisian population deserves our admiration and respect. It is astounding that, with shop-windows bulging with food—a tactless reminder to the half-starved populace that the rich can still procure all the delicacies of the table—they do not smash the windows and knock down not only the merchant, but his merchandise. But, no. At most a joke or a witticism, delivered without a trace of rancour.'

There was, however, one immediate result of the Revolution which had a lasting effect on the eating habits of France. The break-up of many of the great houses of the nobility meant the dispersal of scores of great chefs and their numerous assistants. A large number of them went to England—but many others opened restaurants in Paris.

Men of all sorts started to eat in restaurants. The more liberal nobles and upper classes who had supported the Revolution ate at Beauvilliers. He had been chef to the Comte de Provence, later to be Louis XVIII, and can be regarded as the father of all restaurateurs. The real revolutionaries ate at Méot's; indeed, the 1793 Constitution was drawn up under his roof. He had been chef to the Duc d'Orléans. One writer talks of these champions of equality eating at Méot's 'like kings, princes, ambassadors and financiers,' his menu comprising at least one hundred dishes.

It was not only the chefs who opened restaurants. Luxury traders in more despised fields—jewellers, goldsmiths, embroiderers, haberdashers—all took to being restaurateurs and caterers so that, according to Saint-Aubin, it was not unusual to find a whole street taken up with nothing but their shops.

The greatest of these newcomers to the field of gastronomy was Germain Chevet. He had been a gardener, whose privilege it was to provide flowers for Marie-Antoinette. He risked his neck by sending her seditious notes hidden in bunches of flowers when she was imprisoned in the Conciergerie. Indeed, he was arrested and was only spared from execution because he had seventeen children. Chevet's punishment was to have to dig up his roses, symbols of decadence. He planted potatoes, which were thought to be more egalitarian. They did not prosper. He set up a booth in the Palais-Royal where he sold *pâtés*. They were so good that, although he was arrested again, when he was released he was able to expand his business to sell all kinds of food.

Chevet must have been a talented businessman, because he rapidly secured an absolute monopoly of the first vegetables and fruits as they came into season. But he was more than this. He was an imaginative cook and it was in his establishment that *écrevisses* were first cooked in a *court-bouillon*. His skill with food was such that in time he started a school. Among his pupils was the greatest chef of all time—Carême.

The restaurants quite changed the look and the tempo of life in Paris. In 1789 there had been barely one hundred restaurants in the city; by 1804 there were more than five hundred. This proliferation of eating places and the uncertainty

in questions of manners among the *nouveau riche* both created the need for guides and critics.

We have already met Grimod de la Reynière, but it was after the Revolution and in this new climate that he came into his own. He instituted the *Jurie des Gourmands*, who held regular dinners, usually cooked by de la Reynière's chef, at which they tested the produce of the multitude of suppliers. They also tried out the dishes of the caterers who provided ready-cooked entrées and *pâtisseries*, awarding a sort of academic certificate, which they called a *Légitimation*, to those of which they approved. Their proceedings were published in de la Reynière's *Almanach des Gourmands*, an annual which also included his comments on restaurants. His power was enormous, being sufficient to make or break an establishment. But he was also concerned with the welfare of traders, and came up with happy inventions for their convenience such as the speaking-tube from the kitchen to the dining-room.

His *Manuel des Amphytryons*, published in 1808, was a guide for hosts. It covered everything from managing servants— 'Let them steal a little, it was ever thus'—through the duties of a host in keeping his guests' plates filled, to actual methods of preparing food. De la Reynière may not have been very likeable, with his ugliness and black humour, but he was a lively writer and was unsnobbishly concerned to see that more people could eat better and that the newcomers should not be cheated. In this he set standards for gastronomic critics which have lasted to the present day.

The gourmet-writer, as opposed to the producer of cookery books, is a singularly French phenomenon. The great difference between the two is that the cookery-book writers, of which Britain and the United States have always had a plethora, are prescriptive and dictatorial, whereas the gourmet-writer is descriptive and encouraging; not trampling on the imagination but, by intelligent speculation, prompting it to soar.

The greatest of gourmet-writers was Jean Anthelme Brillat-Savarin. If there are doubts about the good nature of de la Reynière, no-one can fail to love Brillat-Savarin. He came from a family of lawyers and was born in Belley, in the department of Ain, in 1755. He, too, became a lawyer and eventually a politician, ending his career, after various vicissitudes, including a spell of exile in Switzerland, as a magistrate in the Court of Appeal. At one point, the estate which his father left him was confiscated by the State. However, he was compensated and bought another, where he spent two months of the year for the shooting season. There he installed his two sisters, who spent their whole time in bed, getting up only when their brother came for his annual visit. Brillat-Savarin lived well in Paris, enjoying the friendship of his cousin on his mother's side, Madame Recamier, going to Grimod de la Reynière's dinners and moving happily in good society. He never married, though he had a saucy appreciation of women.

Brillat-Savarin's *Physiologie du Goût*, the distillation of his lifelong interest in all matters concerning food, was published a few months before his death in 1826. Apart from a treatise on duelling, this was his only book, yet it stands as an extraordinary testimony to civilized man's concern with sustenance.

THE GUIDE MICHELIN

The first restaurant guides, such as de la Reynière's *Almanach des Gourmands* (1803) and Blanc's *Guide des Dîneurs* (1814), were published in the early nineteenth century in response to the growing popularity of restaurants in Paris. But it was not until a tyre company saw the value to its business of encouraging expeditions by car that France's provincial restaurants began to receive the stimulus of an objective system of rating.

Each year in early March before the new *Guide Michelin* is published, the whole restaurant world of France is in a frazzle of apprehension. Rumours fly: someone's sister-in-law is the printer's cousin; he has hinted that a three-star restaurant in the South is to lose two stars. A girl, whose uncle has had an affair with an inspector's wife, is sure that the Michelin will introduce a fourth star.

The rumours may not be true, but they are a measure of the importance that restaurateurs attach to their ratings, or possible ratings, in the *Guide Michelin*. As Alain Chapel says, 'What other profession is there in which you can be impartially rated, in a manner which you know is just?'

The Michelin introduced a single-star rating in 1926; two- and three-star ratings were added in 1931. The first post-war edition to give three-star ratings came out in 1951, with three in Paris and four in the provinces. Today, there are eighteen three-star establishments. The fact that twelve of these are in the provinces—a threefold increase since 1951—is striking evidence of the way in which the *Guide Michelin* has inspired country restaurants to strive for standards which before were rarely found outside Paris. Another major change is the rise of three-star provincial *chefs-patron*. In 1965, there were only three. Now, eleven out of twelve provincial three-star restaurants are owned solely or jointly by chefs.

The Michelin's main sources of information are letters from the public and reports from their full-time inspectors. The inspectors are usually recruited from the management level of the hotel and restaurant industry and must know how every classic dish should be prepared. Each year, they recheck every listed restaurant.

An inspector eats incognito. After the meal, which is always paid for, he explains who he is and asks to see the

André Michelin, author of the first guide, wrote, 'This Guide appears with the century; it will last as long as the century.'

kitchen and cellar. He is looking for exactly what a discriminating customer would notice—quality, service and imagination. The wine list is almost as important as the menu. In the case of humbler establishments, inclusion rests solely with the inspector.

Three-star restaurants are tested several times a year. Much consultation precedes any promotion or demotion at this level; nothing ever happens quickly. No restaurant can get two stars until it has had one, nor three until it has had two. The Michelin will never advise a restaurant how to improve its rating. The taking away of an award is very carefully deliberated, for Michelin realize that this can ruin a business. If a chef has had troubles, they stay their hand, hoping that any decline is temporary. It would certainly be two years from the first doubts to actual demotion.

The *Guide Michelin* has never taken payment or advertising. They prohibit any mention of Michelin in a hotel or restaurant's advertising, on its notepaper or its signs. Michelin are aloof, cool—and supremely powerful.

The first *Guide Michelin*, published free in 1900, listed 1200 towns. Today's guide lists 4369 localities, 7129 hotels and 3447 restaurants in 1200 pages.

Without the ingenious use of symbols, the information in one year's *Guide Michelin* would fill six books of the same size. The most famous symbols are, of course, the good food stars: one for 'good cooking in its class'; two for 'excellent cooking, worthy of a detour'; and three—'here one will find the best cooking in France, worthy of a special journey.' Crossed fork and spoon symbols rate the amenities: one, plain but good; two, fairly comfortable; three, very comfortable; four, top class; five, luxury.

'What is thirst?' he asks. And there follows a near scientific explanation of the evaporation of fluids in the body at 105°F; the postulation of the idea of three kinds of thirst, one of which is the thirst of the drunkard; an examination of the philological association of thirst with the desire for power, riches and vengeance; the observation that while mild hunger can be pleasurable, even the mildest thirst cannot; the thought that thirst causes death more quickly than hunger. On he goes for many pages, carrying us along with anecdotes, odd bits of information and stray asides about subduing the inhabitants of the New World hardly less by brandy than by firearms; always surprising us and usually making us laugh.

Brillat-Savarin discussed things which had never been discussed before. He asked the simplest questions and answered them with the armoury of a civilized, educated man, who spoke five languages and was interested in everything from medicine to ornithology, history to the design of clothing.

There was nothing lecturesome about *Physiologie du Goût*. Brillat-Savarin was a man of strong opinions and he was full of cautionary tales about such things as the effects of too much coffee, pointing out that a man could do very well drinking two bottles of wine a day, but not survive long on an equal quantity of coffee, which would render him imbecile.

'It is the duty of all papas and mammas to forbid their children coffee, unless they wish to have little dried-up machines, stunted and old at the age of twenty. This warning is particularly commended to the Parisians, whose children are not always so strong and healthy as if they had been born in other parts of the country, such as the department of Ain.'

There is nothing officious about this, merely a desire to be helpful, and he went on to explain how he had been forced to give up coffee, because of its stimulating effect causing him severe lack of sleep.

Similarly his rules for a dinner party: no fewer than twelve guests, 'of divers occupations but analogous tastes and with such points of contact that the odious formalities of introduction can be dispensed with,' well-lit dining-room, 'cloth superlatively white,' the temperature of the room between sixty and sixty-eight degrees; witty men without pretension and 'the women charming but not over prone to flirt,' few dishes, but 'exquisitely choice and the wines of the first quality'; the progress of events should be slow 'for dinner is the last business of the day'; coffee piping hot, liqueurs chosen by a master hand; 'withdrawing room large enough to allow a game at cards for those who cannot do without, yet still to leave space for colloquies apart; let the guests be willingly detained by the pleasures of social intercourse and sustained by hope that the evening will not pass without some ulterior joy; let the tea be not too strong, the toast craftily buttered and the punch mixed with all due care; let the retreat begin not earlier than eleven o'clock, but by midnight let all be abed.' Such instructions were inspired by the hope that people following them would reach the apotheosis of happiness.

What Brillat-Savarin did was to take the subject of eating and lift it from the commonplace and transform it into an art. His work proved that, 'Gastronomy is the reasoned awareness of everything which relates to man when he nourishes himself.'

FEASTING THE EYE

The eye has always played an important part in the pleasure of eating. The first impact of the chef's art is necessarily visual. For grand occasions in the Middle Ages, the 'subtlety' was invented. This was a large ornamental centre-piece, built up from a mixture of edible and inedible ingredients, sculpted to represent objects and symbols meaningful to the guests of honour at a feast.

At the wedding feast of Henry V of England and Catherine of France in

A typical Carême design for a *pièce montée* was this harp, made of *pâte d'office* (pastry) masked with rose-coloured sugar. The strings were made from white and yellow spun sugar, the laurel wreath from green biscuit and the pineapple from caramel. The garnishes around the base were caramel-glazed *choux*, mosaic tartlets and *gâteaux renversés*, glazed in the oven.

1420, there were three subtleties, one for each course served. That for the last course was 'a tyger looking in a mirrour, and a man sitting on horseback clean armed, holding in his arms a tyger whelpe . . .'

In France, the decorative centre-piece to a course became known as the *pièce montée*, that is, a specially 'built-up' piece. The tradition reached a peak in the early nineteenth century with Carême. His *pièces montées* encompassed an extra-ordinary range of subjects, which were in the fullest accordance with the romanticism of the times: Greek and Roman caskets, Gothic towers, Indian pavilions, Chinese pagodas, mossy grottoes and Turkish fountains.

For these and many more, Carême left beautifully detailed drawings, showing the influence of his study of architecture. He wrote that 'a pastry-cook of the present day should possess . . . the skill of the architect . . . the columns that more particularly belong to our style of decoration are the Doric, Ionic and Corinthian.' Carême's *pièces* were chiefly pastry (he had trained as a *pâtissier*) decorated with almond paste and sugar, in a range of colours.

Alexis Soyer, another master-chef produced a sensational pyramid-shaped meringue *gâteau* for a dinner at the Reform Club in London in honour of Ibrahim Pasha, son of the Egyptian Viceroy. The guests were reluctant to spoil the pyramid and ate only the fruit which surrounded it.

The architectural and sculptural side of cuisine has not completely disappeared. The wedding cake of today is a *pièce montée*. Michel Guérard is a sculptor in food who can build cathedrals in sugar. Paul Bocuse's *chef-de-cuisine*, Roger Jaloux, built an olive press out of lard for his qualifying examinations. Louis Outhier is especially noted for his miniature decorative pieces—*foie gras* hedgehogs with almond spines (the almonds relieving the richness of the *foie gras*).

A *grand socle au buisson des homards* (grand pedestal with a 'cluster' of lobsters) was one of many designs published by Urbain-Dubois in his *La Cuisine Artistique*. This elaborate construction, topped by a miniature fisherman with his net, was solely for decorative purposes, the lobster and crab meat having been removed from their shells.

Naturalistic *pièces montées* from Gustave Garlin's *Le Cuisinier Moderne* (1887): sponge cake disguised as a treetrunk and a coiled pastry beehive thatched with meringue. The bees were made from chocolate and meringue, with almond wings.

In the early nineteenth century, then, the mature art of French cuisine finds its literary expression in Brillat-Savarin. We have considered many of the factors in this development, but one more, the scientific and technological aspect, now becomes important. Today, we take the existence of efficient stoves and kitchen ranges very much for granted, and it is perhaps surprising to learn that until about 1800, there were no such things. Even gastronomic masterpieces were still cooked over open hearths—a state of affairs which not only wasted fuel and heat, but 'cooked the chefs as much as the food.' It is interesting that we owe to one man the kitchen range, as well as the beginning of modern mass catering (antithetical to cuisine as this may seem)—and the modern theory of heat.

This man was Benjamin Thompson (1753-1814) or, as he is better known, Count von Rumford, a lively American-born scientist who served George III of England and became the Elector of Bavaria's war minister. His researches into heat, and interest in its economical use, led him to develop enclosed stoves, which were first installed in the military cookhouse in Munich and rapidly spread through Europe. Kitchen ranges based on Rumford's principles were soon in use in France, and chefs took advantage of their even heat production to invent new sauces and smoother *roux*. They also devised the sauté pan, which Grimod de la Reynière welcomed extravagantly, calling *sauté de volaille au velouté réduit* 'the *ne plus ultra* of the century.'

At this stage, it can be argued that French cuisine had reached perfection in all its essentials. All the basic methods of cooking had been devised. All the fundamental sauces had been invented. Carême implied that there were only four grand sauces—*espagnole*, *velouté*, *allemande* and *béchamel*—and that all others were made by adjusting them in an infinite number of ways. This still applies today.

Were a young apprentice from Paul Bocuse's kitchen to find himself miraculously transported to Carême's kitchens, he would feel reasonably at home. One of Carême's pupils making a parallel exchange would see little bewildering, except the lighting, the air-conditioning, the refrigerators and the microwave oven, none of them things which importantly affect the *craft* of cooking.

Since Brillat-Savarin wrote his *Physiologie du Goût*, the patterns of cuisine have not altered. All that has changed has been emphasis and style. Cuisine has developed according to the whims of the time and the tastes of the chefs. Our story, henceforward, is therefore the story of the great chefs.

The names which stand out beyond all others are Carême and Escoffier. The first dominated the whole of the nineteenth century. The second presided over the first half of the twentieth century, until the new age of the *chef-patron* produced the changing climate of cuisine which we are now experiencing.

Marie-Antoine Carême, the son of an itinerant stone-mason, was born in 1784 in the rue du Bac in Paris, the youngest of some say seventeen and others twenty-five children. When Marie-Antoine was eight, the stone-mason made this improbable speech to his son: 'Go, go and fare thee well, my child. The world is large; chances are many. Leave us to our squalid poverty; it is our lot. Die we must as we have lived, penniless.

This is the age of quick fortunes. There are splendid opportunities for all who, like thee, have a ready wit.' Carême's father must have been a flowery fellow. In any event, the boy went. He found himself a job in a modest eating-house and never saw any of his innumerable family again.

Carême must indeed have had his wits about him. 'By 1802,' (at the age of eighteen) 'I was earning quite a lot of money, better proof than all the compliments paid me that there was in my work something original which pleased and upon which was built my reputation.'

What was original about Carême was the breadth of his interest in food and the amount of knowledge he struggled to acquire. After about four years in the eating-house, he went as an apprentice to the *pâtisserie* run by Bailly, who was famous for his cream tarts. The *pâtisseries* used to supply the great houses with people to prepare the pies, *pâtisserie* and sugar, fish-glue and marzipan dishes which the resident chefs left to outsiders.

While with Bailly, Carême first taught himself to read, chiefly, he wrote later, so that he could study cookery books. When their secrets were revealed to him, he found them gravely disappointing and it was then that he determined he would write definitive books for the guidance of young cooks of the future. He took time off from Bailly's shop to go to the museums and study drawings and prints and to learn about architecture. 'Of the five fine arts, the fifth is architecture, whose main branch is confectionery,' he wrote, rather absurdly; but it was his obsession with cooking in every aspect that made him great. Usually he would not finish working until 10pm. Then he would go to his room to read and draw. His draughtsmanship was excellent and it would be difficult to surpass the artistry he brought to the preposterous fantasies of the *pièce montée*. His reading included anything he could find about the cuisines, not only of Europe, but of Turkey, Egypt, India and China.

By the time he was sixteen, Carême was already being sent out by Bailly to the great houses, in particular that of Talleyrand, of whom he said, 'Monsieur Talleyrand understands the genius of a cook. He respects it; he is a most competent judge of delicate progress and his expenditure is both great and wise.' It was with Talleyrand that Carême's name was to be most closely associated, but he was also sent to work for Napoleon, for whose palate he had less respect. Carême's opinion of Napoleon may have been coloured by the death, during the retreat from Moscow in 1812, of nearly fifty of France's best chefs, including Laguipière, for whom Carême had worked at the Élysée Bourbon and whom he regarded as the greatest chef ever to have lived.

Carême was genuinely concerned with the conditions in which chefs worked. His description of a kitchen has a tang of protest: 'Picture a large kitchen at the hour of a grand dinner. See twenty chefs coming and going, moving with haste in this furnace of heat; look at the great mass of charcoals, a cubic metre for cooking the entrées, and another mass on the oven-tops for cooking the soups, sauces, *ragoûts*, for frying and for the *bain-maries*. Add a heap of glowing wood before which turn four spits, one bearing a sirloin of one hundred kilos, another the poultry and game. In this inferno everyone moves quickly, not a sound is heard. Only the chef has a right to be

RUMFORD'S REVOLUTION

Guided by his interest in 'the practical management of fire and the economy of fuel,' Count von Rumford (born Benjamin Thompson) produced a host of useful inventions, including the kitchen range, double-boiler, baking oven, pressure-cooker and drip coffee-maker. He also made important advances in pure science. In Munich he measured the heat produced by boring cannon, boiled water by it and was the first to put forward the modern kinetic theory of heat: it is the energy of molecular motion, rather than a fluid or 'caloric' as had been supposed.

From the point of view of cooking history, the most important of Rumford's inventions was the kitchen range, which he proposed as the remedy for the waste of fuel and singeing of chefs that resulted from cooking on blazing open hearths. A typical Rumford arrangement consisted of a brick range, enclosing and separating a series of fires, above each of which a pot or stew-pan fitted into a circular, iron-rimmed opening. The heat of each fire could be separately regulated by varying the draught through its ash-pit door and the smoke was carried away by flues leading through the brickwork to the main chimney. Any temporarily unwanted fire was capped with an earthenware cover and its draught almost cut off. In this way it could be kept alive, but burning hardly any fuel. The entire arrangement concentrated heat where it was needed, reduced fuel waste and made the chef's work more bearable. Simple as it seems, this invention, together with the baking oven, was mainly responsible for modern methods of cooking and baking.

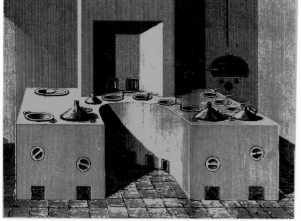

Rumford opposed alcohol and worked to popularize coffee as a substitute. To this end he investigated the source of the flavour of coffee. Having decided that it lay in the volatile oils of coffee and that these were destroyed by boiling, he decided that coffee must be made in a sealed container at a constant heat below boiling. He then came up with several designs for drip coffee-makers, with water jackets to keep the beverage at the right heat. This version offered alternative-size measures for the coffee.

heard, and at his words everyone jumps to obey. Then the last straw—for about half-an-hour the windows are shut so that no air shall cool the dishes as they are served. This is how we spend the best years of our lives. We must obey even when our physical strength fails, but it is the burning charcoal that kills us.'

Napoleon said, 'To dine like a soldier come to dinner *chez moi*; if you wish to dine like an emperor go and eat *chez* Cambacérès.' Jean-Jacques Régis de Cambacérès, Duke of Parma, was the Arch-Chancellor, perpetual President of the Senate and the chief architect of the *Code Napoléon*. Everyone agreed that he kept one of the finest tables in Paris, comparable with that of any house except Talleyrand. But Carême hated him and his food. He was miserly, liked meatballs and insisted that left-overs be used in the next day's dishes. Above all, he treated his staff poorly, thereby flouting Carême's maxims, that 'cuisine is a difficult art; the generous host gives it dignity and grandeur,' and 'the man who knows how to appreciate a good servant is always well served, his home is happy.'

Carême's idea of cuisine was the same as Talleyrand's: that it should be spectacular and expensive and that it was worth more than arms and battles, congresses and assemblies. 'I need saucepans rather than instructions,' Talleyrand told Louis XVIII. To impress the Tsar, Talleyrand arranged for a 'disaster' at a banquet in his honour. A huge, elaborately decorated salmon was brought into the hall. The waiter dropped the dish, and Talleyrand beckoned to another waiter, who brought in an equally large and highly decorated salmon. It was a gesture which would have appealed to Carême, with its implication of invincibility and limitless resources.

This love of the spectacular, which in particular manifested itself in Carême's passion for *pièces montées*, was a reflection of his daring and his inventiveness. 'The chef who is a man of routine,' he wrote, 'lacks courage. His life drips away in mediocrity.' Part of Carême's strength lay in his independence. Nearly all his life, he worked as a freelance, only rarely taking jobs as a resident chef. When he did, they lasted usually for a very short time. At one period, soon after he left Bailly's *pâtisserie*, he toyed with the idea of opening his own restaurant, partly to outdo Beauvilliers, who was regarded as his chief rival. It is interesting to compare the attitudes of the two chefs.

Beauvilliers' restaurant was patronized by those of the *Ancien Régime* who were prepared to come to some accommodation with the Revolution. He was steeped in the old respectable traditions and used to walk round his restaurant with a sword buckled at his side, the privilege of officers of the crown and a reminder of his days in the service of the Comte de Provence.

Beauvilliers despised *pièces montées*. The romantic ruins made of lard and the Grecian temples and statues of sugar, *l'ornement de la cuisine*, as Carême called this kind of work, maintaining that it provided 'the necessary food for mind and heart and filled pleasurably the leisure of modern gastronomes,' was, in Beauvilliers' opinion, so much rubbish. 'The chef's job is not to please the eye but the palate; not to fill one's leisure but one's belly pleasurably.'

The older man's judgement may have been sounder, he may have been a surer man with an entrée and was certainly better at a roast, but he was a defender of a dying style. Carême was an inventor, a man of adventure capable of the sublime. He was seeking a new style and he found it. It is his name we remember.

All his life he searched for adventure in his own particular field. He went to England to be chef to the Prince Regent at the Royal Pavilion in Brighton. It was tough going. No-one in the kitchens spoke French and no-one but the Prince seemed to know what he was about. The Prince sent for him and said, 'Carême, you will be the death of me; you send in such appetizing fare that I cannot help overeating,' to which the chef responded, 'Sir, my duty is to tempt your appetite; yours to control it.' Despite the difficult circumstances, Carême managed to continue with his writing, but he left after seven months, observing later that whereas the Prince usually had pains that lasted days and nights on end, he had 'not during the time that I spent in his service, suffered one attack of gout.'

Carême went to Russia to study the Russian way of doing things, but he disliked the Russian service which came to replace the old French method. He favoured the French way by which everything was put on the table at once and got cold while it was admired. In the more practical Russian service, the carving was done either in the kitchen or on a sideboard; the dishes arrived in sequence and the guests could eat them hot. It was not conservatism that made Carême reject this arrangement, but the fear of losing the drama of his great set-pieces.

He enjoyed the immense banquets which he was called upon to organize: the dinner in 1815 given by the Royal Guard for the National Guard, with 1200 people seated at twelve long tables in the Louvre; the military dinner held in the Champs Elysées for 10,000 men, with tables stretching from the Place Louis XV to the Barrière de l'Étoile; the Grand Bal de l'Odéon, a return

THE RISE OF DINING OUT

Until the late eighteenth century, almost the only public eating places in Paris were inns and the shops of *traiteurs* (caterers). At the inns, guests ate a set meal around the host's table—hence, *table d'hôte* for a set menu.

The *traiteurs* sold mainly cooked meats, *ragoûts* and *pâtisseries*. In 1765 they sued a soup-vendor, one Boulanger, to prevent his selling sheeps' feet in white sauce. He won. Boulanger called his soups *restaurants* or restoratives, and from his rudimentary establishment, the word came to mean a place to eat, to restore oneself.

In 1782, the well-known chef, Beauvilliers, opened what we would recognize as a restaurant, with a choice of dishes served at individual tables. This was called La Grande Taverne de Londres—an indication of how the English, with their taverns, were regarded as pacesetters in eating out.

By 1789, the year of the Revolution, there were about a hundred restaurants in Paris; by 1804, when de la Reynière's *Almanach des Gourmands* first appeared, there were five or six hundred. The *Almanach* suggested three reasons for this increase. First, the English influence. Second, there were many politicians and legislators without homes in Paris, who therefore ate out, encouraging others to do likewise by their example. Third, the break-up of aristocratic houses meant that those of their chefs who did not emigrate were driven to open public restaurants. Another possible factor was that the 'patriotic millionaires', who had enriched themselves during the Revolution, spent their money at restaurants

rather than risk drawing attention to themselves by lavish entertaining at home. In any case, it was by the early nineteenth century that, in the words of one writer, 'the culinary genius of France had become permanently fixed in the restaurants.'

The Parisian restaurant always had about it a certain sauciness. Side by side with the restaurants of the Palais-Royal, there were brothels, gaming-houses and peep-shows. Restaurants were places where men took their mistresses rather than their wives. By the middle of the century this was the practice at fashionable establishments such as Vachette, Foyot and even the Café Anglais, where

the famous Dugléré cooked.

During the twentieth century most grand Parisian restaurants, such as Maxim's, Lasserre and the Tour d'Argent, have been run by *maîtres d'hôtel* who employ chefs. One great exception is Raymond Oliver, *chef-patron* of Le Grand Véfour, whose television programmes did much to revive public interest in cuisine. Oliver's three-star rating was matched in 1978 by Alain Senderens, *chef-patron* of L'Archestrate. On the whole, though, it is in the provinces that the early nineteenth-century pattern of the *chef-patron* has been revived, and with it, the prestige of the chef.

The Boeuf à la Mode, established in 1792 in the rue de Valois, lasted until 1936.

given by the National Guard to the Royal Guard, to which 3000 people came.

Carême's career was as spectacular as his dishes. But possibly his greatest contributions to cuisine were the books he had promised himself to write as a youth. He wrote in all some eight books, having produced five before he was forty—a considerable feat for a man who never took a day off work. In them, he covered history, theory and practice. The *Maître d'Hôtel Français* contained a menu for each day of the year, an essay on the vegetables available in each season and observations gleaned in all the countries where he had worked. Many of the books dealt primarily with *pâtisserie*, but *L'Art de la Cuisine Française au 19ème siècle*, in five volumes, is the most comprehensive, ranging over every aspect of eating and cookery from a study of teeth to the composition of the most delicate

sauces. It set the tone for cuisine for seventy years. He was still dictating to his daughter when he died, a poor man, in 1833, at the age of forty-nine. As he had written, 'The coal kills us, but what matter? Fewer days, more glory.'

Gastronomy had become in France an art, a subject for endless discussion. As Joseph Favre, a great chef and gastronomic author, was to write at the end of the century, 'For the sake of dinner, men of all sorts and conditions call a halt to other affairs. The banker stops counting his hoard of gold. It is for dinner that the musician creates his harmonies, the poet his verses; it is for dinner that the doctor works his cures and it is so that he can himself have a better dinner that Tartuffe adjures abstinence on others . . . for dinner that the charlatan puts on his act, the captain commands and the soldier fights. All these evils . . . have but one aim—dinner.'

A *table d'hôte* in a Paris hotel, caricatured by Thomas Rowlandson in 1810.

Fin-de-siècle interior of the Restaurant Vachette, about 1900.

Les Trois Frères Provençaux was known for its Mediterranean dishes.

One of Paris's oddest restaurants in the 1950s was La Grenouille.

THE ORDER OF EATING

Beauvilliers, in *L'Art du Cuisinier* (1814), gives the courses of a dinner as soups, removes, first entremets, roasts, second entremets and salads (excluding *hors d'oeuvres* and desserts from the menu proper). The soup was 'removed' by light dishes of poultry, game, meat or fish, as the prelude to the entrées: more elaborate preparations of the same foods, usually with white or brown sauces. As relief to this initial climax came the first entremets, of light *pâtés*, galantines or *vol-au-vents*. Then came the second climax, meat, game or poultry again, but always roasted, or in the case of fish, fried. Second entremets were vegetables, fruit, egg dishes and sweets (vegetables were not, as now, eaten with the main courses). Salads were eaten before or after the entremets or with the roasts.

The traditional way of serving, *à la Française* or *le grand couvert*, was to split the menu into two or more parts and to put all the dishes in the first part on the table at once. When the diners had eaten their way through the first, the next course was served in the same manner. The traditional service enabled the dishes to be arranged with artistic symmetry, but resulted in cold food and congealed sauces, and made it impossible for the diners to eat anything that was beyond arm's length. In the 1850s the *service à la Française* gave way to the more stream-lined *service à la Russe*, in which the courses were carved and apportioned in the kitchen and brought to the table in sequence, and diners got their food hot. This is how we dine today.

Service à la Française.

Service à la Russe.

The first written menus were simply lists of what the kitchen staffs of great households were supposed to prepare for particular meals. By the early nineteenth century, as restaurants became popular, menu cards for diners to consult came into use; they were also posted outside to attract custom. The fashion was for highly decorated menus, as shown by these examples, of 1871 (a Siege menu that purports to offer rat, dog and elephant) 1889 and 1903.

As with all arts, cuisine had its periods of flowering and its periods of stagnation. Nevertheless, there is proof of its continuing basic form, set by the time of Carême, in a most popular cookery book of the nineteenth century. While much of Carême's writing was really of use only to professionals, A. Viard wrote a book in 1806 called *Le Cuisinier Impérial*, providing, in the words of the author, 'simple explanations of all cooking operations.' It was to go on appearing in new editions throughout the century, conveniently changing its title with each political upheaval—*Cuisinier Royal* for Louis XVIII, *Cuisinier National* for Louis Napoleon, *Cuisinier Impérial* when Louis pronounced himself Napoleon III and finally *Cuisinier National* again for the Third Republic.

After Carême, there was a decline of cuisine under the constitutional monarchy. The *petite bourgeoisie*, having become interested in food, imposed a certain stodginess on it, while the grander sections of society were more interested in display than in true gastronomy. Under the Second Empire cuisine improved again, in reaction against the drabness of life under the bourgeois monarch, Louis-Philippe. Then the siege of Paris reduced the poor to eating animals from the zoo and was hardly a time for good eating. Gradually, after that, standards rose until the 1890s, when a peak was reached which lasted until World War I.

Again, as with any art, there were practitioners who stood out from their fellows, their skill transcending any wave of fashion.

Louis Eustache Ude, a great contemporary of Carême, was one of the many French chefs who exported their art to Britain. He was employed for a time by the hunchback gourmet Earl of Sefton, who paid him no less than three hundred guineas a year (and left him a hundred a year for life), and worked in London at Crockford's Gaming Club.

Ude was a chef in the grand manner, temperamental and irascible. A member of Crockford's once had the temerity to quibble at a sixpenny surcharge for the exquisite sauce on a dish of red mullet and Ude exploded: 'The imbecile, the damned imbecile apparently thinks that red mullets come out of the sea with *my* sauce in their pockets.' When Ude served grouse out of season, the Marquess of Queensberry reported him and he had to appear in court. *The Times* reported Ude's exchanges with the magistrate, complete with a parody of Ude's accent:

M. UDE: I know nothing at all about vot vent into de room. I never sawed it at all.

SIR F. ROE: Whether you know it or not, the Act of Parliament makes you liable.

M. UDE: Upon my honour, dat is very hard. Ven I got de summons I remonstrated with my Lord Alvanley, and he say 'Oh never mind, Ude, say dey vere pigeons instead of grouse.' 'Ah my Lord,' say I, 'I cannot do better than call them pigeons, because dat bird is so common in this house.'

(Loud laughter)

Sir F. Roe, who appeared greatly to enjoy the scene, said he should certainly put the lowest penalty—namely, five shillings.

M. UDE: Vell, I shall pay de money, but it is dam hard.

Next day in Crockford's, a suspicious looking *salmi* was

served and Queensberry demanded to see the menu. The waiter rushed to Ude, who wrote one out, entitling the dish *salmi de fruit défendu*. Even the pompous Marquess laughed.

Ude believed nothing should come before cuisine. It was long thought that animals killed slowly tasted better than those killed quickly and the practice of whipping pigs and calves to death persisted well into the nineteenth century. Ude maintained that if the taste of the meat was improved, then any supposed cruelty was justified.

There was Antoine Gogué, who tried to persuade everyone that cooking was fun and encouraged people to come into his kitchen 'to witness and enjoy the childish satisfaction of design and decoration.' There was Jules Gouffé who raised the Jockey Club to a shrine of gastronomy. There was Bignon, at the restaurant Riche, who was famous for his sauces. There was Magny, who invented his *petite marmite* and did wonders with *écrevisses à la bordelaise*. Theodore de Banville wrote of Magny's *châteaubriand*: 'Surrounded by *pommes soufflées*, this fillet is twice as thick as an ordinary beefsteak. It is not at all red, but when it is cut, the juice runs out and mixes with the *maître d'hôtel* butter so as to make it a live and vital thing.'

Then, of course, there was Alexis Soyer, who represents so many of the characteristics of great chefs. He spent most of his working life in Britain, as did many famous French chefs; but this is not surprising for Britain was for so long the richest country in Europe and it was there that people of wealth, in a more stable society while political unrest reigned elsewhere, could provide the conditions in which cuisine could flourish.

Soyer was born in 1809, the son of a small shopkeeper. At sixteen, after training for four years at Chez Grignon in Paris, he moved to La Maison Douix. After one year he was made head chef. He was even at that age an extraordinary character, given to practical jokes and riotous behaviour, but evidently a person of almost incredible talent. In 1830, he became second chef at the French Foreign Office. The job did not last long. When Soyer and the other chefs were at their stoves one day in July, insurgents burst in and shot dead two of his colleagues. The other chefs fled, but Soyer stood there singing the *Marseillaise* at the top of his voice. The rebels cheered him and carried him shoulder high into the street. When things had calmed down, the Bourbon monarchy was ended and Soyer realised he was unemployed. He left France for the more placid kitchens of the Duke of Cambridge. He worked in many aristocratic houses in Britain until, in 1837, he married the artist Emma Jones, and was appointed chef at the Reform Club even before it was built.

Soyer worked with the architect, Sir Charles Barry, to design the finest kitchens ever seen in any country. The Vicomtesse de Malleville described them as being 'spacious as a ballroom, kept in the finest order, white as a young bride' and went on to compare Soyer with Vatel and Carême. Soyer's genius may be judged from the fact that many features of his kitchens remain in the Reform Club, 140 years later.

In 1842, Soyer's private life received a severe blow with the death of his wife in premature labour. He was in Brussels when he heard the news and he attempted to stab himself in grief. He did, however, regain much of his gaiety and good humour, but it may be that his personal loss prompted his compassionate interest in the suffering of others. In 1846, Soyer started a huge soup kitchen in the Farringdon Road in London, using equipment which he devised, which fed between 8000 and 10,000 of the poor every day. The next year he extended his operations to Dublin, where, in three months, his kitchens served well over a million rations to the starving.

Soyer was a man of infinite contrast. In his dinners for the rich, he would not hesitate to serve a dish costing one hundred guineas, but he was to give his services free to the British government during the Crimean War. When he left the Reform Club, and that was a major event of public concern, he took to freelance work, roasting on one occasion a whole ox at Exeter over an apparatus he contrived, using gas. In 1851, he had hopes of running the catering arrangements for the Great Exhibition, but was disgusted to find that no alcohol was to be allowed. So he took over Gore House opposite the exhibition site and converted it for what he called a Gastronomic Symposium of All Nations. He proposed to serve food from every country except New Zealand, on the grounds that he did not care to cook 'baked young woman for two or boiled missionary'. The place was an extravagantly decorated collection of restaurants, cafés and bars, one big enough to seat 1500 people. It was not in very good taste, and, after the Exhibition closed, Soyer lost his licence. The venture cost him £7000. Luckily his writing kept him financially afloat. His books would sell 10,000 or more copies even before publication. He wrote for everyone, dividing his famous *Gastronomic Regenerator* into two parts— *The Kitchen of the Wealthy* and *The Kitchen at Home*. It contains 2000 recipes. He also wrote *The Modern Housewife*, *The Poor Man's Regenerator* and *A Shilling Cookery*.

In 1855, Soyer went to the Crimea at his own expense to sort out the appalling chaos of the British army's catering arrangements. In a short time his resourceful ingenuity transformed the confusion into some of the most efficient mass catering yet seen in a distant military campaign. But Soyer's splendid altruism cost him his health; he was seriously weakened by Crimean fever and died three years later, aged only forty-nine. Before his death in 1858, however, Soyer passed on the benefit of his Crimean experiences in two books, *Soyer's Culinary Campaign* and *Instructions to Military Hospital Cooks*.

There is much in Soyer's career and his views that foreshadows the *chefs-patron* who are the subject of this book. 'Publicity is like the air we breathe, if we have it not, we die,' he said. His Magic Stove, the precursor of lamps used for cooking at tables in restaurants, was shown off everywhere—even being demonstrated on the top of the Great Pyramid. He took to marketing bottled sauces, one for men and one for women, at two shillings and sixpence a bottle. He even invented a suit which, at the pull of a string, if you turned up at a party incorrectly dressed, would convert, even while being worn, into a different kind of suit. He was passionately opposed to any cheating in cuisine and disliked over-ornamented food. Believing that there should be no secrets, he happily gave recipes to anyone who was interested. He was a collector of paintings, possessing several fine Chardins. He even tried his

THE RESOURCEFUL ALEXIS SOYER

Alexis Soyer was the first great chef to be interested in philanthropic mass catering. He produced a host of kitchen inventions and sponsored a wide range of branded foods.

For the British army in the Crimea, Soyer designed an economical 'camp and bivouac kitchen' and trained army cooks in its use. Amid great fanfare, he introduced his system with a banquet cooked from the soldiers' ordinary rations.

Soyer's Nectar, made from fruit juice and aerated water, was supposed to 'cool and tranquilize the system.'

Soyer's Sauce (not to be confused with soy sauce), marketed in half-pint bottles, was particularly recommended for meat dishes.

Soyer designed a scaled-down ship's kitchen to produce large dinners in a minimum of space (17×8 ft), with the equipment ingeniously arranged for convenient use. Some of its main features: 1, roasting fire-place; 2, *bain-marie*; 3 and 4, charcoal stoves; 5, drawers and ventilation for charcoal stoves; 6, hotplate and grid-iron; 7, oven with hot cupboard above; 8, pestle and mortar; 9, kitchen table; 10, spoon-drainer; 11, shelves; 12, vegetable boxes.

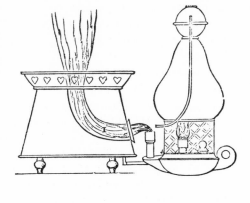

Soyer's Magic Stove was the ancestor of the lamps used for cooking at table today. The stove was fed with a flame of vaporized gas, generated from spirits of wine (purified alcohol) heated in the pear-shaped reservoir by the lamp beneath. The Magic Stove was demonstrated on top of Egypt's Great Pyramid—a publicity stunt equal to any by today's star chefs.

hand at painting, as well as writing plays. All in all he was a curiously modern man.

Meanwhile, in France itself, cuisine proceeded on the lines laid down in the early years of the century. The main changes were not directly concerned with cooking. The fixed-price menu was introduced under the Bourgeois Monarchy, when the famous restaurants in the Palais-Royal found their custom being drawn away by the newly fashionable ones in the Boulevard des Italiens. It was also designed to overcome the problems of those affected by the strict cut-back in public expenditure and the reduction of army pay and pensions. The fixed-price menu brought a certain discipline into restaurant cooking and provided a challenge to which chefs responded with the same ingenuity that they had shown during the restrictions and famines of the 1560s.

The other great advance, *pace* Carême, was the universal adoption of the Russian service. This was largely due to Félix Urbain-Dubois, who campaigned for its introduction in the face of strong opposition from culinary die-hards who believed that anything introduced in the time of Louis XIV must still be right. Urbain-Dubois, who at one time was chef at the German court, also represents the new division which was growing up between *haute cuisine* and *cuisine bourgeoise*. In earlier times good cooking had been the prerogative of the nobles. The peasants were glad of anything to eat. With the Revolution had come the idea, and to some extent the reality, that everyone should eat well. Marin, Menon and Carême had all included advice and recipes for a wider class of people. Now, for different reasons, a new split had occurred. Urbain-Dubois' *La Cuisine Classique* was strictly addressed to professional chefs, as was *Le Livre de Cuisine* by Jules Gouffé. The best cuisine, henceforward, would need a battery of assistants and equipment to which even the most prosperous housewife could never aspire.

One man, however, was to dominate the world of cuisine in the late nineteenth and early twentieth centuries. That man was Georges Auguste Escoffier. The son of a blacksmith, Escoffier was born in 1846 in the small Riviera village of Villeneuve-Loubet, and started his training in an uncle's restaurant at Nice when he was thirteen. At nineteen he moved to Paris and, over the next eighteen years, accumulated experience at three great Paris restaurants, at the Rhine Army Headquarters at Metz and in the grand resort hotels in Nice, Monte Carlo and Lucerne.

In 1883, Escoffier started to work with César Ritz, who managed the Grand Hotel in Monte Carlo; six years later the two men moved to the Savoy Hotel in London. It was here, in association with Ritz, that Escoffier's name became world famous. Together, at the Savoy and later at the Carlton and the other Ritzes, they created the concept of the grand Edwardian hotel, with its splendid luxury and cosmopolitan menu of dishes named after opera singers, dancers and even a ship (the *Jeanette*, which had foundered while exploring the Arctic).

The social status of chefs had risen after the Revolution from the condition of being, with the exception of a few romantic figures like Vatel, just another class of servant. The establishment of restaurants had given such chefs as Bignon, Magny, Catcomb and the haughty Dugléré a certain standing through their familiarity with their customers. But as chefs became more

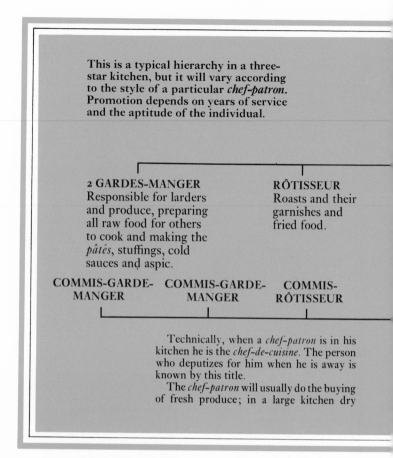

This is a typical hierarchy in a three-star kitchen, but it will vary according to the style of a particular *chef-patron*. Promotion depends on years of service and the aptitude of the individual.

2 GARDES-MANGER Responsible for larders and produce, preparing all raw food for others to cook and making the *pâtés*, stuffings, cold sauces and aspic.

RÔTISSEUR Roasts and their garnishes and fried food.

COMMIS-GARDE-MANGER **COMMIS-GARDE-MANGER** **COMMIS-RÔTISSEUR**

Technically, when a *chef-patron* is in his kitchen he is the *chef-de-cuisine*. The person who deputizes for him when he is away is known by this title.

The *chef-patron* will usually do the buying of fresh produce; in a large kitchen dry

confined to their kitchens by the professionalism of the latter half of the nineteenth century, their status dwindled again. As A. Tavenet wrote in his *L'Art Culinaire* in 1883, 'We have come to be looked down upon as labourers, to be summoned when needed and to be dismissed with a brief nod of thanks when the fancy has passed.'

The conditions in which cooks worked brutalized them. The heat was so intense that they drank copiously, so that as the day wore on, they became drunk, bellicose and unattractive. Their work was dangerous; one doctor maintained that there were more industrial accidents in kitchens than in the mines. Even today in any kitchen at any time there will be two or three chefs with quite serious burns on their arms. Escoffier himself was so short that he had to wear built-up shoes to avoid burning himself on the stoves.

He set about trying to rectify both the working conditions of chefs and their public image. He forbade all alcohol in his kitchens and provided instead huge pots of barley-water, which a physician told him would be beneficial. He banned smoking and shouting. Even the orders had to be spoken loudly rather than yelled out. No chef was allowed to go out into the street in his smelly cooking clothes; he must always put on a suit.

Having set about reforming the atmosphere of the kitchen, Escoffier went on to organize the method of work. The system of *parties*, by which work was apportioned, had already been instituted, but it was confused and slow. The *rôtisseur* might be having to grill fish while the *poissonnier* was idle. Often, one chef would do all the work on a particular dish, even including jobs which would plainly have been more easily done by another

CHEF-PATRON
The owner of the restaurant.

CHEF-DE-CUISINE
Responsible for supervising every section of the kitchen.

SOUS-CHEF
The *chef-de-cuisine*'s assistant.

POISSONNIER
All fish including
fish fried in butter.
Makes his own stocks
and sauces.

ENTREMETIER
Makes soups, cooks
vegetables and
cooks egg and
pasta dishes.

PÂTISSIER
Desserts, ices,
petits-fours
and pastry for
all dishes

2 SAUCIERS
Stocks, *roux*,
sauces for meats
and other entrées.

COMMIS-POISSONNIER

COMMIS-ENTREMETIER

COMMIS-PÂTISSIER

COMMIS-SAUCIER

goods are bought by a store-man known as an *économe*.

Generally, one of the *chefs-de-partie*, a *garde-manger* or *saucier* is the *sous-chef*. Sometimes, however, the *pâtissier* will hold this position. Pastry cooking can be a

lifetime profession and often the *pâtissier* will be the most senior chef in a kitchen, although he has never worked in any other department. Other chefs move between disciplines. In most kitchens there are two *chefs tournants* and they stand in for any

chef-de-partie who is absent.

It is necessary to complete a three-year apprenticeship and qualify for a *certificat d'aptitude professionelle* to become a *commis*. The rank of a *commis* (first, second, third, etc.) depends on length of service and skill.

partie. The *rôtisseur*, for instance, had to make the pastry for a *boeuf-en-croûte*, rather than the *pâtissier*.

Even today, the system is confusing enough, but Escoffier set down a code which rationalized many operations so that several *parties* could contribute to one dish simultaneously. In this way the time taken to make a dish was often reduced by more than half and it was far easier to ensure that a dish was served at the right temperature.

It was not only in the realm of mechanics that Escoffier was a true innovator. In cooking itself he was a questioner of all that had gone before. While stating that the foundations of cuisine were eternal, he believed that with changing times and what he called 'the disastrous effects of hyperactivity on the central nervous system,' cuisine was already being, and would have to be still further, refined to suit the ever-increasing refinement of modern palates.

As André Simon wrote, 'Escoffier denounced the two traditional basic sauces of French cuisine, *espagnole* and *allemande*, both old-fashioned French sauces in spite of their names, the first a *sauce brune* and the other a *sauce blonde*. He substituted for them and their bastard progeny the much lighter and more fragrant *fumets*, the concentrated natural juices of meat, fish and vegetables in water, broth, butter, olive oil or another cooking medium.' As these two sauces were two of Carême's four essential sauces, it was a broad onslaught.

Escoffier was an intellectual, rather than a purely intuitive, chef. He passed sleepless nights thinking up new combinations to satisfy the voracious demands of his fashionable customers. In *Le Guide Culinaire*, he published 5000 recipes—and he

called it merely an '*aide-mémoire de cuisine pratique*.' He did not claim this number of recipes as his own, although he did invent an astonishing amount of new, lasting dishes. He was merely following his usual habit of trying to get everything down on paper in an orderly way. Indeed in all fields, his great distinction lay in having codified almost everything to do with cooking, explaining it in scrupulous detail and bringing up to date much that was old-fashioned. He distilled the experience of a century and added to it his own extraordinary flair.

Escoffier was a kindly man who harboured no grudges. He even looked after Ulysse Rohan in his old age—the very chef whose harsh treatment of Escoffier as a youthful apprentice had inspired his reforms of working conditions. Escoffier's reforming instincts extended to society as a whole; in the manner of Soyer, he was given to working out schemes for a welfare state complete with old-age pensions, unemployment benefit and graduated income tax. In a word, he fully merits Charles Barrier's description of him as a 'visionary'. He died in Monte Carlo in 1935. He left only £335.

As Escoffier brought cuisine to a peak and spread the gospel of French cooking, there was a surge of interest in the subject. Clubs, societies, institutes, gourmet circles, academies, brotherhoods and every kind of group sprang up, to discuss, write about, debate, promote and generally carry on about food.

The gourmet-writer became once more a figure of importance. One of the most considerable was Charles Monselet (1828-1888), who wrote *Le Triple Almanach Gourmand* (1866) and much poetry on the subject of cookery, and gave his name to many dishes which contain artichoke hearts and truffles.

However, Monselet's experience as the victim of a carefully laid culinary trap stands as a warning to critics. When he had proclaimed the excellence of a dinner to which he had been invited, it was revealed that he had fallen for a totally spurious menu. What purported to be swallow's-nest soup was noodles with bean *purée*, brill with shrimp sauce was cod, wild goat cutlets were marinaded lamb, capercailzie was young turkey and so on. He had also fallen for a rigged wine-list.

The one critic who was much too wily to be caught by such a ruse was the extraordinary Maurice Edmund Sailland (1872-1956), better known as Curnonsky (literally 'Why-not-sky')—a name he chose for its fashionable Russian tag. After Brillat-Savarin, Curnonsky was France's greatest food writer, whose practical knowledge and expertise contrasted with the philosophical bent of his predecessor.

Physically, Curnonsky was the gourmet of popular imagination, a huge man with great fleshy dewlaps surrounding his face, who in later years had to be virtually carried into restaurants. His influence was as prodigious as his physique; if he pronounced a favourable verdict on a restaurant it was assured of success. His usual test of a restaurant was to order lamb. When he sat down to eat, very often a crowd would gather; this did not disconcert him in the least. One observer of Curnonsky's lamb-testing described his expression: 'His whole face would be impassive, but when the first slice went in his mouth, a muscle would twitch. Then another slice from the pinker part. Another muscle twitched. He seemed to have muscles all over his vast face, which twitched according to what he was eating. One here for chicken legs, one above the eyebrow for asparagus and so on. The crowd waited to see the judgement spread over his face. When it came it was final.'

Curnonsky's extensive writings covered an amazing range of gastronomic subjects. He studied every different aspect of cuisine, dividing it into four sections. First, *haute cuisine*, 'the concentration of the finest talent and the finest produce.' Secondly, French family cooking—'I have never eaten better than in the houses of the wine-growers of my own locality, the peasants of the Landes, Breton fishermen, Lyon silk-weavers and the workers of Paris.' Thirdly, regional cooking—'The ideal marriage of gastronomy and tourism.' Perhaps his major work was *Le Trésor Gastronomique de France* (1933), a vast labour originally planned as thirty-two volumes, but eventually cut down to one. It contained a catalogue of all the regions of France, with their natural produce and typical menus, listing villages, wines, liqueurs, herbs, game and cheeses. Fourthly, there was impromptu cooking—'. . . done on a pot luck basis, with whatever comes to hand . . . shrimps caught on the spot, fish from the nearby stream, milk from a farm close by, the best parts of a hare just decapitated by a speeding car, fruits from the hedgerows, vegetables "borrowed" from a farm when its owner isn't looking.' In 1927, in recognition of his literary and masticatory labours, a public referendum elected Curnonsky Prince of Gastronomes.

In any art, the influence of great masters can be stifling, the more so if they are fond of codification, as were Escoffier and Curnonsky. Neither man intended to put French cuisine in fetters. Escoffier, in his *Le Guide Culinaire*, could not have been more explicit about the ever-changing nature of cuisine: 'It would be absurd to pretend to fix the destiny of an art which is enhanced by so many aspects of fashion and is equally as inconstant.' Yet such seemingly definitive assessments of cuisine as those of Escoffier and Curnonsky inevitably tended to be accepted as inviolable dogma. As a result, many chefs in the earlier twentieth century tended to substitute the writ of

PAYING THEIR WAY

The great cry of the three-star chefs is that they never count the cost. They buy only the best. They use Limoges china and Baccarat glass. A trained waiter is paid more than a factory worker—3000 francs a month. A senior *chef-de-partie* earns at least 8000 francs a month.

The net profit margin in a great restaurant is about 4·5 per cent. As Jacques Pic says: 'In turnover we are millionaires. In profit, we are nothing of the sort as we must plough nearly everything back into the business.' The turnover of the restaurants in this book range from approximately four million francs to ten million. Nearly half the takings go to buy food and wine. This is a vastly larger percentage than is the case with most restaurants, where 40 per cent would be a high figure. All the great chefs own their restaurants. If they did not, and had to pay a rent, there would be no hope of their being able to operate on so generous a scale.

The French are notoriously unwilling to discuss money. The balance sheet below is based on the experience of several *chefs-patron*. It assumes a restaurant which seats 100 people, employs 35-40 staff, is open 291 days a year and serves an average of 108 people a day.

BALANCE SHEET

EXPENDITURE	francs
Food and wine	3,271,500
Wages	1,530,100
Gas and electricity, including ovens, heating restaurant and display lighting	137,500
Breakages and losses: 3 plates a day @ 65 francs, 10 glasses a day @ 35 francs	158,500
Laundry: tablecloths and napkins	124,500
Insurance, including cover for mishaps to clients, but not breakages	69,000
Flowers, on every table and hall	32,000
Bank interest on loans for improvements	60,000
Transport, car and bringing supplies from market	30,000
Legal and accountancy costs	10,000
Printing	10,000
Sundries (all publicity including free meals; bad debts, thefts, telephone, cleaning materials, etc)	100,580
Repairs and renewals, including new kitchens every 20 years @ 500,000 francs	75,000
	5,608,680
Taxes	975,000
	6,583,680
INCOME	
86 set menus a day @ 150 francs	3,753,900
22 *à la carte* meals @ 200 francs	1,280,400
Wine and coffee @ 60 francs a head	1,885,680
	6,919,980
Less expenditure and taxes	6,583,680
Net profit	336,300

Escoffier for their own imaginations. Cooking stagnated and swiftly became dull, as does any art when performed by rote.

There were, however, a handful of chefs who were important exceptions to this conformity, and it is to their inspiration that the creativity of present-day French cuisine is chiefly due.

First, there was Édouard Nignon (1865–1935), who worked as a chef until he was forty and then became *maître d'hôtel* at Larue and made it one of the most popular restaurants in Paris. Nignon was a free spirit, a poet of a chef, who hated too well formulated ideas. He agreed that culinary art requires strict observance of certain well-established principles (to that extent he was not in opposition to Escoffier), but believed that respect for these principles should never hamstring chefs. 'Routine in cuisine is a crime,' he said.

His great concern was for produce and for honesty in presentation. He wanted a dish to taste of the things it was made of. He also wanted a chef to be free to express his own individuality. The recipes in his *Les Plaisirs de la Table* and in *Éloges de la Cuisine Française* are broad sketches of how a dish should be prepared, leaving to the cook plenty of scope for his imagination since there are no measurements or timings.

It was this kind of thinking which was gradually to move cuisine from the rut into which Escoffier had unwittingly driven it. Between the two world wars there were three men who, while giving all credit to Escoffier, followed more in the footsteps of Nignon. They were known as André Pic, the debonair of Valence, Alexandre Dumaine, the magnificent of Saulieu, and Fernand Point, the marvellous of Vienne.

André Pic was a wonderful chef in the Lyonnais tradition who more than earned his three Michelin stars. But illness prevented him from founding a following, as might have been expected, and his restaurant declined. It needed, as we shall see, all the strength of his son to bring this great restaurant back to its eminence.

Alexandre Dumaine was a chef rather in the grand style. Born in 1895 at Digoin, by 1914 he was working at the Élysée Palace. Then he went to the Hotel de la Côte d'Or at Saulieu, which he and his wife, an adept publicist, made into one of the most famous hotels in France. After Curnonsky had given his verdict, the hotel became a place of smart gastronomic pilgrimage. Dumaine was a leading chef, but he lacked that ability to teach which might have made him of lasting importance.

Fernand Point, a great friend of both Pic and Dumaine, had an astonishing gift for inspiring young chefs and, for that reason, it was he of this talented trinity who was the one who became the father of the movement which has swept across France in the last twenty years.

In the history of cuisine, it is always tempting to attribute change to the character, will or taste of a particular chef. The reality, is, of course, very different. All change is a response to the demands of customers, to the developing climate in other fields and to the altered way of life of the general public.

So many things have happened in this century that it would have been quite impossible for cuisine to have remained static while everything else underwent so drastic a revolution. The motor car came and people suddenly discovered the regional cuisine which had so excited Curnonsky. Then all forms of transport improved and it was possible for a chef in Nice to cook the same dishes as a chef in Mâcon. Curnonsky's divisions became largely meaningless as *haute cuisine* incorporated and adapted regional dishes into its repertoire.

The change of pace, which Escoffier had anticipated, was bound to change the kind of food that people wanted to eat. No longer could they sit over lengthy meals, nor could they afford the time to take the exercise to work off a large meal or alternatively sleep it off. Meals had to be lighter and quicker. The chefs responded, as they had always done, to the challenge. They produced less creamy and less floury sauces. They produced simpler dishes which in turn meant concentrating even more on the quality of the ingredients. The public looked at the modified dishes, liked them, as they were bound to since they were what they needed, and called them *nouvelle cuisine*.

Of course they were nothing of the sort. We had been through it all before. Listen to the reverend Jesuit fathers, Brunoy and Bongeant, in 1739: 'Modern cuisine, built on the foundations of the old, with less fuss, less equipment and quite as much variety, is simpler, cleaner and perhaps more knowledgeable.'

Fifty years later, Grimod de la Reynière said, 'The dishes of the present day are very light, and they have a peculiar delicacy and perfume. The secret has been discovered of enabling us to eat more and to eat better, as also to digest more rapidly. . . . the new cookery is conducive to health, to good temper and to long life. There is no doubt we are healthier and better fed than our ancestors.'

Certainly cuisine develops, but rarely is anything new. Many of the dishes being served today, and hailed as new cuisine, are simply revivals of dishes which suited a moment in history when tastes coincided with ours. It is, as Escoffier observed, a question of fashion.

The one thing which is different is the universal camaraderie of the chefs. Soyer may have been the first who believed that chefs should share their experience, but it was a notion that took a long time to be generally accepted. Until very recently, chefs would disappear to a corner of their kitchens furtively to stir secret ingredients into their sauces. Today they are quite open with one another and the public. Escoffier may have improved the status of chefs in his kitchens, but there are chefs working now who were ashamed in their youth to admit their profession. The banding together of the chefs has enabled them to battle for a real freedom and to raise themselves from being near slaves to being stars. It is quite remarkable that, before the war, any restaurant was nearly always run by a *maître d'hôtel* who employed a chef; whereas the twelve chefs in this book are *chefs-patron*: the owners of their restaurants. If one man can be said to be responsible for this uniting of the chefs and their elevation to the position of jet-setters who travel the world displaying their talents, it is Paul Bocuse.

There may be those among them who favour commercialization and those who disapprove of it, those who stand aside from the publicity and those who court it, those who are more traditional and those who are less so—but this group of men, the three-star provincial *chefs-patron* of France, have brought a new life to their honourable profession.

Madame Point
Restaurant de la Pyramide
Vienne

Among the Roman monuments of Vienne, south of Lyon, is the stone pyramid which once marked the centre of the arena where chariot races were held. Two thousand years later it gave its name to France's most famous provincial restaurant, Fernand Point's La Pyramide, just along the boulevard which has been renamed in his memory. The old pyramid (in the picture, its tip is below the restaurant building) must have appealed to Point: it appeared on his menu and there were pyramidal pastries and butter moulds. He even referred to himself as a pyramid: 'My weight is confidential. But if you wish to obtain my volume, you have only to multiply the surface of my base by my height and divide by three.' Since Point's death, his wife, Marie-Louise, and the staff of La Pyramide have maintained the standards of cuisine which made Point the most influential chef of the century.

How many times, one wonders, had Archimedes climbed into his bath without noticing anything interesting about it. He was quite an old man by the time that morning came when he cried, 'Eureka!' For that matter, why Archimedes? There were plenty of other mathematicians of a cleanly disposition, who might have spotted the water's rising as they settled into their tubs; but they didn't.

Why Fernand Point? Of all the chefs who might have lifted *haute cuisine* from the rut of thirty years, he seems a most improbable candidate. He came from a modest enough background—he was almost pathologically insular, hating ever to be away from home and never even contemplating the possibility of travelling abroad. He had no interests other than food; he never read a book unless it were about cuisine. He saw no point in going to the theatre, saying, 'The theatre comes to me.'

Yet it is Fernand Point who will probably be regarded as the greatest chef of the twentieth century, certainly the chef who had the greatest influence on the style of French cooking. Within this half-shy, half-naive man lay that intangible coil of genius, which made him see those obvious things which others never saw, and led him to question what everyone else took to be settled.

Point was born in 1897. His father, Auguste, was the tenant of the hotel-buffet at Louhans station, where his grandmother and mother cooked reasonable food of a high standard. When Point was eighteen, it was clear that there was only one profession which would ever interest him, so he went to train in the kitchens of the Hotel Bristol in Paris. Madame Point today keeps in a cupboard in her office at La Pyramide, the certificates which he earned there and at each of the places in which he worked over the years—the Hotel Majestic in Paris where he was *saucier*, the Hotel Imperial in Menton, which gave him an additional special note of praise from the chef, Biglie, the Hotel Royal at Evian-les-Bains, where he was *poissonnier*.

In 1922, when his tour of training was done, it was plain that his talents were too great for a modest station-buffet. In any case, the railway company were being awkward and Auguste Point, with the proud spirit which his son inherited, told them he was off to Lyon. In the event, he couldn't find a restaurant at Lyon, but came upon a restaurant at Vienne. Here Auguste Point installed his son, Fernand, in the kitchen and La Pyramide was born. It was a good, sound house; but the decorations were of a gloomy nineteenth-century style favoured by the previous owner, there were no inside lavatories, indeed few comforts of any sort.

These drawbacks Point ignored, but by the time his father died in 1925, they had built fine new kitchens. Point was concerned only with what was put on the customers' plates and, over the next five years, he built up a wonderful reputation in the region and to some extent among gastronomic experts, but it was hardly a luxurious restaurant.

In 1930 he married. The young Madame Point quite simply said that she wouldn't go into the place while it was in such a state. They shut the restaurant, employed an architect to redecorate it entirely and to create a terrace and garden on the new land which Point bought beside the house. It was Point's marriage which finally liberated the singular originality

minute after being uncorked) with several friends.

Point disliked doing large dinners. 'A banquet can be a success, but it can never match the perfection of a meal prepared for a small number of people.' His fame, however, was such that Albert Lebrun, the President of France, came to Point for a banquet in July 1938. There were eight courses including *délices de St Antoine en feuilleté*, which turned out to be a pig's trotters, and the President, a lachrymose fellow, cried when he read the menu. The eating of it revived his spirits so that, as he got later and later for the opera he was due to attend in Vienne, he said, 'I would rather be damned *chez* Point— Faust can wait.'

Nevertheless, it is likely that Point preferred the Aga Khan, who was a regular visitor to La Pyramide. When he ordered a

dish of the famous *gratin de queues d'écrevisses*, Point would cook eight portions, knowing the holy man's appetite, and probably do two *volailles farcies de foies volailles et de foie gras* as well. That was the kind of living he understood.

Fernand Point was still a young man when the war started, but it was for him a particularly taxing time. He was essentially a man of peace and kindness. War and brutality revolted him possibly more than other people. It also meant restrictions which were wholly incompatible with everything on which his life was built.

He disliked feeding the occupying army and was constantly at odds with the authorities. One day a German officer arrived at 2.30, asking for lunch. Point said there was none. The officer insisted, offering him petrol coupons. Point pointed out that he had no car, and took the officer to the kitchen and showed him the empty refrigerators. As a result of this incident, the restaurant was shut down for six months. Point was threatened with imprisonment from which he was saved only by a protest from the Mayor of Lyon. Madame Point was forbidden to attend her father's funeral. Later he was charged with having black market butter, but once again escaped trial.

These strains were enough, but the Points added to them by working with the Resistance and helping escaped Allied soldiers and airmen. Very often, while Germans were eating in the restaurant downstairs, there would be as many as nineteen people hiding in the attics. For a sensitive man who loved his fellow men, these five years were an intolerable misery which undoubtedly contributed to his early death. After the war both Fernand Point and his wife were decorated by the British, and things gradually returned to some sort of normality.

For Point, things could never really be the same. The grand style which he enjoyed, was finished. He came to dislike 'progress.' His wife says that he would have hated to have lived today, but in the last ten years of his life he made perhaps his greatest contribution to cuisine. He had always said that it was the duty of chefs to teach and to train the young. He was a superb teacher, knowing exactly how to encourage enthusiasm while instilling the benefits of experience. He was one of the first to start breaking down the limiting tradition of secrecy among chefs, wanting them to share their knowledge rather than guard it jealously.

So it was that his philosophy came to dominate post-war cooking. First there was his old friend, Raymond Thuilier, the insurance man with whom he spent, he said, more hours talking about cooking than he ever had with a trained chef. Thuilier was the first of his protégées to win three Michelin stars. Then there were his pupils—Bocuse, Chapel, the Trois-gros brothers, Outhier, François Bise, the son of another old friend. Nearly half of the chefs who appear in this book were actually trained by Point, and thus *nouvelle cuisine* was born.

In 1955, at the age of fifty-eight, Point died, remarking an hour or two beforehand that he was so well looked-after that he would certainly die cured.

La Pyramide was too great a house to die with him and Madame Point had played too large a part in its creation to allow it to do so.

Today, it is still a great house fully deserving the three stars which it never lost. For seven years after Point's death, his *chef-de-cuisine*, Paul Mercier, carried on the exact traditions of Point. Then he too died. Madame Point was faced with a great problem. She was reluctant to bring in anyone from outside, so she decided to take a risk. She gave the kitchens to Guy Thivard, a young man of twenty-four, who had joined Mercier's brigade three years before. 'He trembled a lot,' Madame Point says, 'but now he has worked for sixteen years as the chef.'

Madame Point was always a wise women. She sees La Pyramide as a museum dedicated to her husband's memory, of which she is proud to be the custodian. She still works as she has always done, answering the telephone herself, receiving the customers, organizing the financial side of the business, choosing the wine and writing the menus every morning.

Every morning a waiter arranges a profusion of flowers around the restaurant and, during service, each waiter's tray bears a fresh bloom. In the kitchen, a photograph of Point hangs above the order board, always with fresh flowers beside it. Madame Point's salon displays mementoes of her husband—pictures, tributes, his model of the old Roman pyramid. The respect he inspired is summed up by Paul Bocuse: 'There was no-one like him. No-one.'

Madame Point deals with her world-wide correspondence, including reservations for months ahead, thank-you notes from grateful guests and letters from old and new friends. Every day she is sent flowers, often by other chefs. During World War II the Points' aid to the Resistance made them many British friends; to their letters she replies in English. At lunch with a friend in her salon, Madame Point awaits *sommelier* Louis Thomasi's verdict on the wine, although Thomasi considers that her knowledge of wine is greater than either his or Point's. One of Thomasi's morning chores is to groom her dog, Peggy.

Nowadays, she also keeps an eye on the kitchens. She works at least ten hours a day, but she enjoys it. 'I have always loved the contact with the clients, and I have seen so much and so many people like Sir Winston Churchill, the Queen of Holland, the Duke and Duchess of Windsor—always in such an agreeable setting.'

She is still marvellously elegant, belonging to the age of her husband's fame, wearing beautiful clothes and a particularly delicious perfume. She is somewhat saddened by the change of customers, regretting the loss of the aristocrats and sighing discreetly at those who leap up from the lunch table to make a business call on the telephone. She is very much the mistress of the house, fussing over every member of the staff, all of whom run to her with their problems or a cut finger.

She is always a realist. 'People come here for the food,' she says. And it is in this that the wisdom of her choosing Guy Thivard is apparent. She recognized in him a first-rate chef, but also someone with no overweening ambition. He was just the person to preserve the memory of Fernand Point, changing things only little by little, yet also of sufficient talent that, once his confidence was built up, he would be capable of taking over La Pyramide.

Guy Thivard's father was a labourer and his mother ran a little café-restaurant. Before coming to La Pyramide, he trained under Vignard at the same time as Alain Chapel. He is by temperament a traditionalist, believing that experimentation in cuisine has gone far enough and that it is time to consolidate. 'We must remain classic and stick to our specialization. The best thing would be to have just five specialities, but nowadays we have the problem of everyone copying our dishes.'

He is very conscious of the presence of Fernand Point whose photograph hangs in his kitchens. He talks of the many sleepless nights he spent worrying about the responsibility of taking over these famous kitchens. His hands twist nervously all the time he is talking. He did indeed change things very slowly. It was only a year ago that the dining-room was redecorated and that gas and electricity were brought in to replace the old coal ranges. At least half the dishes on the menu are still those of Fernand Point, although Thivard's dishes such as his *rouget* with a *Périgourdine* sauce and his *assiette marée* are adventurous and interesting.

He is a simple family man, who enjoys bicycling and mushrooming and taking his two teenaged sons to a football match. He is a craftsman who looks forward to the six-weekly meeting of the Toque Blanche—a group of seventy or eighty Lyonnais chefs who get together in one of the members' restaurants to discuss their trade.

Thivard, for all that he may not fit in with Point's picture of a chef, being thin and nervous and not even 'formerly fat', has fulfilled everything which Madame Point could have wished for. La Pyramide is still one of the great houses of France and, during her lifetime, it will remain so.

The Points had one daughter who takes no interest in the restaurant. La Pyramide will go one day to Guy Thivard, a family man with two sons which, in Madame Point's view is how it should be. The life-work of a man who did more than anyone else for his fellow chefs, will be entrusted to a chef.

Charles Barrier's glass-sided office, in the middle of his kitchens, is rather like a recording studio control-booth. From it he can talk to the staff by intercom and see what everyone is doing. The only disadvantage, he says, is that everyone can see what he is up to as well —in this case, scanning a trade paper in a lull. He is facing the original kitchen, beyond which are the dining-rooms; to the right is the new, larger kitchen. With all his paperwork meticulously sorted in the latest filing system, Barrier's approach is highly organized. It is also encyclopedic; he has instant recall of the ingredients and measures for almost all the recipes in the pile of cookery books he keeps in the office. The restaurant building was put up in 1953 to replace Barrier's bomb-site barrack hut; it is across the Loire from the centre of Tours.

Charles Barrier
Tours

The scene is a scorched hillside in the heat of the day. There are two men working, breaking stones. Not far from each other, naked save for their shorts and sunburns, they look alike. In their hearts they are very different. One is a convict working out his sentence. The other is a prospector looking for gold.

'That is a story of Saint-Exupéry,' says Charles Barrier. 'One must always analyse the spirit in which any act is done.' The spirit of Barrier is a very different one from that of all the other members of the *bande à Bocuse*. Apart from Thuilier, who stands alone, Barrier is the oldest of the chefs in this book. He belongs, in the circumstances of his upbringing and training, to the times when all but the greatest chefs were little regarded. While he welcomes the changes that have come over the world of gastronomy, they came too late to help him. He reached the pinnacle by a harder route, one which has left its mark on him. Now that the battle for the status of chefs is won, he looks at the world with a kind of embittered tolerance.

Barrier was born in 1916 into a large peasant family near Langeais in Touraine. He was the eighth child and his father was killed in the First War when Barrier was eighteen months old. For his mother life was 'not difficult, it was nearly impossible.' Poverty was general in the villages but the Barriers were the poorest and were known as the Barriers-Misère.

As soon as he was thirteen he had to go to work. 'I had no particular wish to be anything. It did not matter what I did, as long as it was a job in which I did not have to eat at home—a *charcuterie*, an *épicerie*, anything would have done.' This method of choosing a career has left Barrier with the view that

45

All produce enters the restaurant through the delivery door at the back. Nothing gets past this important check-point which is not of the quality or weight specified by Barrier in his telephone orders. The notice states that no deliveries can be accepted after 11.30am.

vocation is meaningless. The only thing which matters is work and success is the measure of the amount of work a person does.

At the thought of this, Barrier launches into a discourse on the irrelevance of vocation. 'What is the link between a man who became a priest a hundred years ago and a man who becomes one today? There is none. They believe different things and do different things. The *curé* of today is a business-man. Anybody can want to be a painter. Anybody might want to be Mozart, but it is no good wanting if you haven't the ability. The only exception is the genius, who is driven, but is predestined. Among chefs there have only been two geniuses —Carême and Escoffier. Nignon was a poet rather than a chef. Point was a purveyor of happiness.' The lecture then wanders on to cover visionaries, among whom he includes de Gaulle and, once again, Escoffier.

In the event, Barrier went to work in a *pâtisserie* in Langeais and, for better or for worse, the die was cast. After two years he went to Tours to work in a coaching-inn, Le Nègre, which stood where his restaurant now stands. Barrier must have been a strange boy, a mixture of nervousness and confidence. 'I could tell that the place was not well run and I told them that one day I would be *le patron*. They all laughed at me, of course, but I knew it.'

Perhaps not surprisingly, he did not stay very long at Le Nègre, but instead went to work in private houses, where he stayed for many years There was Madame Costelle, who owned a stud at Houdan. The chef there was Thuault, who had been chef to King Alphonso XIII of Spain's chamberlain. Then there was the Fouré family, who owned Messageries Hachette, and the Princess Murat. In these houses the life of a chef, however junior, was comparatively easy. 'It was like only cruising in a 300 kilometre-per-hour car.' The standard of cooking was immensely high, far better than in any restaurant. The work came only in spurts and there was both time and opportunity to learn the craft thoroughly. The range of ex-perience was very wide, because when there was a really big party, the staffs from neighbouring grand houses would lend a hand and Barrier saw many different chefs at work. The extravagance was unbelievable and the staff feasted on what-ever was left—and they always saw to it that there was plenty.

The only drawback was the low pay, which eventually de-cided Barrier to work in restaurants. He went to Lucas-Carton in Paris, the Hotel de Paris in Monte Carlo and the Carlton in Cannes. Under the old system, he was still a *commis*. No matter how great his talent and experience, there was no chance for a young man to rise in the kitchen hierarchy. It was depressing and in Barrier's case very lonely. 'At the Majestic we were twenty-four in the kitchen, but I was alone. I felt I was a victim of injustice, being so poor, being unable to get on. I suppose today I would have been a vandal, but we weren't vandals in those days, so I just withdrew and did not talk to anyone.'

This sensation of not being involved with his colleagues has lasted all his life and colours Barrier's view of his own training and of teaching in general. The important thing for Barrier is to be oneself. 'I suppose at school until I was thirteen I was a pupil, when I had no philosophy, but after that I was never anyone's pupil. The whole concept is limiting. You make a

As one of the older generation of chefs, Barrier's route to success was tough, and he affects a certain embittered resignation. But he likes nothing better than good conversation; for him this is part and parcel of the rapport he achieves through his cooking. 'Nothing done for others,' he says, 'is ever wasted.' The present restaurant stands on the site of an old farmhouse which became an *auberge*, Le Nègre, in 1880. The original building was destroyed soon after Barrier took it over in the Second World War, but he kept its name until he won his first star in 1955, when he changed the name to his own. But some of the old clients still know the restaurant as Le Nègre, so, while he does not particularly approve of it, he has kept the name on a plaque.

code, then the schools teach it. It leaves no room for people to be themselves. There is a medical school here in Tours where the young professor is so sure of his rightness that he kills talent. There are only three things to learn: first the technique, second how to organize and last human relations. So I think of no-one as my teacher, of no-one as having influenced me. The teacher does not elevate the pupil, nor does the pupil elevate the teacher. Life has been my professor, a ferocious master— for if a professor is too gentle, he is no good. For one gets nothing free,' he ends gloomily, but somehow benignly, settling back in his chair with his look of embittered optimism.

One may expostulate with him and mention Point and Bocuse—were they not teacher and pupil? 'It is possible,' he says, for, however definite his opinions, he always allows that he could, in this evanescent world, be wrong. 'But really Point was just the detonator. If there had been no trajectory to go on, Bocuse would never have got there.' And what were Barrier's

detonators? 'Kicks,' he says. Then he adds, 'If you were to ask me what was my principal quality, I would say courage. I am not sure, but I would say courage to be myself.'

Barrier is of course old enough to have been involved in World War II. He was in the army from 1939 until the fall of France, when he did various odd jobs, ending up in Tours as a railway-track maintenance man. One day in 1943, by chance, he ran into the woman who owned Le Nègre, where he had worked as a boy. She was looking for a tenant to run the place for her and offered it to him. Six months after he took the place over, the old *auberge*, originally a farmhouse, was blown up and reduced to rubble. The retreating Germans left behind a number of barrack huts, and the mayor offered Barrier one of these to re-erect on the site.

It was one of those perverse bits of fortune which seem to suit Barrier's temperament. They were hard times in any case. Food rationing and other restrictions made it hard to run a

restaurant. At night he used to go out and kill a calf or negotiate surreptitiously with farmers for supplies. His reputation in Tours was as much for having food to eat at all, as for how he prepared it. The locals did not in the least mind eating in a barrack hut, so grateful were they for anything of quality. But the owner of Le Nègre saw no future in her bomb-site, so Barrier was able to buy it for virtually nothing. His prediction that he would own Le Nègre had come true.

For ten years Barrier did nothing to the place, continuing to serve his customers in the barrack while gradually building his reputation as a chef. That, to him, was the truly important side of his business; the appearance of the place was always secondary. But, in 1953, he finally replaced the barrack hut with a modest-sized restaurant, where the tables were crowded together and the kitchens were in full view of the diners. The tables and the ovens had all been in one room in the old barrack and his clients had begged him not to disappear from sight in the new building. Within two years of the rebuilding, Barrier earned his first Michelin star and his second came four years later. As was his way, he ploughed all his profits back into the restaurant. After ten years, he was able to buy the house next door and build another, much longer dining-room. He got his third star in 1965. The name Le Nègre was virtually forgotten. Now it was Barrier.

There was never anything of the publicist about him, nor any ambition to succeed in any other way than by sheer hard work. 'I would never do advertisements or promotions of any kind. For me, it is a choice between money and freedom and I would always choose freedom. Money has no interest for me. I do not want two cars. One cannot be in two places at once so what is the use of two cars? My ambition was always focused on my profession—to be one of the best in the *métier* into which I was thrown.'

48

Barrier's youngest son, François, calls the orders over the kitchen intercom. He looks after the day-to-day running of the kitchens, while his father has overall charge. In the main kitchen chefs work at one of the two 'pianos'; almost all the pots and pans are copper. Within easy reach is the service area, where Barrier is giving a dish the final once-over under infra-red lamps. One of the kitchens' many modern features, these are less to keep the food warm than to bathe it in an attractive light—as well as to show up any imperfections. All being well, the food is on the table in half a minute or less.

Perhaps more than any of the other chefs, because of his independence and his singlemindedness, Barrier's success has depended solely on his abilities as a chef. There has been no element of luck, no advantage from situation, no boost from connections, no help from timing—only his cooking.

'I could say, though I might be wrong, that because cuisine has the image of he who made it, the quality which distinguishes my cuisine is honesty. If it is honest, then it is simple, because one cannot cheat with simple things. I have a great respect for produce. It was Curnonsky who said that cuisine is the taste of things. Marriages, the putting together of different things, are necessary, but they must be happy. I remember seeing an American chef putting paprika on a sole. I asked him what on earth he was doing; he said that he thought it looked nice. What a monstrous betrayal. Truffles and *foie gras* are another unhappy marriage. I used to think it was essential to put them together, that is what I had been taught. Then I realized there was nothing complementary about them. They do not go together, it is a *connerie*. Now I eat one or the other but never both.

'Another way to betray produce is to do too much. You must not put parsley on something if it makes no contribution. A client must know what he is eating. The worst thing is for someone to call over the headwaiter and ask him, "What did I eat?" I think it was Saint-Exupéry who said that art is not when there is nothing more that you can add, it is when there is nothing more that you can take away.

'There is too much talk of presentation of food. Ten years ago, when I was still evolving, I did elaborate presentations, as I thought it was important; now I think it is,' he pauses, '. . . *merde*. One must pay a little attention to presentation because the eyes are important. But I can tell you, in ten years' time Outhier won't be making his hedgehogs out of *foie gras*.

'When I said the eyes are important, though, I meant it. There are colours and patterns which repel you and others which make you hungry. When I chose the pattern for my plates I was very careful to see that it was not too strong. I had them tested for the kind of light they reflected. The manufacturers were very keen to have a second border round the edge, but I refused.

'Naturally, one must also respect the client's taste. It is no use to set an absolute form of one's own; I have learned a lot from my clients. When I was younger, if I had a client who said he wanted a well-cooked duck, I would have refused to do it. Now I would give it to him and shut my eyes. I am not in the business of rectifying wrongs. It is a question of age—I used to think I could teach people things; now I know that you cannot convince them of anything. One cannot do a cuisine to please everyone. When people come here, I often hear them talking about other chefs—people in restaurants always talk restaurants. They say quite rude things about other chefs. I know they are wrong, but it is never any good worrying about what people say. Each man has his own taste.

'That is one reason why I am not interested in criticism or praise. I am completely indifferent to what anyone says about me. Of course, though, nothing that concerns my clients is a matter of indifference.' (Barrier, for instance, re-organized the back entrance of the restaurant for the convenience of one of his

François Barrier displays the ingredients for a house speciality, *saumon frais en papillote*—fresh salmon steaks and a julienne of vegetable strips cooked in an envelope of buttered paper.

The julienne is mixed thoroughly before being cooked in butter.

A piece of the thickest part of the salmon is cut off.

The bone is removed and two steaks skinned and trimmed.

The steaks sit on a bed of vegetables on a sheet of cooking paper.

Generous-sized pieces of butter and a spoonful of fish *gelée* are added.

The final flavourings are salt, pepper and fresh tarragon leaves.

Starting to fold the *papillote* around the salmon and vegetables.

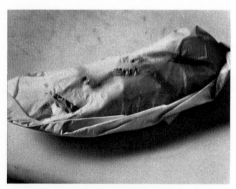

About twelve folds of the *papillote* seal the juices in while cooking.

After fifteen minutes in a hot oven the package is ready to cut open.

Serving up: the tender fish is carefully lifted onto the plate. . .

. . .followed by the julienne, impregnated with buttery salmon juice.

Ready to eat: a simple but happy 'marriage' of the best produce.

regular customers who arrives for dinner in a wheelchair.)

He rambles on, responding to the briefest question with an elaborate answer to the question itself, a digression or two into some quite removed philosophical points and ending with a world-weary reflection in the tones of a more acid Polonius.

It is sometimes hard to believe that this amiable and ruminative, if rather reserved and distant, man can be the one who so doggedly built up a great restaurant, working at the beginning at least eighteen hours a day and even doing the washing-up. It is when he guides you round his kitchen that you recognize that here is a craftsman who has questioned every precept and re-examined every automatic action of his craft until he was satisfied that he could not improve on it.

The kitchens cover at least as great an area as the dining-rooms. They may look rather old-fashioned when compared with the gleaming modernity of those at Troisgros or Pic, but they have long had many features still thought of as novelties.

Everything is essentially practical. Barrier's office, actually in the kitchen, is a glassed compartment where he can do his paperwork and keep an eye on what is happening at the same time. There are separate cold rooms for bread, soft fruits and vegetables, meat and for *pâtisseries* and ices. (Barrier was one of the first chefs to abandon the general storage room.) The fish, which arrives fresh from Brittany or the Atlantic coast every morning, goes into a high-humidity cold drawer, packed with specially rounded ice cubes which do not pierce or pinch the fishes' skin. Above the fish drawer is a marble top which is graded in temperature from very cold to cool. Another cold cupboard is filled every morning with the day's supply of champagne, white wine, spirits and soda water. There are two sets of ovens, one set for the *rôtissiers* and *poissonniers*, who are

A soup of chicken wings with *quenelles* of chicken is served in an unusually shaped bowl—deep, and with its own lid, so that it holds heat well. Chilled strawberry cake, trimmed to reveal a frieze of half-strawberries embedded in cream, is the centre-piece of the sweet trolley. It is topped by an intricate chocolate filigree in a freehand display of the *pâtissier's* decorative skills. A bottle of local Loire red wine, Chinon, may accompany pigeon cooked in a brown sauce and served with baby turnips and garlic cloves.

supervised by Barrier's son, François, and the other for the *entremetiers* and *sauciers*. The ovens are fitted with convectors to maintain an even temperature.

Now, at sixty-two, Barrier does less of the heavy physical work. He has handed over much of the execution to his son, while keeping a firm hand on the organization. One might suppose that his achievements have brought contentment, but it is not so; the way has been too hard. What Barrier has arrived at is a resigned tolerance.

'I am a bit older now and each age has its charms. People used to be more acid with me, but now they dare a little less. I used to encourage the legend about me that I am an aloof type. People have never been free with me because I have always put up a fence, to preserve myself for the future. I never get angry with people, but, by the same token, I have never been great pals with anyone.'

Barrier married in 1945 and had three sons. Now, although Madame Barrier works in the restaurant every day and they eat their meals there together in the smaller dining-room, he lives in the countryside outside Tours, while she has a flat not far from the restaurant. His eldest son, after going to the hotel schools of which he disapproves, runs his own restaurant at Niort, some two hundred kilometres away. In some ways, the father is glad of this, because more than one son in the kitchens, he maintains, leads to strife among the women-folk. His middle son, who seems to have been his favourite, was killed some years ago. François, the youngest, who works with him, is, in his father's opinion, too dependent on him and not given to flights of imagination.

By nature, Barrier is a solitary man. 'I live in the country not for the country itself, but for the silence. François likes skiing and fast cars but I have no hobbies of that sort. I am interested in photography and amateur film-making, but I have never had time. I thought about shooting and bought a dog and a gun and a licence, but when I looked at the birds they were too pretty to shoot. The one thing that has given me

It takes at least three years to grow a good asparagus bed. Barrier's grower is Ernest Raffault, a German, who having served in France during the war and returned to live there in 1947, has found acceptance among the locals. His white asparagus grows well in the sandy Touraine soil. The asparagus cutting-tool digs about twelve inches deep into the soil and cuts off the stalk just above the fibrous roots at its base. This done, the stalks are collected into a trimming-box and sliced to a standard length of about ten inches. In the res-taurant, the stringy outside layers are removed with a potato-peeler towards the thick end. This is snapped off and with it come any remaining fibres. *Chez* Barrier, asparagus stalks are cooked flat, rather than vertically.

satisfaction is literature. I have always read every day, mostly philosophy: Machiavelli, Saint-Exupéry, Sartre and Genou (though he is more poetry). Politics I do not care for. Marx discouraged me; he is too full of contradictions. Politics are never exact. I read not for style, but for sincerity. If a thing is too perfect, I don't like it. I may be wrong . . . .

'I have done some writing—a collection of my thoughts. I could have published it, but I didn't want to; it was too private, the kind of thing understood by someone you love and who loves you.

'I used to believe in God. At one time I needed that kind of morphine, but no longer. I am a Freemason, because I do believe in fraternity. It is not possible, for instance, for me to be influenced in friendship by what people do. It is another reason why I am not interested in criticism or praise. We must respect those around us.

'Lawgivers have a grave responsibility; law should be advice, not prohibition. If I were to pass a law it would be to advise people to bind themselves one to another. It is never wasted to do things for other people. When I am cooking, I imagine the pleasure I am going to give to someone—seeking pleasure for oneself is just masturbation. I may be wrong, but I would say that I am a humble man; and humility is an inexhaustible source of joy.'

Barrier is not wrong; he is a humble man, whose needs are simple and whose outlook may seem narrow in some ways. 'I have no interest in travel as I am not curious about what happens far off. If I had not been a chef, I would like to have been a peasant. I think, perhaps, they live closest to the truth, for nature is never dishonest.'

A narrow perspective, but livened by a breadth of imagination. 'The happiest day of my life was the day I became a *Meilleur Ouvrier de France*. I proved something, not for others, but for myself.'

To peel a carrot can be interesting, Barrier says. It is a question of the spirit in which it is done.

François Bise

L'Auberge du Père Bise
Talloires

The necessary ingredients which make up a superb restaurant, as opposed to merely a good restaurant, are as indefinable and as complex as those which are needed to make an attractive human character. There are no rules. In the same way that a lovable person may be ugly or selfish, so a restaurant may be indifferently decorated or exaggeratedly expensive and yet make us supremely happy. It is never for one thing, not even the food, that we like a restaurant.

The food itself can be Bocuse's Lyonnais-rooted cuisine or Outhier's refined cuisine of polish, but on its own it will not be enough. Even the *Guide Michelin* has never given three stars to a restaurant just for the food, without considering its other qualities. A restaurant can be grand like the Baumanière or homely like Barrier, it can be formal like La Pyramide or informal like Pic. The service can be impersonal as at Le Moulin de Mougins or chatty as at Eugénie-les-Bains. There can be *sommeliers* as there are at Chapel or none as there is at L'Auberge de l'Ill.

In a two-star restaurant, other than one of those rare ones which is destined for triple stardom, there is never any doubt that there is lacking that last magical measure of excellence which would raise it to the ultimate greatness. Often, it would be impossible to say what precisely it was that was missing, just as it is impossible to say exactly what finely judged combination of circumstances it is that makes a particular restaurant one of the eighteen finest in France.

Paul Bocuse, who once said that the best meal he had ever eaten in his life was at Chapel, maintains that if he takes every

Seen from Lake Annecy, with
snow-covered Alps on the horizon,
L'Auberge du Père Bise has the
most scenic setting of all the three-
star restaurants; the chalet building
and trimmed plane trees combine
to give a slightly Japanese look. In
summer, goldfinches and other
birds peck about among the outside
tables. The restaurant has its own
quay for diners arriving by boat.
Madame Bise, a worthy successor
to her late mother-in-law, is responsible for the restaurant's smooth
organization.

57

aspect into account—the setting, the dining-room, the food, the service and all the other details which contribute to our enjoyment of a restaurant—then the greatest of all is L'Auberge du Père Bise at Talloires.

In the beginning, there was only the setting, which must be one of the most beautiful for any restaurant and is certainly the most spectacular among all the three-star establishments. The restaurant lies on the shore of Lake Annecy, according to François Bise, the purest lake in Europe. Round it rise the mountains which are the foothills of the Alps. The village of Talloires is small and pretty, little more than a few houses, originally occupied by lake fisher-folk, together with some half-dozen hotels.

It was here, at the water's edge, that François Bise's grandfather, in 1901, bought a small chalet, which he turned into a restaurant. He was a *maître d'hôtel*, who had worked on the pleasure steamers which plied up and down the lake. In the tradition of the day, his wife worked in the kitchen while he looked after the dining-room. The little place prospered, for this was very much the area for tourism at the turn of the century, before people took to going to the sun and the sea. Grandfather Bise's clients were largely the British, who came over from Aix-les-Bains, and even today many of the most faithful customers come from Britain. At the same time it was a simple place run on cautious lines. One day one of the customers told Monsieur Bise that he was a painter and asked if he could pay for his lunch with a painting. Monsieur Bise considered the matter

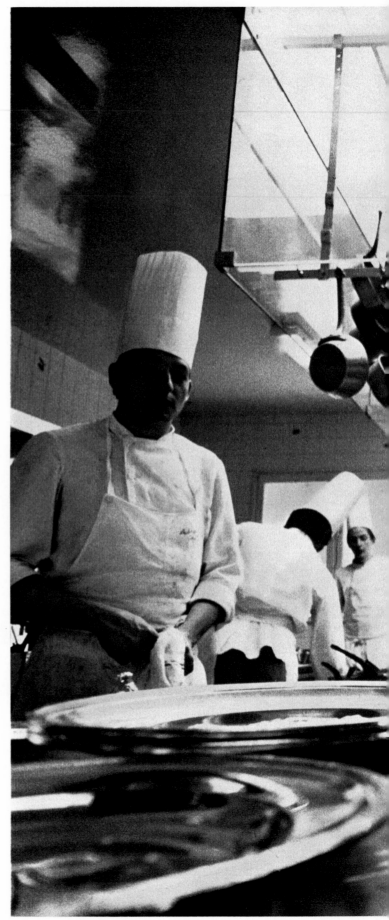

In the days of Mère and Père Bise, it was Marguerite Bise who was in charge of the cooking and Marius Bise who managed the rest of the business. With the son and daughter-in-law, these roles are reversed. François Bise is calling an order in the kitchen's service area. The kitchen, which was converted to gas and electricity only in 1970, is quiet and cool. The 'piano', with a copper *batterie* hung above it, is in the centre, beneath tall skylights which make air-conditioning unnecessary. In all, the restaurant has about forty-five staff, who can serve about 125 covers.

briefly, refused—and Cézanne had to find the cash instead.

Bise had two sons, Marius and Georges. Georges opened his own hotel, Le Cottage, on the opposite side of the road. But it was Marius, who came to be known as Père Bise, who was to bring real fame to Talloires. He was a man cast rather in the same mould as his great friend, Fernand Point. He was large, boisterous and given to drinking great quantities of champagne. Indeed, when the two men were together, they often got through six or seven bottles between them during the day. There was, however, one great difference. Père Bise was not a chef. He continued the pattern set by his father; he looked after the dining-room, while his wife worked in the kitchen. The great dishes associated with the name of Père Bise, the *gratin de queues d'écrevisses* and the *poularde braisée crème d'estragon*, were the creations of his wife. They took over the restaurant in 1928. By 1931, in the same year as Point, they had achieved three stars and it seems likely that Mère Bise was the first woman to earn this distinction. They were a formidable couple. Père Bise was a swashbuckling figure of exuberant charm, given to bursts of temper. Michel Marucco, now the headwaiter, joined the staff as an odd-job boy at the age of thirteen. He well remembers the savage kicks he would get for any misdemeanour. In many ways, Bise was a playboy, loving fast cars and women and spending much of his time fishing. At the same time, he was a genius with the clients, knowing exactly how to please them and flatter them, without any trace of unctuousness—an intelligent and intuitive man.

He was extremely particular about produce. Every supplier knew him for an expert, whose confidence it was hard to win. It took many years before he gave up tasting the butter each morning when it arrived, until he was satisfied that it accorded with his standards and that he could rely on the dairyman's judgement.

The only person he was frightened of was his wife. Whenever he bought a new car, which was quite often, he would hide it at the far end of the garden, forbidding any of the staff to mention it to her. They always did, for in her different way, Mère Bise was quite as frightening as her husband.

In the kitchen, she was a martinet keeping a sharp eye open for any signs of short-cuts or automatic habits. 'Here,' she would shout, 'we don't work like an assembly line at Citroën.' She worked harder than most men, not only doing the cooking,

A winding road from the main village of Talloires leads down to the Auberge, at the end of a promontory reaching out of the lake's eastern shore. Annecy, one of Europe's purest mountain lakes, is the home of the delicately flavoured *omble chevalier* and trout, as well as the gudgeons which Alain Chapel, 100km away at Mionnay, uses for *amuse-gueule*. *Omble* and trout are sometimes cooked together (the dish on the left has a full-sized *omble* and a few smaller ones in front of a trout). By itself, a smallish *omble* might be garnished with herbs and poached in a fish *bouillon*. Trout will often be simply cooked in butter *(truite meunière)*.

During service, Madame Bise patrols the spacious dining-room, making sure that each course arrives as soon as the diners are ready for it. The dining-room, with its unusually patterned beam ceiling, gives a superb view of the lake Madame Bise is highly knowledgeable about wines and is in charge of the buying and looking after the cellars.

but all the flowers and checking all the cleaning. She would be down in the kitchen at 6am to scrub the floor. When her daughter-in-law, Charline, the wife of François, arrived in the family, she was shocked that Mère Bise should perform this menial task. So she got up at 5am to do it for her. When Mère Bise came down at six, she looked at the floor and said, 'If I had got up at five to do the floor, I would have done it better.'

They made an admirable team. Mère Bise virtually never left the house, dedicating her whole life to the kitchens. Père Bise provided the panache which attracted customers of style. Together they created a restaurant which, at one time, was perhaps the most famous in the world.

Of their two sons, it was François who was chosen to become a chef. Naturally, he was sent to train with Père Bise's great friend, Fernand Point. He worked at La Pyramide for three years and Madame Point remembers him as one of Point's quieter but most gifted pupils. After that he went to Paris, to Larue, and came back to join his mother in the kitchens at Talloires in 1951, bringing with him his wife, Charline, whose parents ran a little restaurant in St Germain-en-Laye. In the 1960s many misfortunes overtook the family. In 1965, Mère Bise died, then François' brother, René, in 1968, and finally Père Bise himself, later in 1968.

François Bise was left with an awkward inheritance. He was landed with a restaurant which had one of the best reputations in France. In both the kitchens and the dining-room he had staff picked by his parents, set in their ways. His customers were waiting to see whether he was capable of maintaining the standards they were accustomed to expect.

He had, however, two great advantages. The first was his rather placid nature and traditional cast of mind. The second was his wife, who was, by her nature, admirably cut out to maintain the authoritative style of her in-laws' management of the business.

François, having been trained by Point, was very much concerned to take advantage of the produce of the region. Foremost among this is the fish from the lake—the *omble*, which is not found in any other part of France, and the exquisite trout. There is in Lake Annecy a superabundance of freshwater shrimps which give to the fish a delightful pink colour and a wonderfully rich flavour. François' own preference is for the trout. He has had special tanks built behind the restaurant, where he keeps the *omble*, the trout and the *écrevisses* so that they are absolutely fresh. His meat is local and Bresse is not far for the chickens. It is the country for raspberries and wild strawberries. On the mountainsides grow herbs and mushrooms. With the exception of the lobsters, nearly everything comes from the region and François' menu reflects this, so that in many ways his cuisine is one of the most regional of all the chefs'. Bise gets quite aggravated by the talk of *nouvelle cuisine*, which he regards as a passing fancy. 'Most of what people call new is merely a series of variations on recipes in old cook-books. Things go out of fashion and then come back. There are salads being served today which are really centuries old.'

He says that he has stayed traditional, because he sees no point in betraying the old cuisine. Why suppress something, which was in its own way perfect?

The transition from Mère and Père Bise to their son and daughter-in-law has in some ways been easy and in others hard, because a number of the staff have worked there for many years. Michel Marucco, the headwaiter, who has worked at Bise since he started as an odd-job boy at thirteen, regards his job as a 'marvellous *métier*.' He believes in making guests feel welcome and that they like respect—but not obsequiousness. 'A "bear" arrived the other day; when he left, he was happy.' Madame Bise orders produce over the phone; next morning, Marucco takes the van around the various suppliers, rejecting any produce which is not up to standard. It is deliberate policy at Bise not to have separate wine-waiters; they think that it is easier for the customers to talk to the same person about wine and food.

63

None of this means that he is stagnating. He regards it as essential to search all the time, while never straying from the accepted foundations. His *salade riche* and his *coquilles St Jacques*, marinated in lemon juice and virtually raw, are examples of dishes which would be hailed elsewhere as being ultramodern. He has a great affection for Bocuse, with whom he has travelled to Japan, for Vergé and Chapel and the other chefs. 'They lure me out of my corner.'

Much of his strength comes from not being lured out of his corner too often, for by sticking at home and sticking to the traditions, he has overcome the loss of his father's ebullient personality, which could have meant disaster.

Meanwhile, Charline Bise takes care of practically everything apart from the kitchen. When she was younger, she was extremely beautiful. Today she dresses rather severely, often in black, her hair is gathered tightly back from her face and her

The menu at Bise proclaims their policy of 'always cooking with fresh and natural produce.' The emphasis is on a limited range of perfectly cooked dishes. Pears gently poached in syrup and cream are served with *framboise* (raspberry *purée*)—simple enough, but superbly tempting to the eye as well as the palate. Hand-made chocolates are prepared on the premises by the *pâtissier*. *Carré d'agneau* (rack of lamb) serves two people. Among the suggested *hors d'oeuvres* is *gelée de lapereau*, a jellied *pâté* of young rabbit. An example of the care given to preparation is the carrot balls which are scooped out of whole carrots. *Homard grillé* is simply served with parsley and a decoratively cut half of lemon.

Lapérouse and La Mère Brazier, where he concentrated on the more strictly traditional aspects of his art.

In 1959 Bocuse returned home to face a considerable challenge. His father's little hotel, with its nine tables and nine bedrooms, had been but roughly restored after war-time damage. His rather improvident grandfather had sold not only the original family restaurant, but also the trading name of Bocuse. From this unpromising foundation, how was Bocuse to become the greatest chef in France?

Of course, the answer to this question belies the charges of sensationalism to which his present eminence has exposed him. No amount of mere showing off could be a substitute for the sheer hard work, the unremitting attention to detail and (not least) the ability to organize and inspire a staff, which were needed to establish Bocuse as a star.

Talent he had, but it was solid application, not histrionics, which made him a *Meilleur Ouvrier de France* and won Bocuse his first Michelin star in 1961—just two years after his father's death. As with Outhier, this first instalment of success merely spurred Bocuse to renewed effort, leading to his second and third stars in 1962 and 1965.

But was an infinite capacity for taking pains the whole story of Bocuse's success? Most chefs are hard-working, after all. Perhaps, then, it is in his personal philosophy of food that we can discover the special ingredients of his greatness.

His approach to his calling is one of intense, romantic feeling, rooted in respect for tradition and simplicity, with a strong patriotic pride—and, curiously enough, a certain modesty. When Bocuse talks about cooking he often draws on music for his similes. One analogy between cooking and music is that both the finished dish and the performance depend on an element of improvisation which are never part of the recipe or score. When this goes right, the results are magical. It is the magic that matters. 'For that reason,' he says, 'I would never use electricity. It has no magic. I have gas and the spit because a flame is alive. How could you be a blacksmith with no flame? Think what a poor fellow the Devil would be if all he had was electricity....'

Fernand Point's great contribution to French cuisine was to rescue it from becoming, for example, like Indian food, in which the ingredients are relatively unimportant and spices, sauces and masking tastes become paramount. Under Point, Bocuse learned the true value of produce. Far from claiming novelty, Bocuse regards his mission as encouraging a return to the natural, intrinsic taste of produce, and the chef's role as being, at best, the enhancement of that taste by ingenuity and subtle skill. He maintains that a great chef is one who finds two new dishes in a lifetime, and that the number of chefs who leave a mark on the history of cuisine is strictly limited. In his view, a truly great chef is one who, like Point, inspires a generation of pupils. 'People speak of Point and Dumaine in the same breath. You hear of the pupils of Point—*les petits Points*—but never of the pupils of Dumaine.' And he adds, for good measure, 'You may one day hear of the pupils of Troisgros or Chapel, but never of Thuilier.' Bocuse's own pupils are a source of immense pride to him. They number about eighty, and include four two-star and four one-star chefs—among them not only Frenchmen.

For Bocuse, the integrity of French cuisine is absolute, and

On their way to the upstairs dining-room, diners get this view of Bocuse's kitchen, where he can switch on extra lighting to improve the quality of their snapshots. Polished pans, trays and utensils frame Madame Bocuse as she pre-pares the daily cheese tray on top of the kitchen's plate-warmer. To the right of her, a junior hurries to the *garde-manger*, where meat and fish are prepared for the chefs. Cooking is done on the 'piano' behind her. The open glass door on the left fronts the oven where Bocuse's celebrated truffle soup acquires its golden topping. This stylish kitchen reflects Bocuse's view that kitchens should be spacious. 'Architects destroy *cuisine bourgeoise*—they make kitchens the size of pocket handkerchiefs.'

Bocuse has a taste for rough peasant cooking, so he makes *pot-au-feu*, albeit on a grand scale, for a family lunch. Into the pot go rib bones, shin and other cuts of beef; veal shin, bacon, a truffled chicken, marrow bones, carrots, onions, garlic, leeks, heads of celery, turnips, potatoes, tomatoes, green beans and cabbage, with water, seasoning and a *bouquet garni*—herbs wrapped in the leaves of leeks. Some three hours after the dish started it is ready to be served, on this occasion to Bocuse, a granddaughter, his daughter, his wife and his mother. The soup is a side dish, in a tureen. If it were a bigger party, turkey, pheasant, partridge, neck of lamb and oxtail might be added to the pot. *Pot-au-feu* is cooked with more than one meal in mind, and its stock is valuable for other dishes.

he rejects all suggestions of foreign influence. (It is simply not true that he serves raw food in Japanese style, although he might produce fish marinated in lemon juice.) Cooking, he says, is not influenced; it is dictated by the land. 'Have you ever noticed that good cuisine goes with the places where there are vineyards? That is why I do not like Chinese food. What can you *drink* with it?'

His mother claims that as a child Bocuse used to sulk if given plain ham rather than some elaborate dish. But his tastes are really quite simple. He says he can make a good meal on a sardine. If he cooks for a friend rather than for clients, he will conjure up a simple peasant dish. 'My dream is to have a chicken from the yard and a leek from my garden. That is what the stage-coach hotels had—the produce and the wine of the region, literally the "table of the host." If you have guests you want them to sit in your kitchen and dip their fingers in the food. In many ways that is the kind of restaurant I would like to run, a little one where people eat in the kitchen.'

Bocuse stresses the importance of knowing the whole range of techniques of a craft. 'How many *charcutiers* today know how to kill a pig, or butchers how to kill a calf? They just sell them . . .' and, 'Apprentices in the kitchens today are too specialized. There would be no point in giving most apprentices a live eel. They would probably just shriek. But a real chef knows how to make a cheese, how to cure a ham, how to clean a frog.'

To Bocuse, eating is to do with enjoyment, not with tricks or fancy embellishment. 'A meal starts quietly and ends in liveliness—unless it is a family meal to discuss a will, when it will end in a fight! A meal is a poem; when we give a meal with Roger Vergé, it is like a concert.' Enjoying food is part of living life to the full. That is why Bocuse has no time for Michel Guérard's slimming meals. 'Life is too short for *cuisine minceur* and for diets, it is for living. Dietetic meals are like an opera without the orchestra.'

One has only to see Bocuse eating to realize that his love of food is entirely natural and unaffected. It is the one activity which actually stops him talking. He attacks a bowl of soup with great zest, the level sinking rapidly as his spoon flashes up and down, every part of him relishing every mouthful.

Any craft remains unchanged, in essentials, so long as its purpose remains the same. Modern man still has an appetite: he likes to eat well once a day. Accordingly, Bocuse points out that there is nothing new in cuisine. The difference lies in the cooks, who, instead of being slaves who never emerged from the kitchens, are now people who have been to school and who have copies of Apicius on their shelves. 'Did you know Apicius talked of *nouvelle cuisine* in the first century AD? Also, the French have given up worrying about motor cars and are now turning to the kitchen garden again. All this makes for one thing—a greater honesty in cuisine.'

Such are the attitudes and the spirit of the man, which have enabled him to build up a great restaurant from humble beginnings. The building is improbably situated, a matter of yards from a railway line. Every so often when a train goes by the whole restaurant shakes. Immediately below the dining-room windows a busy road runs along the banks of the Saône. Before it was built up the situation must have been delightful;

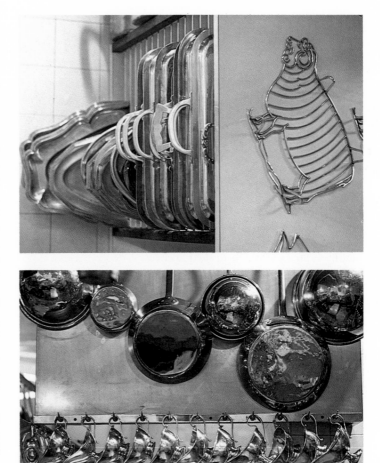

A sheep fashioned from metal makes the trivet for a lamb dish. Other caricatures have similarly appropriate assignments on the serving tables. Bocuse's kitchen is rich in highly-polished displays of pots and pans, trivets and trays, sauceboats and ladles. He is replacing the classical copper pans for cooking in favour of nickel. 'They are beautifully heavy, they need no lining and they last.'

today, with the encroachment of Lyon, it is distinctly suburban.

The house itself is not pretty, despite the alterations Bocuse has made as his business has prospered. It has ended up looking awkward. The downstairs dining-room is in two halves, one being the original restaurant of the old house, aggrandized by a huge, armorial stone fire-place with a spit, and decorated with rather florid wall-coverings. A section with long glass windows has been added to make it bigger, and this section matches the other half of the dining-room, which has somehow the air of a well done-up old paddle-steamer. There are delightfully comfortable chairs, some fine pieces of furniture and then bursts of a different taste—old beams, some of them painted in a Bavarian style, 1930s mirrors, and two huge portraits of Bocuse, one making him look like an emperor-chef painted by Annigoni.

The upstairs restaurant is perhaps more elegant, but is used mainly as an overflow from the lower room. Nevertheless, there is in all the building an atmosphere of friendly industry. It is a house of *grande cuisine*, yet not pompous or forbidding.

The mistake is to suppose that this was achieved by anything but the hard work of a dedicated artist. The flamboyancy only blossomed after his success. The myriad pictures of Bocuse going around the markets of Lyon are not just for show. He still goes there every morning, not to pose but to choose and buy for himself. It may be that people fly from Spain just to lunch in his restaurant and he may enjoy the thought of that, but in many respects it is a much simpler place than one might have supposed. Bocuse assures you that he thinks of it as a *restaurant de route*, used by people driving north or south. He encourages drivers and does not mind if they only eat one course and drink only water. 'One can make a very good lunch drinking water.' There is no formality; there are no rules: 'Red wine goes perfectly well with fish. It is silly to drink *pastis* with food, because it kills the palate. But it's up to the customer. I suppose I would rather people drank Coca-Cola, which harms only them, than smoked a pipe, which can annoy others. Here it is like an opera. Some people may prefer one act rather than another. Why should everyone have the same tastes? What I make are the things I like.'

Such unpretentiousness is at variance with the popular picture of the man, but it is confirmed by the reality of the restaurant. However, it is in the kitchens that one always sees the true character of any chef. Bocuse's are the only three-star kitchens where the décor is more than functional. The ovens have on them a large brass B, the ceiling is painted red and there are strips and spots and fancy lights. The walls are hung with old-fashioned scales and ancient knives. Many of the copper pots are as much for decoration as for use. It is a kitchen of style, in which taste is far more in evidence than in the restaurant.

Even more important is Bocuse's relationship with his staff. No kitchen can work without a team who give unquestioning loyalty to their leader. There, for twelve years, has been Roger Jaloux, the *chef-de-cuisine*, himself a *Meilleur Ouvrier de France*, a man who could set up on his own and prosper, yet who prefers to remain with Bocuse. There is no staff more loyal, or, for that matter, better cared for. As a result, the kitchen ambience is imbued with a quiet assurance which is almost tangible.

Yet there is no complacency. When Bocuse is in his kitchens

'*La volaille!*' Bocuse is angry. The chickens have been incorrectly prepared; the legs have been cut too short, the neck not close enough. Bocuse gathers his team to demonstrate how the job should be properly done. But he trusts his staff and knows how to delegate. When he is away, specialists run each department and the feeling of his pursuit of perfection pervades the entire kitchen. He is a formidably successful teacher: four of his ex-pupils cook in two-star restaurants, four more are one-star chefs.

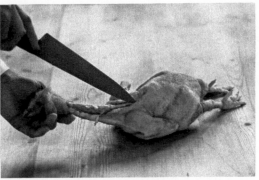

The right way to do it. Turn the chicken onto its breast and slit the skin on the back of its neck.

Cut off the head, then the neck where it joins the body, leaving a long flap of neck skin.

Make an incision big enough to allow the entrails to be removed. Trim the wingtips.

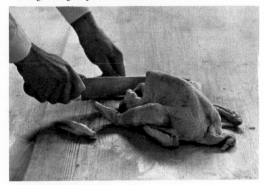

Cut off the feet well below the knee joints so that the skin and tendons will not shrink in cooking.

The Abbaye, the original restaurant
of the Bocuse family, (sold by his
grandfather; rebought by Bocuse)
is now used on *jours de fêtes*—
which may be a party for the
children of Bocuse's staff, a wedding
or the launch of a new car. The
prize of Bocuse's collection of steam
organs dominates this room. Now
electrically operated, it can be made
to play various national anthems,
depending on the occasion. Festive
food may be served from the
Abbaye's spit, where two whole
sheep can be cooked at once, over a
fire of faggots—bundles of chopped
wood—rather than logs, which burn
more slowly. There are further
spits in both of the restaurant's
dining-rooms, and a chicken cooked
on one of them may be brought to
the table on a dish containing
glowing embers from the fire.

Visitors are met by a bellboy bearing the name 'Paul Bocuse' on his cap, who opens car doors and takes coats. Bocuse's name also appears on the plates, in a pattern designed by his grandfather in 1912. Madame Bocuse does the flowers and the wine glasses are by Baccarat, the most notable French glassmaker, 'for the glass serves as a remembrance of the wine.' Another remembrance is match-books: 50,000 a year are taken from the bowl in reception.

the staff keep a wary eye on him—for he may suddenly pounce upon a man who is cutting up a chicken and do it himself at twice the speed, just as he can perform any task in the kitchen better than anyone else. I remember the first time I visited his kitchens he said, 'Look at that sauce, it's too salty!' A man who can *see* that a dish is over-seasoned is surely a phenomenon and one who can command the respect of any staff. The sheer force of the man's personality still reigns in his absence—herein lies the answer to those who criticize his excursions. No doubt such carping will continue while Bocuse remains the public figure that he is, but I have yet to hear that the standards of his cuisine have ever varied.

Thus it is that popular mythology has tended to eclipse what should be the obvious truth about Bocuse—that everything rests on a solid basis of sheer talent and application. There are no short cuts to stardom in *haute cuisine*.

All the same there is certainly no greater self-publicist than Bocuse. There seems no end to his activities and still less of an end to how much one hears of them. Eagerly he will press into your hand the postcards he has had made from the magazine covers which have carried his singular features in a dozen countries. He will show you any number of press cuttings about himself. His face beams from advertisements for mineral waters. Wine bottles bearing his name sit on shelves in London and New York. He has a half-share of a Tokyo restaurant and another in Osaka. Bocuse is a one-man multi-national business and a television star to boot.

'While the tap is running,' he says 'I might as well sit under it'—and the fact is he adores every minute of it. The exuberant, boyish enjoyment of this natural showman is aptly symbolized by the huge collection of fairground steam organs which he has lovingly assembled over the years. These are housed in the Abbaye—the original Bocuse family restaurant, which he naturally bought back and uses on *jours de fêtes*.

Behind the panache, the self-publicity, is a disinterested desire to spread the gospel of French cuisine—and an unselfish readiness to share the credit for it with his *confrères*. Bocuse's demonstration trips are rarely solo acts; usually he takes Roger Vergé, or another chef. 'I go to publicize French cooking and to spread the name of Bocuse,' he says airily; but it is the first half of the statement which is truly important to him. Similarly, he really meant it when he said, on being made a *Chevalier de la Légion d'Honneur* that he was accepting it on behalf of French cuisine. The pleasure which his fame gives him, while undeniable, is in fact the simple pleasure which fame gives to anyone. He says that his profession is the best passport in the world, and tells the story of a friend who, when travelling in California, was let off a speeding fine because he knew Bocuse. 'The doors now open more readily for chefs than for bankers.'

Bocuse's fondness for gesture, and his real generosity, characterize his daily dealings, with friends and strangers alike. Out one day, he happened to overhear an argument between two women, one saying to the other 'If I were rich, I'd bet you a dinner at Bocuse that I am right.' He could not resist inviting them to dine. If Bocuse sees a young couple in his restaurant who obviously understand food, he is quite likely to give them their dinner gratis. Such public generosity is matched by many thoughtful, private kindnesses, informed by an instinct for others' needs—which, indeed, may be part of the natural make-up of a chef. In fact, he loves people, and declares that the thing he most hates is to hurt anyone. 'In the short passage through life, why should we hurt others?'

Bocuse is a prankster, whose practical jokes are legion (in this, too, he is not alone among chefs). Driving from Paris to Lyon, he arranged to meet his friend and fellow-chef, Jean Troisgros, just before the final motorway toll-gate. His toll was about fifty francs, having come all the way from Paris, whereas Troisgros would only have to pay about three francs. As they met, Bocuse managed to swap tickets, and then let Troisgros drive ahead. When he got to the toll-gate, there was Troisgros protesting at the demand from the tollman. Troisgros said 'Here is my friend who will tell you I only got on at Belleville.' 'I have never seen this man before,' said Bocuse, 'He looks like a crook to me.' And he drove away.

Any great specialist is a fund of knowledge. In conversation, Bocuse conceals this behind a façade of pleasantry, preferring not to risk boring people or wasting his erudition on a barren listener. When he detects real interest, however, he will pour out information, revealing the more serious side to his character and a remarkable gift as a teacher. But he does not take himself too seriously. 'Life is a farce. That is why I like jokes. Imagine, when the President of the Republic invites the President of the United States to dine, he also invites me. It is ridiculous.'

Bocuse is a man of simple relaxations; he most enjoys walking through the countryside with his dog. He used to like shooting, but as he grows older his love of nature grows and he takes little pleasure on killing things simply for sport.

His impeccably beautiful wife works beside him in the restaurant, greeting the customers with a polished smile. When he is away she coolly assumes the mantle of authority. Their daughter, Françoise, is married to Jean-Jacques Bernachon, a prosperous confectioner whose factory provides many of the excellent chocolates and sweetmeats for the restaurant. Bocuse has two granddaughters and a grandson born in March 1978. With his vocation and his family, his life seems to be as complete and fulfilled as he could wish.

Financial greed plays no strong part in his make-up; his attitude to money is strictly practical: 'We live in a world in which we need money. I started with nothing, I must end with more. If I can leave something I'll be happy, for one is fond of one's children, you know.'

Yet Bocuse is driven on and on. Partly it is his overpowering energy, enough for four ordinary men. There remains, however, a mystery as to the inner compulsion which harnesses this strength and determination. Here are some clues. His friends say he can never sleep alone; he would rather sleep on a chair in a friend's room. Then he is a physical man, much given to saucy chat and to kissing girls and pinching their bottoms. Finally, he refuses to play any games—'because I hate to lose.'

Taken together, these aspects of his character perhaps reveal a certain loneliness, also suggested by his hesitation in revealing his serious side and apparent fear that intimacy may lead to a loss of control over a relationship. It is the loneliness, perhaps, which goes with the quality of leadership.

Bocuse's main commitment is to spreading the gospel of French cooking, and he has been the prime mover in getting top chefs to travel the world. In Osaka, Japan, Bocuse lectured to 1500 students at a hotel school. 'I think that I also learned as much as I taught,' he says. He has an interest in two restaurants in Japan and visits the country regularly.

79

Alain Chapel
Mionnay

It is a problem to decide in what spirit we should go to a three-star restaurant. Is such an occasion a pilgrimage to a shrine of gastronomy, to be undertaken with solemnity and reverence? Is it a rare opportunity for a blow-out, an abandonment to pleasure and self-indulgence? Or is it an everyday event, writ a little larger?

There are those in this gallery who make no demands upon us, being content to give pleasure and those who, to a greater or lesser degree, seem to ask that we should show a respect due to their art.

Alain Chapel, perhaps more than any of the others, engenders a kind of awe, inspired by his strength of character and his singleness of purpose, which seems to give him such physical stature that he has been described as 'a man of huge physique, a sort of giant,' which is hardly apt for a man of less than six feet.

This strength, real enough when it comes to his cooking, pervades the whole of his restaurant. From the outside the establishment has little to distinguish it from a thousand other such places anywhere in France. It is a low stucco building at the end of the small flat village of Mionnay, grey and unprepossessing, lying right on the edge of the road to Lyon, twenty kilometres away.

It is only when you go inside, across the courtyard with its small garden and into the rather cramped entrance hall, that you realize that this is a place of a different order. It is not that it is grand or elaborate. Indeed there is a certain severity about the place—a stone-flagged floor, rough plaster on the walls, some beams, plain wooden doors. What strikes you is that,

although it is pleasant enough, nothing is overdone. There is no wasted space. There is a kitchen and a dining-room. You are here to eat. To eat, you may reasonably expect, the very best food in France; but there hangs in the air the suggestion that in doing so you will conform to the ritual.

Until recently, for instance, there was only a tiny space with about eight chairs where you might have an aperitif. That aperitif should not offend the sensibilities of the *maître d'hôtel*. Were you to order a Bloody Mary, it might be refused on the grounds that it would numb your palate.

On the tables there is no salt. You are expected to have complete faith in the chef's taste. If you wanted a dish saltier, then you would be wrong.

There lies behind this not the arrogance of a dictator, but a belief in perfection. Unlike Raymond Thuilier, who believes that we should strive for perfection yet know that it is unattainable, Alain Chapel believes that one day he will achieve his *verité* and, meanwhile, what he produces is the best that can be had and should be respected as such. He knows that he has given to you all that he can give and in return asks that you should recognize it.

Strangely enough, this has nothing to do with his being a cook. It would not have mattered what profession he had adopted. His is the genius of solid bourgeois application, not the genius of ambition. His achievement is the summit of dedication and honesty, and cooking the one art in which these count equally with talent.

It just happened that his father had a restaurant, which he bought in 1939—a one-star establishment, run by one of those Lyonnaise mothers, La Mère Charles. Alain grew up in the profession. He was a studious child, taking his *baccalauréat* at fifteen, and a dutiful one. His family had all worked to build up La Mère Charles and he, having no other particular inclinations, was naturally anxious to contribute. At that age he had no idea of what he might achieve, no passion as he puts it. 'After a while one discovers the passion,' he says. But with him, one feels the passion would have come in whatever field he had chosen.

First, he proved himself in his father's kitchens, then he was apprenticed with Jean Vignard, one of Fernand Point's closest colleagues, and later at La Pyramide with Paul Mercier, who took over as chef after Point's death in 1955.

Alain Chapel returned to La Mère Charles when he was twenty-nine and took charge of the kitchens. His father belonged to the older school of French restaurateurs who managed the front of the house and employed a chef. Within two years Chapel's skill had won for him a second Michelin star. Shortly afterwards his father died and Chapel became one of the newer style of chef-owners. In 1973 he gained his third star.

Chapel's training, indeed his whole life, has been rooted in the bourgeois, provincial tradition of the Bresse-Lyon area. However grand the ingredients of a dish, Chapel always brings it down to earth by introducing some simple vegetable. With his *foie gras de canard* comes a salad of forest mushrooms and artichokes, or a turnip; with pheasant come lentils, with scallops, leeks.

'Mine is a provincial auberge and it must remain so,' he says. No restaurant of this class or calibre could survive without tourists and foreigners, but Chapel takes pride in the fact that,

partly because of its geographical position, it is in no sense a snob restaurant. It is not a place to which people go to see or be seen. Sixty per cent of his clients are local. They come to eat the traditional cuisine of the area, elevated and enhanced by his skill and imagination to a level which no-one else has ever attempted. One of Chapel's favourite phrases is 'the standards of my profession,' which, when he uses it, implies not only rigorous discipline but also the basic everyday meaning of standard, 'not elaborate' fare. His is the cuisine of a simply poached chicken, of the turnip and the carrot, but in his hands these mundane things acquire a refinement of which we have never dreamed.

If one asks Alain Chapel whence the inspiration comes at the moment of his creating a new dish, he replies, 'It is when I look at the produce.'

For Chapel, the produce is possibly the most important thing in his business. When he talks of cooking, he says merely that it is easy. Everything is easy if you know what you want to do. For the winner of the Nobel Prize it is easy. Everything is simple, given hard work and rigorous application. He allows, in

his conversation, nothing for talent; it can be taken for granted.

In giving advice to young chefs, he spurns talk of the new cuisine or Japanese influence. The Japanese, he says, create a snobbism. Cuisine is a reflection of life. In France there is better produce than there ever was, if you know where to go. Why look to any other country?

Of course, Alain Chapel knows where to go. His policy of buying differs very markedly from most of the other chefs. He does not wander in the markets, as does Bocuse, spying out the best buys of the day. His policy, in keeping with his character, is to find one man for each kind of produce and then place all his confidence in him.

Chapel will only use pullets for his chicken dishes, and his menu indicates this. His chickens come from Bresse, from a farm which has won the highest award in seven different years. It is no accident that it has also won diplomas as a 'flowered farm'; excellence in just one field might not be enough.

The wild strawberries, raspberries, currants and cherries come from a Monsieur Jasserand who claims that Chapel is most exacting, but he likes that and sells virtually only to him.

Old Monsieur Lancelot provides most of the flowers for the dining-room tables, some small vegetables and herbs. These people are truly Chapel's friends and he often asks them to dine in his restaurant, but they rarely come, regarding him as someone beyond their reach for social pleasure.

'I go to the best, people with whom I am bound in friendship after four or five years. I don't deceive them, nor they me. It is a daily relationship. I am a believer in trust.'

This is not to say that he is not forever searching for better produce. He will journey as far as Brittany to talk to the fisherman, for produce to Chapel is all.

Of course, in reality, produce is not all. It is what both inspires Chapel and keeps his feet on the ground, locked, as it were, in the soil of his native province. Produce may be the basis of his stability, but it is in his kitchen that one sees what is built upon it, his strength in action.

Chapel's kitchen, where he spends six or seven hours a day, is different from any of the others in this book, not in appearance so much as in atmosphere.

The first impression is of unexpected quiet. As the orders are

Perfectionism in action: Chapel, the tip of his tongue sticking out with concentration, puts the finishing touches to a dish. The order board has one square for each table. Among its functions is to make the master plan of timings so that main courses may be served the moment they are ready. Perhaps the most intense of the chefs, Chapel stresses the need for hard, meticulous work —talent alone is not enough. Equally, he attaches importance to personal relationships—with his customers, at one end, each of whom he likes to meet as they arrive so that he can gauge their personal tastes and match them to the menu, and at the other end, his suppliers. Thus, he preserves the integrity of produce at each stage from the soil to the palate.

called out, and the replies of '*oui*' come in acknowledgement, no-one has to raise his voice. There is an air of unhurried composure, of earnest control.

One boy stands by a pile of tiny, floured fish and springy parsley—the materials for the little *amuse-gueule* which are given to the guests with their aperitifs. The order comes. Calmly the boy turns up the gas and waits for the oil to reach its heat. In they go. A pause. Then the parsley in another pan. You look away for a moment. When you look back they are gone. The waiter is carrying them down the passage to the dining-room— the boy has resumed his sleepy pose.

So everybody moves, calmly and without haste; yet all is done at amazing speed. Gradually you become aware of the power of this kitchen. It is like one of those beautiful nineteenth-century pumping-engines, moving majestically and silently, seemingly without effort, yet delivering immense power, smooth and everlasting.

A man's kitchen is a reflection of himself, Chapel says with considerable accuracy. This kitchen is like a sanctum of inner mysteries yet, in another sense, its spirit pervades the whole place. There is no other restaurant where the connection between the kitchen and the dining-room is so emotionally close.

In the first place, the dishes are finally dressed by the chefs on the oven doors which open downwards. From there they go

Downward-opening oven doors serve as plate-warmers while dishes receive final preparation before serving. *Chef-de-cuisine* Guy Gateau pours a sauce on a dish of *ris, cervelle et amourette d'agneau à l'estragon et aux fèves de printemps* (sweetbreads, brains and lamb's spine marrow with tarragon and broad beans). After this, the dish is on the diner's table in half a minute flat. In summer, guests can dine on a terrace. A light *apéritif* wine of the region is the rec-ommended accompaniment to the *amuse-gueule* ('taste-tickler') of small fish freshly caught in Lake Annecy—usually gudgeon. They are fried and served with parsley, lemon quarters and sometimes an oyster, in folded napkins.

Generosity and variety of ingredients mark Chapel's cooking; he is expansive as well as meticulous. A cream of country tomato soup is accompanied by vermicelli noodles with cocks' kidneys (difficult to obtain when few birds are allowed to mature). For the *écrevisses 'pattes rouges' au cerfeuil et petits mousserons de près* crayfish are served with chervil and baby agaric mushrooms. *Foie de lotte au vinaigre et petit ragoût de bettes nouvelles* consists of angler-fish roe with vinegar and stewed young beetroots. (The French do not spurn the angler-fish for its ugliness—on the contrary it is a prized delicacy.) The rich array of *gâteaux* and sweets is the responsibility of *pâtissier* Jean Audouze. It takes two waiters to carry the tray.

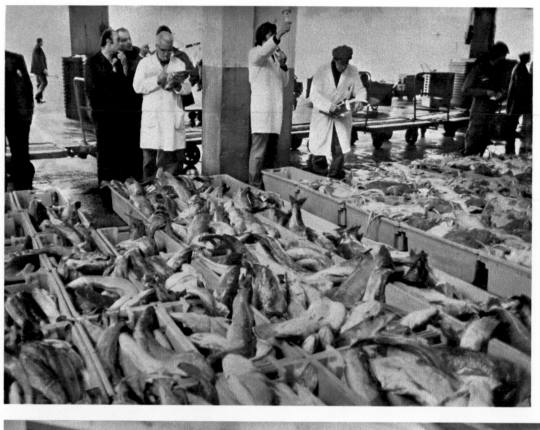

Repect for produce dominates the *nouvelle cuisine*; of all the chefs, Chapel possibly places the most emphasis on this. Consequently he spends much time seeking out the best suppliers. Besides, as he says, 'One must not always be in the kitchen, because it undermines the chefs.' Dissatisfied with the quality of the fish he had been receiving, he made a trip to Brittany to arrange new supplies.

From the boats the fresh catch is unloaded into trays and is immediately auctioned in the covered market on the quay. The auctioneer calls out the bids over a cordless microphone as he walks up and down the rows of trays. Having placed his contracts, Chapel orders by phone several times a week to ensure that the best fish of the moment arrive at his table. Truck deliveries are made four times a week; thus, fish caught one day are served the next.

straight onto the trays of the waiters, who stand by the counter. A dish, leaving the oven door, is on the customer's place within thirty seconds, making Alain Chapel's the only restaurant in the world where you are likely to burn your tongue.

Secondly, there are few three-star restaurants where the customers can see the chefs in their kitchen and the chefs can see and hear the customers in the dining-room. This connection is vital to Chapel's philosophy. He is as sensitive as a piano-tuner to the noise which comes from the dining-room. If it is a *jour de fête*, he says, the tone of the voices is a holiday one and he can hear that the customers have no spirit of rapport with his cuisine. A man's cuisine is a reflection of himself—of his love, his humour, his boastfulness, but he needs the response of his customer.

It is not enough for Chapel to send through to the dining-room a perfect dish. It must be the perfect dish for the person who is going to eat it. For this reason, he likes to meet everyone as he arrives. Everyone arrives in a different state of mind. If he can meet them he can judge what they expect of him. If they demand the maximum, then he is challenged to provide it. The customers are no longer table number three; they are people he knows, who want this or want that. It was his father who inspired this feeling, for he was a man who believed that everything must be done for happiness. If it was a cloudy day, he said they must redouble their efforts to make everyone feel it was a sunny one. Alain extended this view to measuring the mood of each person. It is his pride that his restaurant is highly personal, but 'it is very exacting and nervously exhausting for the cook.'

It is dishes which are particularly requested that give him the greatest pleasure, for the enemy of a chef is monotony. He wants to give constantly and yet it is this essential generosity which is so exhausting for a perfectionist. The two characteristics could perhaps only co-exist in a chef, for perfectionism is by nature a rather narrow, almost selfish trait, which accords ill with the expansive '*acte d'amour en permanence*', which is how Chapel describes being a chef.

Nevertheless, his generosity of spirit is very real. 'Ours is a profession of love and giving. One must never count the cost.' In fact, he never does count it. In financial affairs, he says, one cannot be the judge and jury, so he has a team of three people, including his mother, who have total control of the finances of the business, the restaurant and several bedrooms.

He claims not to be interested in money and certainly for him it is not an aim in itself. 'If this business were to turn over twenty million francs a year, I would sell it and go and start another little restaurant.'

The evidence of this attitude is everywhere—in his absolute refusal to serve more than seventy covers at any meal, and he prefers it to be fewer; in the rapid succession of sweets and *pâtisseries* and bon-bons which are showered on every diner; in the sheer extravagance of the kitchens where he deplores only waste of good produce which might have fed hungry people, but never lavish use of expensive material to foster perfection.

The conflict between the perfectionism and the generosity is perpetual if unconscious. While the customers may not have salt, Chapel is uncritical of them, professing not to mind if they do not understand about food. After all they may learn tomorrow.

Chapel inspects shellfish at the market in Audierne.

Spiny lobsters	Lobsters	Great crabs	Spider crabs

These are animals with hard and stiff shells of different colours.
Nevertheless, when cooked they all become red (except the great crabs).
To mature, they have to change, entirely shedding their shells:
    this is a long and painful process during which the creatures are very vulnerable (from which, the account of the Conger Eel and the Lobster).
The new shell takes one month to harden.
Moulting takes place every year.
They grow very slowly:
    a lobster of 1kg is 10 to 15 years old.
    a spiny lobster of 1kg is 25 to 30 years old.
    a spiny lobster of 3kg ought to be 100 years old.
This is why it is impossible to breed them in tanks.
Crustaceans lay their eggs (in spring):
    the lobster from 20,000 to 30,000.
    the spiny lobster about 100,000.
    the crab from 1,000,000 to 3,000,000.
They feed on shellfish, molluscs, young fish and plankton.
They filter from 10 to 15 cubic metres of water each day.
Their great enemy is the octopus.
When they suffer, or to free themselves, they are able to discard a leg or a pincer (immediately healing). This explains why lobsters and crabs sometimes have one claw.
They are able to grow a new claw.
Kept in the cool, crustaceans can live for three or four days out of the water.
Largest weights on record:
    red lobster of 7kg 200g (imagine his age!)
    lobster from Britanny of 9kg 500g.

'What matters is that I should evolve and search for my *verité*.'

He is particularly aware of his youth. He needs time and, alas, money or, as he puts it, financial independence. For this reason, he is perhaps less well-known outside France, because he wants to concentrate more on his restaurant than, for instance, Bocuse who travels for a large part of the year. 'On the other hand,' Chapel adds ruefully, 'I find it impossible to say no.' So he does occasionally accept invitations to cook abroad.

However, he does concentrate his energies on the restaurant, getting up at 6.30, planning till 7.00, marketing from 7.30 to 9.15, and so on throughout the day and night until he goes to bed at 1.30. He compares a restaurant to a ship, using nautical terms to describe the operation; a good captain must promote every little part. He checks the cleaning of the rooms, the welcome (usually performed by his wife), the table-settings, the linen.

'We are a crew and not one member of the crew must falter. Even the washers-up. The dining-room one has to be wary of. Working there, it is all too easy to succumb to facility. Anyone can smile and be charming, but the waiters have to present the work of the chefs. It is pointless for the cooks to produce their best dishes only to have them ruined in the dining-room.'

His staff or crew hold Chapel in the highest regard, accepting his occasionally fierce reprimands as holy writ, and sometimes the loyalty and respect which he inspires serves him ill. If there is any criticism to be made of this restaurant, it is that the service in the dining-room lacks the anticipatory polish, of say, the Baumanière. There you are never aware of wanting or waiting for anything. At Chapel's restaurant the waiters are so intent on fulfilling the master's words about presenting the chef's food that they may quite forget to fill your wine glass or fail to bring the cheese trolley for an age.

The concentration is wearing for Chapel. The endless vigilance, he says as he ticks off a boy for bringing a coffee flask with barely more than dregs in it, means that he will die young. In some respects he restrains himself. He has, for instance, no apprentices; it is too personalized a restaurant for that. He wants to concentrate only on his crew. But the hours tell on him. 'I don't want to die an idiot.'

It is partly the nature of the business which creates the worst problem. Chapel closes one day a week. That day costs two million francs a year. One solution to his problem of stress would be to close two days a week, but unfortunately that would

Provided one looks for it, Chapel says, French produce is better than ever, and he makes it his business to search out and build a personal relationship with the best supplier for each product. Monsieur Jasserand, of Thurins, supplies soft fruit—direct to the restaurant. (A day too late and the raspberries may become *sirop de framboise*.) Monsieur Lancelot grows salad and herbs in his walled garden in Lyon. Chapel buys daily from his stall in the market.

Chapel's Hervé Duronzier has the special responsibility of buying goat's cheese from Madame Jouffet, taking it away in metal containers. The Jouffet's farm, a château in Tramayes, has fifty goats and also breeds rabbits.

Bresse chickens, farmed north-east of Lyon, are the most highly rated by French chefs. Madame Marinette checks to see if one of her prize-winning chickens is ready for killing. This is done by parting the breast feathers and blowing onto the breast. If a certain vein bulges slightly the bird is ready for the table. For their first month, Bresse chicks are fed on ground maize and powdered milk. For the next three months, they are given free range twice a day to develop their flavour. For their last month, they are cooped up and fed with rice and milk.

not be economically feasible. So his intense labours continue.

Chapel maintains that as a profession the *chefs-patron* are paddling upstream. Any business which employs forty-five or fifty people, as he does, should have a turnover three times greater than his. Of course he could commercialize, but that he fears would undermine his standards. He doesn't like to talk of the possibilities, though he toys with vague plans such as a technical consultancy or selling his name in ways that would leave him free to concentrate.

Another problem is rising prices. There must be a ceiling to what people are prepared to pay for his food, but in a labour-intensive business in which the raw materials have to be the most expensive, will the ceiling rise as fast as the cost of labour and the cost of the raw materials? Experts already say not, says Chapel gloomily.

But he is driven on, despite the tiredness, despite the pessimism. Like the crew he must not falter or he will not be the champion. And to him to be the best is the most important thing in the world.

'The runner who broke the world record in Mexico, he did it once. Then nothing. But twice a day I have to be champion of the world.'

The challenge is always with him. He sees the great chefs as the last professionals, purveying *le beau et le bon*. Theirs is the last industry which can conjure dreams, he maintains, airily ignoring all such things as films or television, let alone the arts. His pride in the profession is probably what makes him appear larger than he is. When doing anything unconnected with his work, he looks somewhat of a fish out of water. Let him put on his chef's coat and hat and he stands differently, proudly, and is himself.

It is interesting what fame has done to Alain Chapel. There is, of course, a measure of arrogance about him. He professes to appreciate criticism, adding, as do all who are in a position to be the victim of critics, that it must be constructive. Then he goes on to describe how he deals with critics. He asks their profession. If they have criticized the garden, they always turn out to be gardeners, if the dining-room décor they are builders, the lighting, electricians and so on. No-one, it seems, ever criticizes the food and, if they did, it is doubtful whether they would receive a soft answer. Similarly he refers to his restaurant as Mionnay as though he were the whole village.

At the same time the fame came too late, even at thirty-five, to disturb the simple, bourgeois honesty and sense imbued in him by a traditional upbringing in his native province. His tastes are quiet ones. He likes walking with his Labrador, listening to Mozart, reading a good book—the tastes of a reserved and private man. But all the time one feels that there is in him a bubbling spirit which he keeps severely controlled, as though fearful of letting go, lest that should interfere with his work. His real friends are few, but those few see in him a different man, warm and humorous. With them his irascible defences disappear. Most of them are the other chefs—Haeberlin, the Troisgros brothers—and they are surprised that others think of him as a rather sad man. He recognizes that to others he is a difficult man. 'I am a Capricorn, a very difficult sign. Me and Stalin and Mao Tse Tung.' He is, in fact, too practical to let astrology really have any influence on him.

His deep respect for work, his perfectionism, have, in a way, stolen from him that part of his nature which would otherwise have been more exuberant. When he speaks of his hobbies, he says they are much neglected.

He bought, in a moment of ebullience, a shiny racing bicycle. It sits in the garage unused.

He has the notion that one day he might, like Haeberlin and Thuilier, be Mayor of his village, but politics must wait. There is too the smaller matter of the electors who rejected him when he stood as a prospective councillor. This was a sore insult for him and he muttered of prophets unrecognized in their own country. But more probably they recognized his worth and realized that so dedicated a man would not be wheeling and dealing in Lyon when he had a restaurant to run.

There is also the infinite sadness to him that he and his wife have no children. There are holidays, of course, and his interest sparkles when he talks of his travels to China and to India, but dominating everything is his 'passionate profession.'

The impression he makes is of a man who has much more affection and love than he has the opportunity to give; instead he gives it to his work. So, perhaps, when we go to Alain Chapel's restaurant, we should go with awe, tinged with some sadness and more than a little gratitude.

Chapel visits the cellars of Monsieur Ramonet, vineyard-owner of the Meursault area, and samples a local wine. The taste varies with the level in the barrel from which it is taken; Ramonet uses a long glass pipette to draw off a sample from the top of the barrel. Chapel consulted Ramonet on the construction of his new wine-cellar; for instance, on what stone is best to keep the cellars at the right temperature.

Chapel owes much to his parents, Roger and Eva Chapel, who gave him a secure grounding in his profession. His father bought La Mère Charles in 1939 and placed Alain in charge of the kitchens when the son was twenty-nine. Roger Chapel's confidence was rewarded within two years by the restaurant's second star, shortly before he died in 1970. Even now, when the rare mistake is made, Chapel's invariable reaction is 'My father would never have allowed it.' Chapel's mother also had much to do with providing his solid foundation; it was her cooking which maintained the restaurant's reputation during the difficult war years. Today she is still in charge of the *caisse*—in the true tradition of family restaurants.

Less of a publicist than some other *chefs-patron*, Chapel nevertheless obliges his clients by signing his menus and copies of a book about him, *Croque-en-bouche*, by his journalist aunt, Fanny Deschamps. He is happy that the basis of his trade is local: 'Because of our geographical position, we're not a snob restaurant. We're practically an *auberge*. People don't come here to be seen.'

91

Michel Guérard

Les Prés et les Sources d'Eugénie
Eugénie-les-Bains

If there are, inside all the fat chefs, thin chefs trying to get out, they are remarkably docile in their attempts. The exception to this rule is Michel Guérard. Not only has he positively changed his appearance, but his whole character seems to be the outcome of a battle between two disparate natures contained within his adjustable frame. A battle in which there is, as yet, no winner.

In the last few years Guérard has become almost as famous as Bocuse; certainly, in the world of cuisine, a person of endless controversy, the acme of modernity. Yet Guérard's beginnings were ordinary enough. He was born in 1933 in Vétheuil, north of Paris; his family had a *boucherie* at nearby Mantes-la-Jolie. They were in a fair way of business, with a spread of hectares near Deauville where they bred the beef for their shop. The young Guérard enjoyed food but had no particular ambition to be a chef. At one time he wanted to be a priest, 'actually a bishop was what I had in mind,' then later an actor. It was only at seventeen, 'already a bit late,' that he decided on his career and went to work at Mantes-la-Jolie for Kléber Alix, who had a *pâtisserie* and take-away catering business. Alix was a fierce taskmaster who, if he was going to make veal *vol-au-vent*, would buy a whole calf, kill it himself and prepare the meat and likewise expected his apprentices to be able to do absolutely everything. It is to him that Guérard owes his skill in *pâtisserie*, which he believes is the best starting point for a chef, requiring as it does great exactitude and a knowledge of the physics and chemistry of its materials. After three years apprenticeship, Guérard passed his *Certificat d'Aptitude Professionelle* in 1953 and started on the usual rounds of a trainee chef, working in Rouen, Dieppe and a two-star restaurant at Tôtes.

It was during this time that he met Jean Delaveyne, who now runs the Camélia in Bougival, whom he regards as his 'spiritual father.' 'We both felt that cuisine needed a push to get it out of the codified strait-jacket imposed on it by the followers of Escoffier.' The point was not that Escoffier was wrong (indeed Guérard believes it impossible to create cuisine of any quality without having studied Escoffier), but that chefs, thinking to put on a particular dish, merely looked it up in Escoffier or Saulnier and slavishly followed the recipe. To vary it was to fall from grace. Delaveyne, who was largely self-taught, inspired Guérard to question such dogma and to speculate on the possibilities of a freer cuisine.

It was some time before he could put his theories to the test. First came more than two years of service in the navy, then a refresher with Kléber Alix and a spell in grand restaurants—Maxim's, Lucas-Carton, the Meurice and the Crillon in Paris and the Normandy in Deauville. In 1958, he earned the gold medal of a *Meilleur Ouvrier de France*. By now his traditional grounding was complete and his impatience correspondingly great. He took the unusual step of going to work for a private family: the Clericos, who owned the Lido cabaret in Paris. In their home he was able for the first time to start experimenting with a lighter, more natural kind of cuisine.

After five years Guérard decided to open his own restaurant—the Pot-au-Feu in the insalubrious Paris suburb of Asnières. At first he was fearful that, if he were to follow his own inclinations, his restaurant would be too expensive, as he had little hope of luring customers to drive ten awkward kilometres from

Guérard, an international celebrity, deals with the morning mail in his office. He and his wife, Christine, share a taste for antiques and he is a keen collector of old books, especially on cookery. They buy china for the hotel at Della Torre, off the rue Paradise, Paris. Her office at the hotel, where she is sitting correcting the proofs of one of her husband's books, overlooks parkland. Christine Guérard, *née* Barthélémy, manages the restaurant and hydro, and has created the décor for the whole Barthélémy chain of spa hotels.

the centre of Paris. But Delaveyne, reinforced by Bocuse and Troisgros who had become friends at Lucas-Carton, persuaded Guérard to stick to his principles and to do the cooking he wanted to do.

The Pot-au-Feu was a tiny place with room for only thirty people, crowded together—really nothing more than a bistro. Yet it became proof that for the French no inconvenience is too great in the pursuit of good food. Soon it was impossible to get a table less than a month ahead and those who did get them were ministers, film stars and socialites.

What they were responding to was the absolute purity of Guérard's cooking. His *foie gras frais* at the Pot-au-Feu was a totally new experience for me and one which was never repeated until I went to Eugénie-les-Bains. His vegetables had the superb quality of being cooked, yet tasting as if they were raw.

By a rather different route, largely by his own imagination, Guérard had arrived at much the same point as Bocuse and the Troisgros brothers—a free and imaginative re-interpretation of French cooking. In some ways he was able to be more revolutionary, because he was less firmly entrenched in a region and had less conservative palates to cater for.

The little bistro had earned him two stars and made him famous. But there were problems. The turnover of the Pot-au-Feu was really too small to cover the costs of Guérard's exacting standards. Guérard was getting fat and unhealthy. He used to go to bed at two in the morning and have barely three hours' sleep before going to market. However, he was freed from a potentially vicious circle by a bureaucratic stroke: the Pot-au-Feu was compulsorily purchased to make way for a new road.

Guérard's reputation was now secure, and he was offered scores of jobs, including taking over the kitchens at Maxim's. He toyed with the idea of buying a place in the Champs-Elysées. Then a happy combination of circumstances occurred. Pierre Troisgros happened to introduce him to Christine Barthélémy, whose father owned seven hydros, spa hotels, dotted about France. They talked about slimming. She invited him to the hydro she ran at Eugénie-les-Bains, a small village in the rural peace of south-west France.

The visit had a double outcome. He and Christine fell in love and married in 1972. He acquired an interest in her hydro and they worked together to revive the rather tired watering-

place once patronized by the Empress Eugénie. Guérard's own weight problem had already made him think about slimming food, but everything in him had revolted against the grated carrots and the other sad items of traditional slimmers' régimes. Eugénie-les-Bains gave him the stimulus to elaborate a whole new range of dishes which not only enabled people to lose weight, but also tasted like real food.

In some ways it seems a little too pat, the invention of *cuisine minceur* coinciding with the lover's acquisition of an interest in a health spa. Certainly, it would have been difficult to establish a restaurant of three-star quality in so remote an area and, equally, a slimming place which served only rich *haute cuisine* would have been impossibly incongruous. *Cuisine*

minceur and the publicity which went with it overcame both these problems. It is easy, therefore, to dismiss it as a gimmick, but it is also unjust.

Michel Guérard makes no extravagant claims for it. *Cuisine minceur* is for slimmers. Some other chefs are inclined to dismiss it as if it were meant to replace 'real' cuisine. This is not so. It is merely an attempt to produce something more palatable than the usual slimming foods. It has no scientific basis, but is founded on the common-sense exclusion of fats and sugar. With some exceptions, its taste cannot compare with real cuisine, but it tastes a lot better than the ground-up ping-pong ball flavour of many dietetic preparations. One has only to compare the lettuce sauce which Guérard puts with his

It was Guérard's *cuisine gourmande*, rather than his slimming *cuisine minceur*, which won him a three-star rating in the 1977 *Guide Michelin*. Served hot or cold, his *soupe aux écrevisses de rivière* (soup with fresh-water crayfish) blends vegetables and herbs with cream, butter, dry white wine, Armagnac and port—a richness of ingredients definitely not for those who are slimming.

Le marché du pêcheur en cocotte (fish-market stew) is a mix of sea bass, sole, red mullet and prawns, together with scallops, oysters and mussels. The fish and prawns are steamed with seaweed.

Volaille 'truffée' au persil (Guérard has the ingredients before him in the photograph at his kitchen window) is one of the most celebrated specialities of *cuisine minceur*. In deference to slimmers' sensibilities he trims the fat from inside the bird, uses no butter or sauce and even discards the fat from the roasting pan.

Preparing parsleyed chicken. First, fresh parsley, chives, tarragon, shallots and mushrooms are chopped.

Fromage blanc, a mild cheese with a low fat content, will be used to bind the flavouring ingredients.

Guérard mixes the chopped herb and parsley garniture with the *fromage blanc* to make the stuffing.

minceur steamed fish with the *gourmande* lettuce sauce to recognize that the *minceur* version is not even pretending to belong in the same category.

For all their criticism, one may wonder how many of the other chefs would, or indeed could, have invented *cuisine minceur*, even given the convenient promptings of love and a spa. Moreover, it may be that, because it is so inventive, there are in it aspects which will have their effect on ordinary cuisine. There is no doubt that, among the new generation of chefs, Guérard is the most imaginative.

It is here that confusion may lie. Because he is so much associated with the exploratory side of what is called *nouvelle cuisine* and has invented *cuisine minceur*, people think of them

as one and the same. *Cuisine minceur*, as we have seen, is an ingenious solace for the weak-willed slimmer. *Nouvelle cuisine* is a name given to the present stage of evolution in the long history of French cooking. At Eugénie-les-Bains the two co-exist in the surprising hotel devised by Michel and Christine Guérard, but nowhere else.

Les Prés et les Sources d'Eugénie, as the hotel is called, has, like its chef, two distinct characters. First, the baths with their disgusting sulphurous waters, the pamphlets with unappetizing news of the water's diuretic properties, the sad outlines of nature's unfashionable shapes, the unrepentant self-absorbed chatter of the over-indulgent—all the paraphernalia of taking a cure. Then, the three-star aspect of the hotel, with the lavish

Baron de lapereau mange-tout is boneless strips of young rabbit cut from the *baron* (back and thighs), cooked in butter and chicken bouillon. It is served with a sauce and baby turnips and noodles.

La pêche au granité de Pomerol, a peach on a bed of crushed Pomerol ice, is a typical Guérard sweet with a minimum of artifice. Pomerol is a rich, young Bordeaux wine with a deep colour.

The skin of the chicken is gently loosened from the breast meat to make space for the stuffing.

The stuffing goes in under the skin so that its flavour is cooked into the meat by direct contact.

The chicken, in a copper pan with a lid, is roasted in a hot oven until its juices run clean.

The finished chicken is served with a simple garnish of young carrots, baby turnips and chives.

97

menus of Guérard's *cuisine gourmande*. It is this aspect which, in fact, dominates. While many of the bedrooms have a certain austerity more appropriate to those who are endeavouring to exercise restraint, the public rooms, the arcade and the terraces are both luxurious and pretty.

The décor is largely the responsibility of Christine, who chose all the materials and even the rather trendy, long dresses worn by the waitresses. Guérard himself likes antiques and collected many of the old clocks, pretty stoves and paintings, including one of Eugénie's aunts, which hangs in the small, rustic dining-room where Tito ate when he stayed at the hotel. For some tastes it is all rather over-decorated, with two different kinds of chairs in the main dining-room, two sorts of table-cloth and, throughout, a general air of too much planning, too calculated an atmosphere.

This ambience vanishes as soon as you step into the kitchen. Then you feel only the bustling energy of this spirited chef. It is a very small kitchen and reveals several things about Guérard. At one end is an open fire, burning fruit wood. To him a flame is as important as it is to Bocuse. 'If there is one thing more than another that I would teach a young apprentice, it is how to cook on an open fire. There you can see what strength someone has. When you provide a person with every-thing—whether produce or machinery or utensils—it can make him lazy. Faced with the restrictions imposed by an open fire, the imagination soars.'

When Guérard went to China, he found that the food was often over-sophisticated, both in the produce and the combina-tion of perfumes. The one thing that really interested him was a restaurant where the whole meal was made up of different dishes of duck. There was no part, from the feet to the head, which was unused. It was a lesson in economy and imagination which appealed to him.

Produce is of supreme importance to Guérard, as it is to the other chefs. Isolated as he is, his vegetables come either from his own garden or from local peasant-farmers with whom he has slowly built up a close relationship. There are good chickens in the area and, of course, the department of Landes is famous for its *foie gras* and for its Chalosse beef. His fish come from St Jean de Luz and his oysters from Marennes. Just outside the kitchen are two tanks, one filled with sea-water in which he keeps lobsters, the other with fresh water for his crayfish.

Guérard works extremely hard during the service, flitting about and involving himself in every part of the operation. Partly, this is necessary because, unlike the rest of the chefs, he has no permanent *brigade*. The hotel is open only for seven months of the year. With the exception of four kitchen staff, he has to recruit nearly the whole complement of seventy people afresh each spring. There are some local casuals and a few faithfuls, such as his excellent young *sommelier*, who like to come back each time, but otherwise everyone has to be trained in the ways of the house. But more than this, Guérard dislikes specialization. 'My principle is to remain eclectic. All cooks like doing fish, simply because it is easier than meat, but apart from that natural preference I try not to allow myself to fall into the habits which likes and dislikes encourage. There is much talk of the quality of provincial cooking, but often

Guérard dances cheek-to-chest with a typically dead-pan Bocuse at the 'Beginners' Ball'—a parody debu-tantes' dance arranged a few years ago by Bocuse. His wife says that Guérard is a comedian who missed his vocation. Certainly, a love of horseplay characterizes more than one of the master-chefs.

Armagnac is a brandy made in the Gers region, east of the Landes. The best kind comes from the area of Bas-Armagnac in SE Gers, and it is there, at Barbotan, that the Guérards have their own Armagnac vineyard. Guérard tests the *bouquet* of a sample drawn from one of the oak casks in which the brandy is matured for a decade. The newly distilled spirit is put into already-used casks so that the wood passes on its experience to the brandy.

provincial cooks are set in ways which are wrong. There is no merit in saying: "That is the way we have always done it." '

There is no specific way in which Guérard's behaviour in his kitchen differs from any of the other chefs but, observing him, one is conscious of an additional quality. When he looks at a chef working, he is not merely seeing whether the job is being done correctly. Some part of him is wondering whether it could, with advantage, be done differently. When he looks at a dish on its way to the dining-room, he is not only checking that it is all right, he is each time assessing the dish anew, in case some variation occurs to him. All the chefs acknowledge that they learn all the time, but in none of them is the process so plainly manifest as it is in Guérard.

It took only five years from the day that Michel and Christine Guérard relaunched the old spa hotel for it to be awarded three stars in the Michelin. That the accolade was merited is unquestioned, but there remains the contradiction between the fat and thin chefs within Guérard, which in turn leads to the controversy which surrounds him.

Guérard is, in many ways, the most popular within the group of chefs. They do not have the same feeling for him that they have for Bocuse; that is more of a veneration. But if they are talking of camaraderie and pranks, they all laugh when they think of Guérard. There is much in him of the comedian that he once wanted to be. At the Paris launching of his second book, he dressed up as a woman singer and mimed to some pop-songs. No-one knew it was him on the stage, but he thought it was fun. He has a wholly infectious irreverence, which makes him the best possible company. At the same time he manages to arouse the suspicions of his colleagues. However obliquely, they give an impression of disparaging his work. This stems to a considerable extent from what is, superficially viewed, the greatest contradiction in his behaviour. While he is one of the most inventive chefs, he does not hesitate to betray what his *confrères* consider the inviolable traditions of their profession.

His latest venture is to produce with Nestlé a range of frozen food. The whole question of packaged and pre-prepared foods interests him greatly and, with Nestlé, he is studying several different methods of preserving food. Far from being forced by Nestlé to put his name to the products, he was anxious to work with them.

'I believe that chefs must intervene because we can offer so much for the customers' protection. I put my name to these things to stimulate the others to get involved. I regard it as a duty, because the creative people in the field should work with industry. In return I have learned a great deal from them.' Guérard has been much impressed with the integrity of the food industry. He was amazed when they condemned a large consignment of what seemed to him perfectly acceptable-looking lobster soup. Under a microscope they had discovered some harmless black spots, invisible to the naked eye.

Guérard also plans a chain of delicatessen shops, selling his jams and ready-made dishes, such as fish *en croûte*. All this is anathema to many of his colleagues who believe that their profession's mystique should be jealously preserved. There are plenty of rumours put about, for instance, that Guérard already uses a deep-freeze in his restaurant and that he achieves the

In contrast to most other three-star establishments, where the décor and ambience may have evolved through decades of family ownership, Les Prés et les Sources d'Eugénie has been completely remodelled since 1974, when the Guérard-Barthélémy régime commenced. Both inside and outside, Christine Guérard's influence is in evidence—from the rough orange stucco of the room where President Tito dined and the antique chic of tiled stoves and old carts, to the flowers and greenery and oft-repeated pumpkin motif. The hotel is open only for seven months a year, which means that most of the staff have to be recruited again each season.

The river beside the restaurant no longer provides fresh fish. Supplies now come from Brittany, except for salmon imported from Scotland or Denmark. Fish is cleaned and prepared on a slab outside the kitchen door. The bones, deftly removed with an ordinary potato-peeler, may be set aside to be used in stock. Inside the kitchen, Paul Haeberlin involves himself in every task from the menial to the most creative. Although a shy man, he is articulate in the kitchen, instructing and advising his team of fifteen, although 'they have to have a natural passion before you can teach them,' he says. His own inspiration often comes from his collection of old cookery books.

scripted and worked as a chef, but was released through the influence of one of his aunt's lodgers, who was the mistress of a German officer. He eventually joined the Free French Army and thus came about the absurd situation of two brothers fighting on opposing sides.

The old *auberges* had both been flattened in 1940 when the French blew up the bridge over the Ill, and it may be that the necessity of rebuilding their *auberge* spurred the Haeberlins, with Jean-Pierre's talents, to be more ambitious than their riparian opposites at La Truite. In any event, in the freer atmosphere after the war, Paul went off to Paris as an apprentice at La Rôtisserie Périgourdine. He then went to train under Edouard Weber, a former chef to the Tsar, the Kings of Greece and Spain and the Rothschilds. Weber had opened, in his last years, a small restaurant at Ribeauvillé, not far from Illhaeusern.

Meanwhile Jean-Pierre had gone to the École des Beaux Arts at Strasbourg and done courses in architecture and painting. When he had finished, Paul was already installed at the temporary building which had replaced the old *auberge*. Whether it was apparent to Jean-Pierre at that time that Paul, if he were to succeed, would need a driving force behind him, or whether joining his brother seemed the simplest solution to his problem

is not clear, but, over the years, it has become obvious that neither could have achieved the eminence they now enjoy without the help of the other.

They toyed with the idea of starting a restaurant of their own, but their father and their aunt Henriette, whom they described as the '*gendarme*', said that first they had to rebuild the old family *auberge*, then they could go off and do what they liked. Naturally, in the process of rebuilding, they gave so much of themselves that it never again occurred to them to leave. It was, as Paul puts it, hard graft. He was always up to light the fires at six in the morning. Their only time off was half a day on Sunday. To start with, it was essentially the same establishment as it had been before the war—a bistro *du coin* in a remote Alsatian village.

Paul added his new dishes to the traditional fish stews and *choucroute: le potage aux grenouilles, les goujonnettes de sole,*

venison *Saint Hubert, le gratin de framboises 'Laetitia'*, but it was Jean-Pierre who, after doing two stints as a *maître d'hôtel* elsewhere, added the important ingredient of style. The character of the two brothers is essentially different. Paul gives the impression of a largish, sleepy man. His movements are slow, his handshake limp. With strangers he hardly speaks at all, being remarkably shy. He has no interest in meeting the customers and is never seen in the dining-room, unless it happens that some of his old village cronies are there late and lure him out with talk of politics or football. Indeed one might be inclined to think of him as rather wet, were it not for his single-minded passion for cooking which, since his childhood days with Aunt Henriette, has driven him on and on to create better and better dishes.

It is puzzling that Paul Haeberlin does not seem to fit in with any of the assumptions which one might make about great chefs from the study of the others in this book. Each, by the very fact of being human, has a distinct personality of his own, but they all share to a greater or lesser degree some characteristics which one could suppose syllogistically to be an essential part of the make-up of a great chef. They are all spurred by a need to express themselves in generosity, but not Paul Haeberlin. This is not to say that he is mean. Far from it. But for him the act of giving is no part of his motive in cooking. They all have about them a certain shrewdness, but not Paul Haeberlin. He is rather a simple character, who leaves anything to do with money to the rest of the family. When he was younger and actively resisting the pressure to run the family holdings, he could not bear to get rid of the family horses, but kept them well-fed without ever working them, so that for the villagers of Illhaeusern the illustration of a life of ease was a Haeberlin horse. The other chefs need encouragement, praise and recognition; Paul seems indifferent or, at any rate, satisfied merely with achievement for its own sake. Perhaps the only quality he has in common with the others is immense endurance.

Paul Haeberlin's kitchen provides part of the solution to the puzzle. It is not like Bocuse's or Pic's or Troisgros' or Chapel's, the carefully planned workshop of a master craftsman. Instead, it resembles an overgrown, everyday kitchen of an ordinary housewife. A large Bertrand mixer, looking like a machine-gun, lies casually on one shelf dripping a bit of ice-cream on the floor. Paul calls out the orders in his high-pitched voice, but no-one bothers to answer with eager cries of '*oui*'; they just get on with it. There is a fair amount of chatter. There seems to be no insistence on discipline, but more an air of informality and simplicity, so that you begin to wonder whether Paul was joking when he said, 'Before we ask new employees if they can cook, we ask if they can play football, because we are proud of our team.' There is a man wearing clogs, the washers-up are girls in ordinary clothes. Old Mrs Haeberlin makes the coffee. There is a tin-opener screwed to one bench, where a boy opens a tin of duck livers for the *gratin de nouilles au foie de canard*. Paul has in some ways an easy-going air. It will be all right, he says to his son who fears that they haven't cooked enough chickens. Later it appears that it isn't. 'See how many we have sold,' says the young Marc reproachfully. Yet somehow, in the end, it is all right. Yes, this is a kitchen run on homely lines.

From this kitchen comes much that is traditional. Alsace is famous for its game, because after the Franco-Prussian war of 1870, when Alsace was yielded to France, the old German hunting laws were retained. Ten-year game-leases are the minimum permitted, so that it is worth the lessee's while to preserve the game. The arrangements are controlled by the mayor to protect the farmer against damage. Game, then, was a natural part of the menu of the old L'Arbre Vert and it still is of L'Auberge de l'Ill. As Paul points out, many of the dishes might have been on a menu two hundred years ago. Indeed his preference is for the produce of the region; he likes to cook game and is still fascinated by fish, although this now has to be imported since the local rivers became polluted.

Paul has no feelings about *nouvelle cuisine*. 'Weber gave me his handwritten recipe book, with many things in it in Russian. Among them was *salade Catherine la Grande*, a salad of *foie gras* and *haricots verts*, which people talk about now as if it were a new idea.' All that is happening, he maintains, is that chefs are simplifying things, because people cannot eat so much nowadays. 'But if you want a good sauce, you have to use cream and butter.' However much lighter the food is, the traditional basis remains.

Against all of this we have to set one plain fact. Paul Haeberlin is a genius and, like all geniuses, he is unique. Although all that he has done, in one sense, is to plod logically and methodically on, just like his mother, grandmother and great-grandmother, producing the best food he can from his home kitchen, the fact is that everything he touches is tinged with magic. His very method of creation is prosaic. For him creation is not a cerebral affair; he is inspired only in his kitchen, at the moment of working. 'When I am working with some scallops and oysters, I think why not try them with some basil. Ah, there's an idea.' Just like a housewife, you may think, until you come to eat them and realize that this is a perfect dish no housewife could have dreamed of, in the same way that she would never have combined a peach in champagne sabayon with a pistachio ice-cream.

Such is his genius, but one cannot help feeling that had he been left to himself, his essentially pedestrian nature would never have allowed it to flower. In his kitchen, the talk is completely bilingual with jumbled cries of, '*Ist das bien cuit?*' If you ask him whether he feels primarily French or German he says, 'First I am Alsatian.' He is rooted in the ambience of the stork and the gnome and the crooked beam, and were it not for his brother he might never have emerged from it.

For the other part of the solution to the puzzle he presents is Jean-Pierre, who provides all those characteristics which seem

Three generations are involved in running L'Auberge de l'Ill—from Mère Haeberlin who makes the coffee, to Paul's son, Marc, who has 'the flair and the patience' to be a fine chef, according to his uncle. The restaurant building, seen here from the bridge, has been extended over the years with additions of ancient and modern pieces. The family vegetable patch has been transformed by Jean-Pierre into a carefully landscaped garden, overlooked by a terrace where only coffee is served, not meals. Their menu mixes old with new. The saucepan contains the celebrated *matelote*, a mix of fish, formerly from local waters, cooked in wine with herbs and vegetables; the dish in front is *matelote* served on a bed of fresh noodles with a cream sauce. The pot bearing the Haeberlin name is of the kind once used for the traditional *beckenoffe*—a family casserole cooked in the cooling ovens of the local bakery. Round the table anticlockwise are *brioche de foie gras* made in the Alsatian style, which is different from the Périgourdine where there is no crust, *saumon soufflé 'Auberge de l'Ill'* and *mousseline de grenouille 'Paul Haeberlin'*, two dishes devised by Paul, and *terrine d'écrevisses* a new creation by Marc. On the board are the ingredients for two veal dishes, *médaillon de veau aux truffes et aux pointes d'asperges fraîches*, and *rognon de veau à la moutarde*. The bird is a woodcock, an example of the game which has contributed to the Haeberlins' fame.

Jean-Pierre recommends Alsace wines, such as Riesling, Gewürztraminer and Tokay, although their most expensive wine is a famous burgundy, Richebourg '37. Also on the wine list are fifty champagnes, including six pink ones. Their collection of antique decanters is in regular use.

to be missing from Paul. The contrast between the kitchen and the dining-room is probably more marked at L'Auberge de l'Ill than at any of the other great restaurants. While Paul's kitchen is a homely affair, Jean-Pierre's dining-room and the garden of which it seems to be a continuation are highly sophisticated.

Jean-Pierre is in every way the opposite of his brother. He is a small, fussy kind of man with darting movements who, when he talks to you, is constantly watching what else is going on in the room. He is as voluble and confident as his brother is shy. While Paul is quite unable to explain his passion for cooking, Jean-Pierre has his philosophy pat. 'My ideal is *le beau*. I am a perfectionist.'

His whole policy is to create an environment. His skill has lain in judging over the years exactly how much to change the restaurant and when to change it. 'We are still the same as when we were a bistro,' he maintains, in plain contradiction of the manifest fact that they are a luxury restaurant. Yet there is truth in what he says. L'Auberge de l'Ill has developed carefully step by step, never denying its origins but, instead, building on them imperceptibly, so that although the old fisher-folk may never set foot in the place, finding La Truite more familiar for their tastes, they have no resentment against the Haeberlins, taking pride in their success and the fame it has brought to Illhaeusern.

When the brothers first took over, it was certainly still a bistro and today one room is kept in the Alsatian style, with rude dressers and check cloths, partly to reassure old customers and

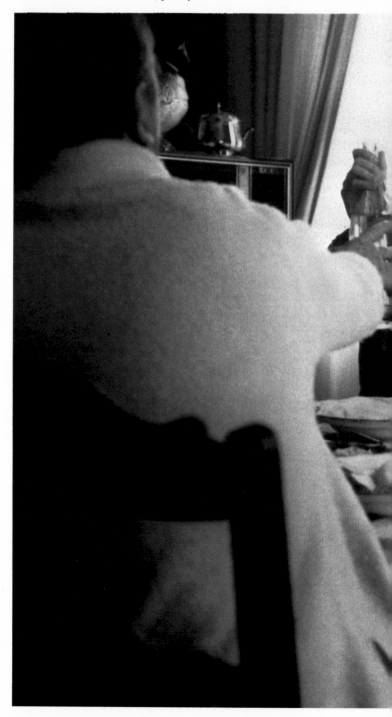

The Haeberlin family—the two brothers, their mother, Marc and his sister, still at school—eat their lunch at 11.30, half an hour before the restaurant service begins. The food is brought from the restaurant kitchen, the only one in the building, and served in their family dining-room, which is also the office where Paul and Jean-Pierre sometimes take reservations.

Marc's inheritance will be a menu closely associated with the region. He is already responsible for buying all fresh food for the restaurant, marketing at Colmar at 6am. The Haeberlins believe, 'Our strength is to buy fresh daily.' Game is bought from individual farmers and meat comes from Paris twice a week. Fish arrives by overnight truck from Brittany.

partly for the rustically inclined tourists. Onto this Jean-Pierre built a grander room, furnished with Directoire chairs and modern water-colours, indulging his own taste without alarming his customers. This room still contains a neat collection of Strasbourg pots and a tall earthenware stove. When they won their first star he judged it to be time to dig up the comforting, old kitchen-garden and create a riverside lawn with weeping willows, where people could sit and have coffee. The third star coincided with a large extension with modern plate-glass windows, still having Directoire chairs, but nothing rustic. This last ingredient was provided by the saving and re-erection in the garden of a little timber-frame cottage from Colmar.

Now that they have had ten years of triple stardom, Jean-Pierre is going to be able to indulge his fantasies a little more. He has bought a large, eighteenth-century timber-frame building which he has dismantled and wants to put up to make a grand salon where people can sit when it is too cold in the garden.

If one can forgive such coyness as writing Adam and Eve on the lavatory doors, Jean-Pierre's decorations are polished and stylish. Similarly his organization of the service is superb. The waiters are some of the best in France and there is the additional friendliness of there being two waitresses. It seems that while the French, in particular the Parisians, prefer men to wait on them, the Swiss and, to some extent, the Germans like women. He is opposed to separating those who serve food from those who serve wine, therefore all the waiters are taught about wine,

L'AUBERGE DE L'ILL
des
Frères Haeberlin

68150 ILLHAEUSERN

Jean-Pierre is a water-colourist inspired by the Alsace landscape. His paintings adorn the walls of the restaurant and one is printed on the front of the menu. He also holds exhibitions in Paris.

and the customer only needs to discuss the meal with one person. Everything Jean-Pierre does is most carefully calculated in this fashion.

He greets every customer. Special ones he takes to the table himself, and for extra-special ones he will even take their order. A most precise judgement of the customers is the hallmark of his success. Illhaeusern is an out-of-the-way spot, in undistinguished countryside, but it is harder to get a table here than in almost any of the three-star restaurants. Of course it is on the way to the South for many Germans, the Belgians and the Scandinavians. Yet even in winter, they turn away anything up to sixty clients a day.

Jean-Pierre maintains that his prices are lower than in restaurants of equivalent standing and also that people come for the family atmosphere. It is more likely that if anything other than the food is the source of success, it is the proximity to Germany which accounts for the amazing popularity of L'Auberge de l'Ill. There is no other three-star restaurant within reach of the Germans, who have recently become interested in food more for the quality of its taste than its nourishment and volume.

It is for them that Jean-Pierre, with his infinite sensitivity to the needs of customers, caters. Apart possibly from the Belgians, he regards the Germans and the Swiss-Germans as the best customers. The English he finds demanding and about the Americans he has little to say.

At heart, he is perhaps a little more like his brother than one might expect, in that they both share the insularity of a minority

113

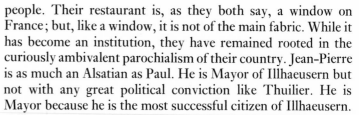

people. Their restaurant is, as they both say, a window on France; but, like a window, it is not of the main fabric. While it has become an institution, they have remained rooted in the curiously ambivalent parochialism of their country. Jean-Pierre is as much an Alsatian as Paul. He is Mayor of Illhaeusern but not with any great political conviction like Thuilier. He is Mayor because he is the most successful citizen of Illhaeusern.

'I am not political. It is true I am not left-wing, because I fear government interference and a levelling down in the name of equality. I stand for the maintenance of tradition. I am the Mayor because I love my village and here we vote for the man and not for the party.'

As with Paul, so with Jean-Pierre. One may judge from his competent but uninspired watercolours, that he probably would have been an adequate decorator and not much more, without the genius of his brother to give a peg to which he could attach his talents.

This is not to deny their astonishing achievement. There is no doubt that their restaurant is one of the best in France. They maintain traditions, persisting in what Jean-Pierre calls 'purity of line', and they create a 'harmony which is everything.'

Jean-Pierre is most insistent that restaurateurs should stick to their stoves. Because their restaurant is full every day all the year round, they have none of the problems of which all the others speak and which drive them to commercialization. 'If you do branch out, it must be a local thing. You must not, as others do, put cards in the bedrooms, selling wines like a merchant,' he says waspishly, though he might consider promoting Alsatian wine. Perhaps it is a part of their strength that they have never made that leap from their peasant inheritance which they planned as youths.

It will be interesting to see how new times affect the new generation. Paul's son, Marc, is now just at the age at which they might have made that leap. He is already arguing in the kitchen with his father, but at the same time has created new dishes for the menu, for example, his *terrine d'écrevisses*. In the precise words that his father used about his own career, he says that he wants nothing else but to be a chef. 'If I had to choose again, I would do it again.'

While it was difficult for Paul to move around in the conditions of his youth, Marc has trained with Bocuse and the Troisgros and in Germany. In the French army he was cook for the Minister of Defence. His world is a broad one.

He is a handsome young man with a pretty wife who, like the rest of the family, is involved in the restaurant, helping in reception. They have a baby daughter, Laetitia. Marc seems to combine the talents of his father and the spirited energy of his bachelor uncle. It is he who goes to Colmar market every morning at six. He is bursting with desire to find new things to cook and new ways of cooking them. 'A few years ago we couldn't serve fish so lightly cooked, but we must not plunge to extremes. We have to have a balance.'

It seems that he has just that balance which in the previous generation it needed two people to find, and there is little doubt that the combination of talent and energy, which lifted L'Arbre Vert so far above the simple bistro which used to be its twin, will carry L'Auberge de l'Ill well into the next century.

Collecting is a Haeberlin hobby: their china, silver wine-coolers and antique decanters are displayed and used in the restaurant. Jean-Pierre searches out old timbers to ornament the restaurant, and even whole buildings to tack onto the Auberge. Their antiques come from shops in the area like this one, which they visit regularly, in Riquewihr, heart of the best wine-producing area in Alsace.

Alsace, bordering the Rhine, has always been a Franco-German battleground and the Haeberlins' scrapbook reflects the turbulence. The inn was bombed to rubble during World War II (photograph on far right). Photographs and postcards show the village and inn before the war. Signatures are collected in their *livre d'or*, or visitors' book, next to which is the photograph of the President's lunch to mark Bocuse's *Légion d'Honneur* award, which Jean-Pierre attended, and at which one of the Auberge's dishes was served.

Louis Outhier

L'Oasis
La Napoule

The palm tree gave L'Oasis its name. A menu is posted outside— a rare habit for a restaurant of this stature—and the gastronomically curious gather to read it. L'Oasis is close to the harbour at La Napoule, a village west of Cannes, where the crescent of beach ends and the rockier coast begins. Many of Outhier's clients arrive by sea, although in more luxurious vessels than the one he uses for fishing.

For all the talk of *nouvelle cuisine*, of progress and modernization, there is in the profession of chef so much that is founded on tradition and a romantic view of the past. In the days of fast food, convenience food, portion control, cost effectiveness, labour relations and all the rest of present-day catering, there is something almost antique about the concepts which are the basis of *haute cuisine*. There is no other surviving business which, by its nature, is obliged to defy the accepted rules of economy, to take always the hard route rather than the easy one. *Haute cuisine* preserves the nineteenth-century values of hard work coupled with dreams of excellence.

Of the chefs in this book, Louis Outhier is the one most inspired by these two archaic notions. His family were country people, millers in the Franche-Comté, living beside the River Doubs. As a boy, he used to watch the farmers arrive in the morning with their wheat and leave again in the evening with their flour. His grandfather was a true countryman who knew the ways of the fish in the river and the game in the woods. He enjoyed catching things, never for the pleasure of killing but always for the pot. He knew just where a hare would be lying at just the right time and he knew the pools where the pike would be; but he would catch one only for a wedding feast. They kept pigs which snuffled about in the mill, eating the grain that had fallen to the ground, which gave their meat a rare taste, enhanced by being smoked in the chimney over a special wood. Food had a great importance in the Outhier household and ecology was natural to them, although it was not called that. And when his grandparents died, his mother kept the traditions alive in the family, talking always about cooking and the advantages of country food, even though they lived now in Belfort where his father kept a garage.

Under the influence of all this, Louis Outhier decided on his career at the age of nine. When the war was over and he was sixteen, his father sent him to work for Denis Michalland, the chef at the Grand Hotel du Tonneau d'Or in Belfort, hardly expecting that much would come of it. As soon as he got there Outhier was fascinated by both the man and the work. Michalland had been a chef to the King of England and Outhier describes him as a man of quite extraordinary presence and appearance, with the hands of a magician. A man of great wisdom and encyclopaedic knowledge. It was like a drug to Outhier, and in the three years he worked at the Tonneau d'Or he was only away from the hotel for a total of four or five days.

When Michalland died, Outhier felt that he had lost a great teacher, but then he found Fernand Point. Although in the three years he had been 'formed', as he puts it, when he arrived as a *commis* at La Pyramide, he suddenly felt he knew nothing. Point, albeit in the classic tradition, had a completely different approach to cooking from anything he had seen; but it was an approach which struck a chord in the country-loving boy. The difference lay in the deep respect for the taste of the basic ingredients of a dish. Point endeavoured to free the quintessence of what he was cooking, wanting things to be what they were. It began with the suppliers. In those days, there were no official standards of quality and Point maintained a constant communion with the suppliers. He insisted on knowing exactly where everything came from, who had grown it. He

taught the young Outhier that success depended on the way he treated produce all the way through the process of cooking—the temperature it was kept at, exactly how it was cut so that the juices stayed in it, the kind of pot which suited it best. After that it was time to consider what went with it.

It was the last two years of Point's life, but in the eighteen months that Outhier was with him, he absorbed the principles which were to lead him to what he is today.

Then this happened. Outhier was doing a two-week stint at the Carlton in Cannes. He happened to run into some friends, called Lalloz, from Belfort, who had a house at La Napoule, which they wanted to turn into a *pension*, and were looking for a manager to run it. Outhier suggested that he and his wife should take it on.

It was logical enough, for how else was he to start? He had no money; unlike so many of the other great chefs, he did not have a chef for a father from whom to inherit a restaurant. He could have gone on working in the great restaurants of France

until he had saved enough to buy a little place of his own, but that would have taken years and would not have suited his energetic and independent temperament. Nevertheless, it must have called equally for a deep sense of modesty to exchange the luxurious atmosphere of La Pyramide, where he had cooked for such people as the Aga Khan, for a simple *pension* with about ten rooms and there cater for rather impoverished boarders who paid a few francs a day for lodging and two meals.

They called the *pension* L'Oasis. They had only a maid and a boy to help them. Madame Outhier had been to a hotel-school and took care of that side of the business. Outhier did all the cooking. There was no menu, just a set lunch and a set dinner—ten dishes a day, for he fed them in grand style on simple Lyonnais cooking. He says that it did him good, working out well-balanced meals twice a day for people who were staying for three weeks. He learned a lot about buying, although it was easier for a set number of people, and how to make the best of cheaper materials than he was used to. The work was prodi-

As the daily *gâteaux* are made, the large weighing-machine is a reminder that *pâtissiers* must measure more precisely than other chefs. All the restaurant's pastry—for fish and meat dishes as well as desserts—is made in this upstairs room. Its wooden work-tops and open-windowed warmth are in contrast to Guérard's refrigerated *pâtisserie*, where the staff work in a temperature of 45-50°F. Desserts are particularly important to Outhier. 'One must never neglect the exit.'

His daughter, Françoise, here discussing a special order with her father and the *chef-de-cuisine*, is an important and respected member of the team at L'Oasis. The clients she welcomes may be European nobility, fastidious gourmets or vacationers there out of curiousity. These she patiently helps, with a detailed explanation of the menu.

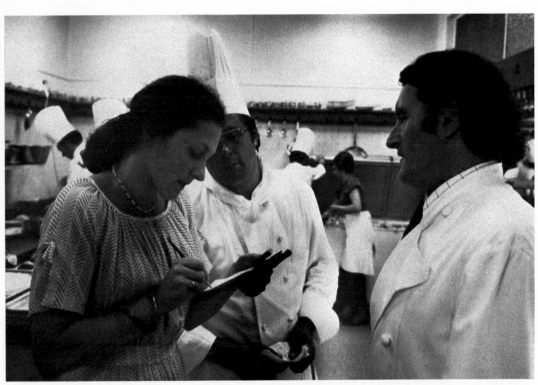

giously hard. Outhier used to work eighteen hours a day. Madame Outhier did all the washing. The season lasted only about four months, but during the rest of the year he made alterations to the building. When they started, there was only one bathroom, so he learned about plumbing and installed more. After two years, in 1956, he offered to buy the house on the grounds that he would rather pay interest to the bank than a share of his profits to the landlords, however agreeable and friendly.

Outhier's boarders soon spread the word around La Napoule of their luck at finding such remarkable cooking in a *pension*. People started to come to ask if they might eat there and, once he agreed, it grew and grew. The place was still small and he arranged two sittings, one for his boarders with their napkin-rings, cautiously re-corked wine and little packets of medicine all stored in the dining-room, and a second for outsiders who came to eat and drink more lavishly. He had just about become a restaurant.

In 1963 Outhier got his first star. This first one was a source of immense satisfaction and pride, and Outhier reacted with characteristic modesty. They were still extremely poor. The cutlery was stainless steel. The plates were rough earthenware with a green glaze which chipped easily. Each evening after setting the tables, they would go round with a little pot of green paint, touching up any pieces which had been knocked. The star had been unexpected and Outhier says, 'I wanted to deserve it, to do everything to live up to it.' So they felt they must improve everything and make tremendous efforts to maintain the standards which they considered a star represented. The result, as anyone else might have foreseen, was two stars in 1965.

'Then we made the same mistake again.' They went in for more improvements, to be worthy of the second star. He enlarged the kitchen and in 1968 finally got rid of the bedrooms and boarders. Even the Michelin were a little startled by his reaction and told him that all they asked was that he should keep on doing what he was doing, not do any more. Five years later, a few weeks before the 1970 Michelin was published, Outhier's daughter, Françoise, was told by a journalist, who had got a rare leak from somewhere, that her father was to get his third star. When she told him, all he could say was '*merde*'.

'Nowadays, everyone chases three stars, but to us it was a disaster.' Once again, despite the Michelin's assurances, everything had to be redone. New cellars, new decorations, always the desperate effort to keep ahead of the honour he felt had been done him. In reality, there was no doubt that he deserved it; but it was an astonishing achievement. Outhier was the first person under forty ever to reach that height. Moreover, it was without precedent for a first generation chef.

The curious thing is that Outhier is not a person of strong ambition, unless making the best of oneself, as he puts it, is ambition. When he says he is not proud of his success for himself, you find it quite believable. He is proud for L'Oasis and the team to whom he gives nearly all the credit. 'One must fight every day for survival,' he says. But why? Why go against all the odds, when it takes so much out of you? He has no answer. Outhier seems to be driven by some religious force to give more and more of himself.

He is a person of a nervous temperament, shy and insecure. 'When I see somebody else's kitchen, I know it must be better than mine.' He is thin and he is one of the very few great chefs who smokes. At times he has made himself quite ill with worrying and his health is not remarkably good. Yet he is a man of simple tastes with a very fundamental approach to life. He likes to get to the very base of anything he does. Having had to create L'Oasis, he has become fond of the actual craft of building. 'What we do in the kitchen is gone in an hour, so I need to do things which cannot be destroyed easily. Somehow one *must* make them remember.'

So, even today, he spends the greater part of the six weeks during which the restaurant is closed working at improvements. The remainder he spends with his wife and daughter, staying a little longer at table, lying a little later in bed. But if you ask what his hobbies are, he pauses. 'Fishing, a little . . . really I

The first delicacy is Outhier's own *amuse-gueule*: smoked-salmon sandwiches, as thin as a coin, picked from a hollowed-out loaf decorated with a ribbon bow.

As a resort restaurant, L'Oasis is open comparatively late: last orders may be taken at 10.30, the last customers returning to their cars—or boats—in the small hours. Service under the plane trees, or in the dining-room, which is used in the winter and whenever the weather forecast is dubious, is by *head*waiters only, and Françoise. Outhier is frustrated by 'working blind'; perfection would be to have a tiny restaurant where he could discuss every meal with every customer.

can't think.' He is a man concerned only with his family and his profession. Politics have no interest for him. 'I don't understand the word.' Anyhow, to be a councillor or the mayor would be impossible. The meetings are at hours incompatible with his profession. This is not to say that he is limited in his outlook. He has travelled, making a world tour with Bocuse and Haeberlin. His restaurant is highly sophisticated. He takes an energetic part in the doings of the Grandes Cuisines Françaises. He is an easy and engaging conversationalist, despite his shyness. The fact is that his profession at so personal and intense a level leaves no time for anything else. While he is not so strictly independent as Pic, he eschews anything which might be construed as publicity, believing that hard work and good cooking are the only routes to success.

Fantasies with *foie gras*. Peaches of startling realism are modelled from goose liver, with truffles as their pits. Real peach stems and leaves complete the effect. Or, for a *truffe surprise*, *foie gras* is coated with finely-cut truffles and served on a collar of chopped aspic. Outhier's devotion to presentation—and pastry—shows in his *loup en croûte*, presented in a gondola fashioned of starched napkins.

As he says, a *chef-patron* has to have two personalities—the head of a business and the man who cooks. 'The cook must be quite separate, thinking only of what is going to be on the plate. For the Haeberlin brothers there is no problem. One sees to the business; the other spends sixteen hours in his kitchen. The difference between those who are chefs and those who are not is their answer to the question as to which comes first: the kitchen or the dining-room?' He does not even bother to answer the question. What it means to him is that, having devoted everything he has to the kitchen, he then has to find some further store of energy for the rest of the business.

The restaurant itself is a surprise and a tribute to Outhier's intelligence. When one considers the influence of his rustic upbringing on his ideals of cuisine, it must have been a con-siderable leap of imagination to achieve so sophisticated an atmosphere. As his daughter, Françoise, points out, there was no natural setting to develop. They had to create something out of nothing, in a place which was just a holiday town. The result is a delight—all pink and orange indoors, with large tables somewhat crowded together; elegant, comfortable chairs covered in a goldish cut-velvet; masses of orange roses; some silver pheasants and stags (for the more important customers' tables); a plain brown carpet; some fine Chinese vases in niches. Outside, the shaded terrace is a mass of flowers, even in winter. In an inland town, it would be florid; in the country, absurd. At the seaside, it strikes just the right holiday note in perfect taste, unless you find fault with the piped music and the gold doilies. Every aspect of the restaurant, indeed of the whole

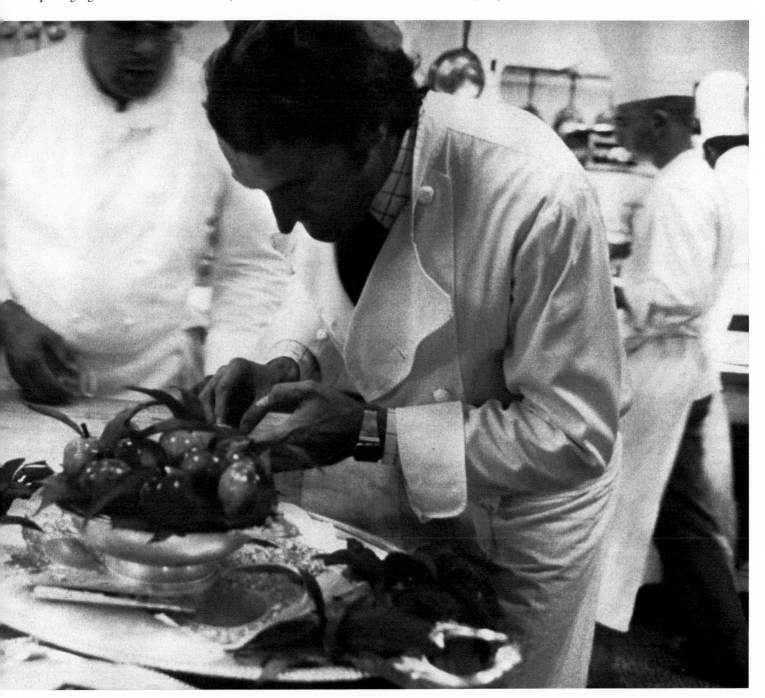

house, was designed by Outhier, who understands every function of the building.

It is Françoise who now greets the customers. She is a pretty girl in her twenties, who at first was not particularly interested in the restaurant. She went off to study business, and when that was done, Outhier built a small boutique for her at the entrance to L'Oasis. It didn't prosper and caused them more anxiety than it was worth. By now Françoise had overcome her initial hesitation which had stemmed from an inherited shyness. Feeling that they needed a little more personal contact with the customers, Outhier persuaded her to take on the all-important job of welcoming people. Madame Outhier now does a little less though, in true tradition, she is in charge of the *caisse*. Outhier, of course, is in the kitchen from which he rarely emerges.

The distinctive aspects of Outhier's kitchens are threefold. First it is happy. The hatless Outhier is perpetually smiling. There is spirit of infinite courtesy in the way the *brigade* of eighteen or more treat not only the boss, but each other. Secondly, it is extremely well-planned, with many imaginative touches. Each work point where the preparation is done has its own water-supply and its own marble spot. There are long wood surfaces, which he believes are better for the produce, washed twice a day. (Wood is illegal in British kitchens because of the danger of harbouring germs and may soon be banned from France). Three bright and hot brass spotlights hang over the point where Outhier may examine each dish before it goes to the dining-room, without its getting cool. Thirdly, the finishing touches which everyone gives to the food are most impressive; the delicately curled bits of lemon peel, the careful ring of fractured aspic round the *foie gras truffe surprise*, so that it looks like a black pearl set in jewels, the pink bow on the loaf of bread containing his *amuse-gueule*—smoked-salmon sandwiches, which are so thin you think they are one slice, somehow impregnated with salmon. They are actually made of rye bread, allowed to go slightly stale and sliced with a bacon slicer. It is

'The first dish should captivate the audience. . . . The palate, the eyes and the ears should all feast.' So *foie gras* becomes a hedgehog in *hérisson de foie gras*, with eyes of truffle and spines of almonds—the flavour of the nuts serving to relieve the richness of the *foie gras*. The flower decoration is, in fact, a sculpted turnip. Some chefs suggest a rich, sweet Sauternes wine with *foie gras*, others vermouth or a light red wine.

Outhier's *mille-feuille de saumon au cerfeuil* is a 'double-decker' sandwich of poached salmon and thin pastry in a sauce with chervil.

124

a meticulous kitchen, satisfying Outhier's belief that, at the very first sight of a dish, the customer must see that he and his team have done their maximum. It is small wonder that, in the summer, when they open the kitchen doors onto the side-street to try to get a little cooler, a crowd of fifty or more may gather to watch, for it is pure theatre.

From first to last what counts is the concentration. Outhier, naturally, does the buying, going to market three times a week, keeping that faithful 'communion' with suppliers that he learned at La Pyramide. 'There are two ways of buying. Either you ask the price or you inquire about the quality.' The local products are only of limited help to him, except in the way of vegetables and fruit. Provençale cuisine, apart from fish, he says is a poor cuisine. So, as with nearly all the other grand provincial restaurants, it means keeping contacts with suppliers all over France.

The food which 'empassions' him most is game. Again there is little to hand, except for some rather special little hares, which feed on the Alpine herbs. In any case most game is not suitable for his busiest season. As with the décor, so with the menu. He has had to create it for a holiday resort—magical salads, a great many fish dishes, chicken, duck and kidneys rather than a lot of meat, and finally his *pâtisserie*. He has built a whole *pâtisserie* kitchen upstairs, next to his flat. There he makes up one of the most elaborate sweet-trolleys in the country. 'One must never neglect the exit. It must be in grand style.'

Whenever one produces anything, he says, it must be the best one has ever done. It has to be honest. If one succeeds it is because one is perpetually anxious; ever to be satisfied or complacent is fatal. One has great enthusiasm at the beginning for an objective, but it never really is reached. For this reason, he has no fears about the future because he is happy to go on trying to prove that he can always do better.

There is an irony in having proved what he has proved so far. Before he got his third star no-one knew the name of Outhier. They knew his restaurant as L'Oasis. He could have

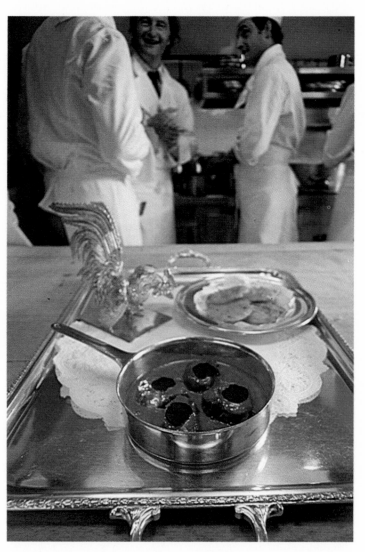

Noisettes de chevreuil, overlooked by a silver cockerel, has a red wine sauce and a side dish of slim potato pancakes. There is a hot spotlight over this work-top to keep the food warm while Outhier applies the finishing touches. An often-open door to the kitchen is one of the tourist attractions of La Napoule, and chefs taking a breath of air will often discuss their performance with admirers.

Suprême de volaille Jacqueline is fillets of chicken in a wine sauce, served with grilled apple and rice, and decorated with truffles.

There is a cigar-lighting ritual at L'Oasis. Once chosen, the cigar is warmed by being passed slowly through the candle-flame. When it is aglow, the waiter blows the tip into a complete ember.

sold a going concern. Now he is a personality, he couldn't sell it. He can no longer make a fortune, unless he adopted the ruses and ploys of Bocuse and Vergé. This he could never do. 'I made it without publicity, by hard work and word of mouth. The young are confused by all the brouhaha. Twelve years ago, no-one wanted to come into the profession. Now there are floods. The publicity has had a bad effect because the young think that is all that is needed. Apart from anything else, they do not realize how fickle the Press are. Fashion moves too rapidly and the Press are eager to slash people too soon.' At the same time, he admires Bocuse who, he believes, has done battle for the chefs with great courage, changing their conditions and improving their standing in the community.

As for the future of L'Oasis, he is happy now that Françoise has come to enjoy the business. He is a long way from retiring, but one day he believes she will run the business with a chef, on the lines he has set down. Of course, she could never be a chef. 'It is not that women could not do it, although it is physically unbelievably hard work. It is that, in order to do it, a woman would have to erase her femininity. She could not wear make-up. The steam would destroy her complexion. Her hair would be ruined. She would develop awful muscles. It simply is not compatible with being a woman.'

Against that, he is delighted with the resurgence of interest which housewives have shown in cooking for themselves. In the old days, women were better cooks because they had more time. Outhier believes that they must relearn some of their grandparents' skills. The first thing is care in buying. Marketing is something one needs to learn. One must question and find out everything one can about where a particular thing has come from, and when and what has been done to it. One must learn to recognize a tired chicken, a chilled vegetable, a wrongly cut piece of meat. One must spend time and make comparisons, not buy the first thing one is offered.

Women, he says, do not nowadays work out exactly what happens when they cook. They make a *soufflé* and it works once. The next time it is a flop and they give up, whereas if they thought about it they might remember the little thing they did differently.

Next, he recommends that housewives should buy professional implements, the best they can afford. It is no good complaining about the results if you cook in stainless steel pots, in which food tends to burn. It is much better to buy copper ones. It is also important to remember that there is a reason for all the different implements. One general purpose whisk is no use. You need one kind to whip white of egg, another kind for *crème chantilly*, a third for sauces.

After that, it is reading and sense and not being too ambitious to start with, rushing in to make elaborate recipes before you have learned the basics. Finally, generosity, the desire to please.

And it is that desire to please which sums up Outhier's philosophy. His work and dedication have but one end. 'Method, order and organization are nearly sacred matters for me. One could say that this is the most inconvenient, the most arduous and demanding profession in the world, but it is the best. The best because one is conjuring up a sensation of pleasure—a moment of dreams and magic.'

126

Outhier checks a melon for ripeness. Personally he eats little, but very often. A fastidious man, his working dress is unusual for the lack of a hat, the visible presence of shirt and tie, and the length of his apron. Also a practical person, he is knowledgeable about building construction, plumbing and decorating. Here he is explaining the motif he wants over the fireplace in a room undergoing renovation.

Jacques Pic
Valence

Tolstoy was probably right when he said that unhappy families were unhappy in different ways, while happy ones were happy in the same way; yet truly happy families have become so rare that today they have the appearance of individuality.

It may be that the social conditions in a provincial town in France are, by virtue of their solidity and their slightly old-fashioned rigidity, conducive to familial happiness. Even given these circumstances, the family of Pic in Valence is singular in the quality of its happiness and closeness.

The restaurant Pic is a family restaurant in every possible meaning of that phrase. Even its creation, or rather its re-creation, was a matter of family pride.

The name of Pic has stood out among restaurateurs for forty years or more. André Pic, who is now in his eighties, inherited the family *auberge*, Des Pins, and built it up during the 1930s until he ranked, with Point and Dumaine, as one of the three greatest provincial chefs of France. Des Pins, which had been in the family for three generations, stood in the hills above Valence, but André Pic decided that he would do better to move into the town. Already he had plans for his three-year-old son, Jacques, to whom he wanted to leave a prosperous establishment. In 1935, he bought an antique shop with a large garden, and converted it into a restaurant. By 1939, this new enterprise, with its clutter of small rooms, had been given three Michelin stars. It had become not only the most important restaurant for the people of Valence, but a famous stopping-place for travellers on their way to the South of France. Everything seemed to be going according to plan.

Unfortunately André Pic's health could not stand the strain

of a chef's life. In 1946, he lost one of his stars and from then on the restaurant declined even more rapidly. Monsieur Pic could no longer stand for any length of time and, in his exhaustion, he was unable to teach his staff the niceties of his cuisine. He was too tired to supervise the buying. In addition to all these problems, his son, Jacques, did not much want to be a chef. His grandmother had told him that he would never make a cook; he wanted to be a garage mechanic.

In 1950, another star went. André Pic was discouraged to the point of contemplating selling up. It was then that the sense of family unity began to work on the eighteen-year-old Jacques. He was deeply unhappy to see his father, for whom he has a great admiration, so cast down. So, although he had worked in the kitchens, he set off to gain experience elsewhere. He tried to go to both Dumaine and Point, but they had no room for him. He worked in Geneva, Beaulieu, Deauville and Paris. His instruction was not perhaps in the mainstream followed by his colleagues of today, which may account for the difference between him and the others of the *nouvelle cuisine*. He travelled for four years and, during the last one, did his military service in Algeria—an experience which even today adds a little spice to his cooking. Then he returned to Valence and became engaged to his wife, Suzanne, who was training to be a nurse.

For three years he hesitated, divided between his own inclinations and his anxiety to please his father. It was his fiancée who encouraged him to stick it out. In 1957, he took the plunge. He got married and at once took over the restaurant. It was typical of the Pic family that he could not have embarked upon it until he had a wife to complete the team.

Having finally made his decision, Jacques Pic set about rebuilding the fortunes of the family restaurant with amazing energy. He is, as he says, an impulsive man, who might on his own have been tempted to sweep everything aside and rush into too violent a reorganization. His wife calmed him and respect for his father contained his revolutionary spirit. Sensibly, he concentrated, to start with, on the dishes which had made André Pic famous—the *poularde en vessie*, the *gratin de queues d'écrevisses*. Of course, his father's style had belonged much more in the tradition of Escoffier. Jacques Pic lightened the sauces in keeping with the modern trend. At the same time he devoted much attention to improving the produce. He also started to redecorate the restaurant and reform the garden. Within five years he had won back the second star.

Jacques Pic maintains that he was lucky with the timing of his takeover. De Gaulle had created a more stable climate. There was social progress, which meant that more people had enough money to go to better restaurants. He also gives credit to Raymond Oliver of the Grand Véfour in Paris, who stimulated interest in cooking in a series of television programmes, and to Gault and Millau, who 'took up the relay stick' by advising housewives on how and where to buy good produce, and then went on to produce an authoritative guide to restaurants. He admits that the loss of his father's stars was perversely beneficial. 'It made me unhappy and gave me the incentive to raise the house up again, whereas a place which was running perfectly might not have inspired me.'

The two things which he would never mention are, of course, the two which count for far more than any chance of timing—his talent as a chef and his and Suzanne Pic's magic in creating a wholly beguiling atmosphere of contentment and well-being.

The restaurant Pic is totally different from any other three-star restaurant. In every other one, as you go in, you feel to a greater or lesser degree, a pricking of awe. You have surely heard of Paul Bocuse and his showmanship, the Baumanière you know about if only because the Queen of England went there, Michel Guérard hardly hides his light under a bushel. But Pic? His is a name known only to gastronomes, for he shuns publicity. He does nothing but cook; certainly nothing to advertise himself or build himself up as a star. Vergé, Chapel or Troisgros, you might run into them in Persia or Los Angeles, Helsinki or Osaka. Pic you will find only in Valence.

The fame of the other chefs often infects their staff, not exactly with superiority, but with an expectation. Their welcome, however friendly or polished, is always tinged with the implication that they expect something of you. 'Here you are,' they seem to say, 'in a great man's restaurant. Mind you enjoy it.' As you go into the Pic restaurant, you feel nothing of this. That is not to say that it isn't grand. The hallway is all marble and beautifully plain, but any formality is instantly dispelled by the genuine warmth of the way you are greeted by Madame Pic or Madame Odette, who has been with the Pics for

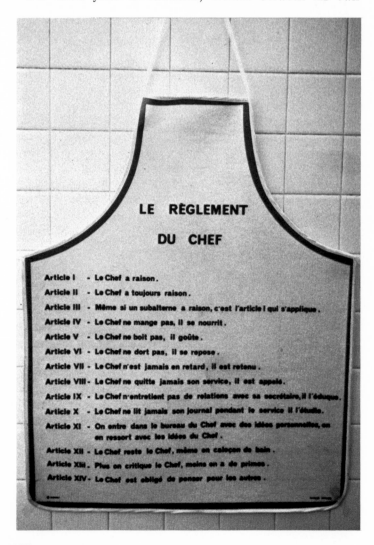

LE RÈGLEMENT

DU CHEF

Article I - Le Chef a raison.

Article II - Le Chef a toujours raison.

Article III - Même si un subalterne a raison, c'est l'article I qui s'applique.

Article IV - Le Chef ne mange pas, il se nourrit.

Article V - Le Chef ne boit pas, il goûte.

Article VI - Le Chef ne dort pas, il se repose.

Article VII - Le Chef n'est jamais en retard, il est retenu.

Article VIII - Le Chef ne quitte jamais son service, il est appelé.

Article IX - Le Chef n'entretient pas de relations avec sa secrétaire, il l'éduque.

Article X - Le Chef ne lit jamais son journal pendant le service il l'étudie.

Article XI - On entre dans le bureau du Chef avec des idées personnelles, on en ressort avec les idées du Chef.

Article XII - Le Chef reste le Chef, même en caleçon de bain.

Article XIII - Plus on critique le Chef, moins on a de primes.

Article XIV - Le Chef est obligé de penser pour les autres.

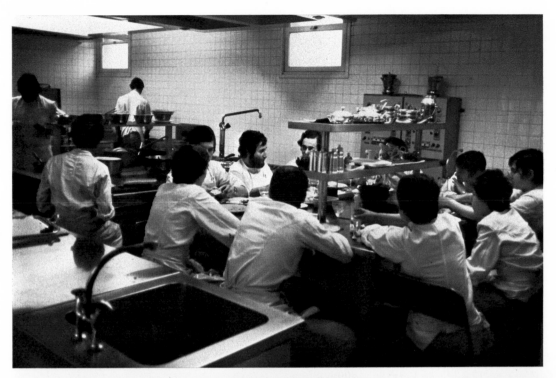

As his father lunches upstairs *en famille*, Pic's bearded son eats with his colleagues of the kitchen *brigade*. Earlier, Pic has briefed them on the day's menu. 'Working as a chef is not a private act,' he says, and he shares in the chores of preparation. Other restaurants of this class usually avoid novices, but exchange promising trainees. Pic disapproves of 'birds of passage.' He employs local youngsters, trains them—and keeps them. He is the great chef least likely to apply the rules displayed on the apron decorating his kitchen wall.

thirty-five years. You know at once that no-one is going to ask anything of you. A huge black dog, called Giankin, romps across the hall. It takes three people to sit on him. There are apologies and laughter. You recognize that this is someone's home and they are pleased that you have come to it and hope you won't mind if there are any shortcomings.

The dining-room bears out the feeling one has had on arrival. As with everything the Pics do, it is wholly unpretentious, but absolutely satisfying. Of the original three small rooms, only one remains. The others have been knocked together and then enlarged. The overall effect is pink and yellow. One side gives onto the garden where, in the summer, one may eat out. While there is nothing sophisticated about the place, Pic's purpose being to make you feel 'très chez-vous,' the attention to detail is very noticeable. The plates are not blazoned with coats of arms or even the name of Pic; they have a pretty floral pattern, specially designed for him by Limoges. Each one costs 65 francs. The glasses are plain but good. Again, each one costs 35 francs. The object is not to show off, but for each thing in the restaurant to be just right.

It is interesting to compare the service with that of other three-star restaurants. It is at the same time more natural and a little more old-fashioned. The waiters, who all look surprisingly young, although the majority, as with most of the staff, have been there for ten years or more, are all dressed in dinner jackets. The wine-waiters wear the long green aprons of the *sommelier* and stand to attention as they taste the wine from your bottle. At the same time, his waiters enter more enthusiastically into your enjoyment of the food, not with the formal enquiry as to whether everything was all right, but

The family favourites of the Pics. His wife chose *salade de pêcheurs au Xérès*—lobster, crayfish, shrimp, scallops and truffles in a dressing containing sherry vinegar. The leaves are *mâche*—lamb's lettuce or corn-salad. *Filet de loup au caviar*, Alain's choice, is a fillet of sea bass, lightly cooked, coated with caviar and served with a cream sauce. Anne's preferred dessert is *oeufs à la neige*, steamed egg-whites floating on a cream and egg-yolk sauce and sprinkled with caramel. For himself, Jacques Pic made *truffe de grignan en chausson*—truffles cooked in pastry, framed by starched pockets of parsley. The plates are made in Limoges.

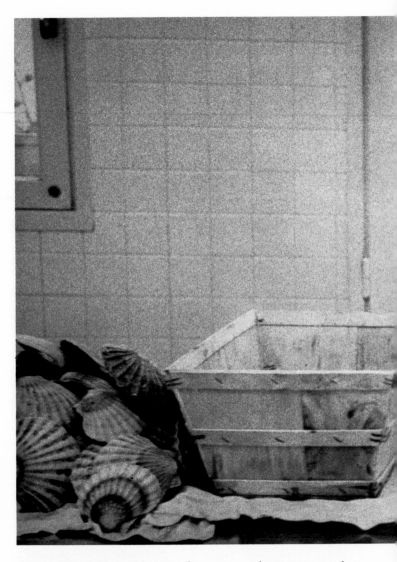

Pic does his paperwork on a cool hotplate, amid the produce that he must necessarily order by telephone as there are few markets nearby. He and his secretary do have a tiny office, but it has more of a controlled 'piling' system than a filing system. His business is run from the kitchen, and his policy is to serve generous portions at prices lower than those of his peers. 'We don't take a pencil to work it out. We don't double on our costs. We are absolutely mad.'

more of a happy discussion of personal tastes. The naturalness stems from Pic's policy of choosing young boys of the town and training them himself as opposed, for instance, to the Haeberlins who never take on untrained staff. The more old-fashioned element comes from his firm principle that, while a restaurateur must be close to his clients, he must never be too close. When once, lightheartedly, I said to him that a waiter had teased me about something, it took me ten minutes of fast-talking to preserve the amiable young man from a severe dressing-down. For Pic that was far more serious than, for instance, one of the wine-waiters giving me some wildly inaccurate information. An honest mistake he can easily forgive, a betrayal of his philosophy is nearly unpardonable.

The centre of Jacques Pic's philosophy is the client. It is a commonplace among chefs that part of their satisfaction in their work comes from giving pleasure, or just giving. It is noticeable, though, that many of them can be quite beady about taking. They enjoy, as well as anyone, the material benefits of their stardom. In this Pic, and probably Outhier, stand alone in seeking absurdly little for themselves.

This real generosity, which amounts to selflessness, runs through the whole organization of the business. By the nature of things, it starts with the buying. For Pic this is some-

thing of a problem, because there are no important markets near Valence. With the exception of fruit and some vegetables, nearly everything has to come from a distance. As usual the ducks are from Challans, the chickens from Bresse, the meat from Paris, the fish from Brittany. The cheeses come from one or other of two cheese factors in Lyon. Nearly all the ordering is done by telephone, but Pic has established a sound relationship with his suppliers, gently persuading them that their reputations, as much as his, depend on their providing him with the best produce. His policy is best exemplified by his relationship with the truffle man with whom the restaurant has dealt for forty-five years. The truffles arrive from Haute-Provence, most carefully brushed so that there is no chance of their being white ones disguised by earth, nor poor ones un-strengthened by frost. Pic loves truffles, though he believes that old-fashioned chefs went mad with them, putting them in everything, and he and the truffle man have the highest regard for each other. Pic sighs at the thought of how much he spends on truffles—more than 80,000 francs a year. 'Each year we say we will buy fewer; but each year, of course, we buy more.'

His particular area of generosity is in the kitchen, for it is there that he feels more at ease. 'I am a man of the kitchen-range because I love it, but also because I am a shy man and

do not really like being in the dining-room. It is in the kitchen that I can express myself best.'

The kitchen at the restaurant Pic is new and large, possibly the biggest of all the three-star kitchens. It occupies nearly the whole of one side of the garden, so that the clients, eating out, can see the chefs at work. The first thing that strikes you is its sparkling cleanness. It might be an operating theatre, except for the whimsical touch of a large stuffed goose standing above one of the work surfaces. Like a surgeon, Pic washes his hands after almost every act he performs. Next, you think it is a friendly, youthful kitchen, the spirit quite denying the clinical appearance of the place. You see here what Pic means when he says that this is where he can express himself. Outside the kitchen, he appears to be rather a short gentle person, covering his shyness with an almost apologetic geniality; always smiling, certainly not in any way commanding. In his kitchen, he relaxes and then you see his strength for he, just as gently, dominates the young men who treat him as a respected friend. It is in character that he stands out from them, not by wearing a larger hat, but by wearing none at all.

The third distinguishing factor of this kitchen is the precision with which everything is done. Pic is a very precise man and, to achieve his effects, he does more of the actual work in the kitchen than many others, who are content to create, instruct and then supervise. He likes to slice the fish himself for the envelopes of *turbot aux morilles*, because he cuts them so much more delicately. He likes to put the finishing touches to the dishes, often like a guilty schoolboy adding a little more caviar to the already smothered *filet de loup au caviar*. 'It is no good half-giving,' he says, 'one must give all that one can. Our popularity lies in doing our job properly.'

If there is a fault in Pic's cuisine, it is that he overdoes the generosity. His food is richer than is now the case with most of the others, partly because he remains aloof from their grouping together. He respects them and they him, but he has a stalwart independence. 'If we copy our neighbours, we are finished; but naturally we look at their ideas and adapt them to do other things.' He also simply gives you too much to eat. No-one else would think of producing his Menu 'Rabelais', with its eight rich courses of *huitres à la ciboulette, cassolette d'écrevisses aux morilles, feuilleté de bécasses, suprême de saumon frais aux poireaux, aiguillettes de caneton en salade, rognon de veau à l'oseille, loup et langouste sauce oursin, filet de pigeon bohémienne.*

At the same time, his food is exciting in its originality, because his imagination is always at work and he has the courage to make mistakes. 'If you read enough, you will see

that everything has been invented or tried, so all one can achieve is new marriages. You are at the stove and you feel something is lacking, or perhaps you really have run out of something, so you cast around for that little extra which will make up the deficiency. That is how I find dishes, while I am working and looking for that extra touch.'

Trained by his father and by more traditional chefs, Pic has a solid base which gives him a certain additional confidence. Valence is where the South begins, so Pic draws more than his less carefree *confrères* at Lyon on a broader cuisine; his North African memories inform such dishes as his *St Jacques sultane*. For all his quietness and modesty, he is as adventurous as anyone cooking today. 'One never arrives,' he says, 'It is an eternal beginning.' It is for this reason that he accepts criticism.

None of the other chefs is quite so honest about his dishes. Take his *safari de poisson aux oursins*. It consists of small pieces of eight different fish, with a sauce flavoured with sea urchins. Pic says he does not think it is quite right yet, because some of the fish cannot quite stand up to the sauce. It is delicious but soon, no doubt, it will be better. 'What manual worker does not make mistakes? Look, I am the cook, not a man of pomp. I am here to please the clients.'

Who are the clients? 'We are in a provincial town. We must have the people of the town. We like the tourists who pass by, and most of all we like those who come and say that their parents came here thirty years ago, but we must always keep faith with the people of Valence.'

There is evidence that the Pics do more than that. In the

Pic's personal values sustain a menu of traditional quality and a loyal dedication to catering for local functions. In the upstairs dining-room, a wedding party may find their table decorated by a cone of shellfish with a speared lemon and truffle in its side; a festive menu might include *poularde de Bresse en vessie 'André Pic'*, a Lyonnais dish which he credits to his father, of truffled chicken cooked in a pig's bladder.

hallway are the boards of the clubs which meet for their lunches in the upstairs banqueting rooms—the Rotary, the Round Table, the Lions, the Soroptimists, the Kiwanis. Valence is certainly the town in which to join such organizations, for what other branches can meet in a three-star restaurant? Naturally, it does not pay Pic to have such meetings; they could never afford the economic price. He gives them exactly what he is serving downstairs, say, *fricassée de poisson*, *gigot d'agneau*, cheese and a sorbet. All at a much reduced rate. 'These people helped me when I was beginning. How could I abandon them? Just because we have a little success, we mustn't swell up like frogs. One cannot change one's nature, so I can never be a man of money.'

A man of money is precisely what Pic is not. The butter comes to the table in pretty miniature copper saucepans, lined with silver. People are always asking if they can buy one. Pic could do a bit of business, selling them for two or three hundred francs. Instead, he has been known to give them away.

As with everything else, he views the bill from the client's point of view. 'The prices must be reasonable, because the customers aren't dupes. Our principal concern is that they should come back.' Already he thinks the restaurant is too

expensive, so he keeps his prices as low as possible; consequently the profits drop all the time. His costs have quadrupled in the last five years. His is a slightly larger restaurant than some of the others, capable of doing over a hundred covers at a meal, but he regards anything over ninety as dangerous and a hundred and twenty, for some exceptional reason, as an absolute limit. He employs a total of thirty-five people and, even allowing for the lower wage rates in a provincial town, one can estimate his wages bill as being not less than 900,000 francs a year. That alone could be a quarter of the gross, which gives some idea of the problem.

At the same time, Pic is by no means rash. All the time he is wanting to drive on with that same impulsiveness that he had some twenty years ago. He wants to enlarge the staff dining-room, to get rid of the last of the little rooms, to create a new garden. 'It is not ideas we are short of. We have seven or eight different plans. If we are not actually doing something, then I feel we are going backwards.' As a counter-balance to this love of rapid progress is the sagacity he has learned from his wife. He is never prepared to borrow more money than he has and he talks always of securing a solid base from which to operate.

At the back of his mind there is the family tradition. As

At the end of a 'working' holiday, Pierre Troisgros dropped in for dinner at Pic's restaurant with his wife and architect. The 'work' was toward finalizing plans for the new kitchen at Les Frères Troisgros. Pic's work area has white-tiled walls, stainless steel surfaces, and is larger than most of the kitchens that can serve a hundred three-star meals at a time. It is particularly well organized, and great care has been taken with functional details. His cooking hobs are mostly electrically fired; the new Troisgros kitchen has also adopted electricity.

his wife puts it, 'Our goal is always that Alain should be inspired.' The Pics have two children—Alain, who is nineteen and a younger daughter, Anne.

It is when one sees the Pics as a family that one understands the difference between him and the other chefs. For the others there is the spur of glamour and excitement. For the Pics there is no need of outside stimuli. They are interested, not in fame, but in achievement. They remain, essentially, the proprietors of a provincial restaurant, with the solid and simple values of the liberal French bourgeoisie. They describe the day when Jacques Pic was asked to fly to New York to cook a dinner for the shoe manufacturers, Charles Jourdan, for the opening of their first shop in America, on New York's Fifth Avenue. (The Jourdan factory is just outside Valence). Their instant reaction was to suggest that Bocuse should go. Eventually Jacques was persuaded, partly by Suzanne who felt he should see America and, when he went, she lay awake all night worrying about so unusual an adventure as a plane flight.

If one goes with them to dinner in another restaurant, it is almost comic to see his puzzlement at the respect with which he is treated. Their pleasures are simple ones. The restaurant is shut on Wednesday, not because that is a quiet day, but because that is the afternoon of the rugby match. If there is no rugby, Jacques and Suzanne go for a walk in the country with the romping Giankin. In the winter they go to the snow for a fortnight, for Alain to ski. For three weeks in the summer, they go to the hinterland of the Landes with lots of friends. 'I don't like to be alone. It is nice for two or three days, then we need friends.' They don't do anything. 'My wife and I cook, or the friends do it, and we spend hours and hours at the table, laughing and talking.' The pleasures of an unassuming man.

That is all that he wishes, except that Alain should be inspired. It is touching to see the conflict which this produces in him, for Alain is going through similar doubts to those which beset his father at that age. A bit of friction with youth, Pic feels, is a good thing to push one on. 'With my son there is plenty.' He does all he can to restrain his natural desire to see Alain follow in his footsteps. One half of him wants to nag at the boy, the other half knows he must leave him free to choose.

I would judge that Alain will choose in the way that his father hopes, for what the Pics regard as friction is what anyone else would call astonishing amity. And if he doesn't, that amity will still prevail. For, however narrow the compass, there is nothing that is small about the family of Pic.

139

Raymond Thuilier

L'Oustau de Baumanière
Les Baux-de-Provence

Les Baux was once the centre of a medieval fiefdom famous for its Cours d'Amours. As a city it flourished until 1632 when Louis XIII, feeling threatened by its power, ordered its destruction and left its 6000 inhabitants destitute. Les Baux now provides the setting for the Oustau de Baumanière, nestling in the valley. The rock, crowned by a ruined castle and dominating the countryside, was reproduced as a cake at Maxim's for Thuilier's eightieth birthday party. Thuilier was fifty-one when he opened his restaurant. He still attends to every detail, while finding time to paint the surrounding landscape and its flowers. One of his paintings is on the front of his menu.

There are wild places in the world which seem to respond to civilization with a disdain that, at the same time, enhances both the elegance of what man does to them and their own savagery. Such a place is Les Baux. It is like a tame panther held on a silken leash, tame only for as long as it chooses to acquiesce in the game of being a pet.

To an inelastic imagination, there can be no less likely spot for the flowering of courtly love. Yet it was here, in the thirteenth century, that the millenium of the hopeless passion began. And, on reflection, the very ferocity of the place—fierce columns of rocks, sudden cliffs, arid hillsides—perhaps gave an edge to the sentimentality, so that the concept of courtly love could survive to colour our loves even today.

Similarly on a day in 1941, in time of war, it was no ordinary imagination which could look at this wild, lost place and think it was the right situation in which to establish a restaurant of infinite elegance. There were the rocks, the ruined castle of the crusaders, the crumbling renaissance façades of the village and, far below, an abandoned olive-oil mill, which had sunk to being an ordinary farm and then been abandoned again. It was this building which was to become world famous.

Even more improbable, the imagination belonged to Raymond Thuilier, the son of a railway engineer, who had spent twenty years of his life in an insurance company, first as a salesman, ultimately as a director of the company.

To Raymond Thuilier, there seemed nothing strange in the decision to become a restaurateur in so neglected a place, at the age of fifty-one. The combination of his experience and his nature dictated it as a logical progression of his career.

In the first place it was in his blood. He speaks little of his father, who died when he was young, but on his mother's side his family had been *aubergistes* for three generations. '*Aubergiste* is a nice old-fashioned word,' he says. '*Aubergiste* means a family welcome while *hôtelier* means a less personal hospitality. I like *aubergiste*.'

When she was widowed, his mother took over the *buffet de la gare* at Privas and, as a young boy, Raymond watched his mother working in the kitchen. She was an excellent cook and, he maintains, really his only teacher. In his youth he promised her, rather against her wishes as she knew the arduous nature of a chef's work, that he would one day revert to the admired profession of her family. A handsome young man, intelligent and ambitious, almost any career seemed open to him.

Then came the first war in which he served as a sapper. Thuilier has a passionate resentment for the years which the two wars stole from him, but it happened that after World War I he was demobilized in Provence, and the artist in him was so attracted by the light there that he decided that this was where he would ultimately settle.

First, he had to make a living. He joined a life insurance company. It might seem a strange choice for an artistic person whose two passions were painting and cooking, but there is in Thuilier a measure of fascination with commercial success—though not in any way vulgar.

He says that his work with the insurance company gave him insights and understandings which he might otherwise have found difficult to acquire. Human contact was not altogether

Jacques Picart, the *chef-de-cuisine*, has been at the restaurant since it started. He checks every dish before it leaves the kitchen, in this case duck with peaches, prepared by Thuilier's grandson, Jean-André Chariel.

Chariel has been trained for his inheritance by Chapel, Haeberlin and the Troisgros brothers; he has also attended business school. At the Baumanière he works in each section of the kitchen. Below he is at the 'piano'—one large gas-fired hotplate with areas at different temperatures, which is the kitchen's cooking surface. Above it is a warming plate and taps for speedy pan-filling. The pans are of tin-lined copper, which is used by most of the great chefs.

The Baumanière is unusual in having women among its waiting staff, and trolleys rather than trays, perhaps reflecting that the elderly Thuilier has a long-serving, older team. The waitress is Thuilier's sister-in-law, wife of the *sommelier*. Thuilier welcomes friends backstage.

easy for him. In selling insurance policies he learned to understand people. 'You have to go to the customer.' What he learned then, he later applied in his restaurant.

In a sense, the whole of his life was a preparation for the fulfilment of his pledge to his mother. Wherever he was working, whether in Lyon or Paris, he cultivated the company of chefs, in particular Fernand Point, and spent as much time as possible in the best restaurants. He cooked all the time for his friends.

It may have been no coincidence that Thuilier made his final decision in 1941, the year after his mother died. Naturally it was a decision that alarmed his friends. Even the *Commissaire de Tourisme*, Georges Pompidou, later to be President of France, said to him that for an insurance man he had little sense of security. However much they might share a love of Les Baux, it was a dead city. Thuilier replied that as an insurance man he understood risks. Having a vocation for cuisine, he never contemplated the possibility of failure. It was, in fact, a risk which he had calculated most carefully.

Les Baux, although dead, had known two periods of great prosperity. It lay near several centres of tourism. He saw no reason why it should not become famous once again. He also reckoned that, by the time he had managed to restore the ancient mill, the war would be over. In times of austerity he would stand a better chance against the opposition, who were limited by the restrictions of food shortages and rationing. The timing, indeed, struck him as particularly favourable.

He formed a fifty-fifty partnership with Madame Moscoloni who, rather in the background, worked side by side with him to build up the business.

The restoration took six years in times of great practical difficulty. France was occupied, labour was short, materials hard to come by. There were the Germans to contend with, particularly difficult for Raymond Thuilier who is given to voicing his opinions. He was accused of being a Gaullist. 'If General de Gaulle represents France, then I am a Gaullist,' he told the Germans. They said he was trying to harrass them. 'You took away the spring of my life,' he said, 'and you took away the autumn of my life. All I want is that for the winter of my life you should get out of my country.'

The winter of his life began without them, and it was to be a long, long season of happiness that really became his whole life. In 1946 the Oustau de Baumanière opened. The restaurant today still has the air of a castle dining-room from which the owners have slipped out for a minute. It is grand without being formidable, friendly without being familiar. There are huge stone fireplaces, tapestries and a sculptured Roman lion, but the table-cloths are bright and pretty and Thuilier's own decorous pictures give colour to the grey stone.

All his calculations had proved correct. The war was over. There was a whole new generation of young Frenchmen who had never known what good food could really be. The age of rapid travel and tourism was beginning. Within two years he had earned his first Michelin star. In eight years he had achieved the summit of three stars. So rapid a rise requires either a remarkable skill or some unusual characteristic.

In Thuilier's case it would seem to be the curious blend of an artistic nature with a shrewd worldliness. To talk to him about

143

Jean and Pierre Troisgros

Les Frères Troisgros
Roanne

We have an image in our minds of chefs as roly-poly figures full of *bonhomie*, as if the Michelin man also did the cooking. However, the image is a false one. It is cooks who whistle at their work, while chefs cry. The exceptions to this rule are the Troisgros brothers.

From no other three-star restaurant would you see a superior-looking customer emerge, with a cork trailing behind him, tied by a string to the back of his raincoat belt. His friends laugh at him and, when he realizes why, back he comes to the restaurant. Pierre Troisgros looks grave. Jean looks pained. How could such a thing have happened?

But, of course, it could happen, for almost anything can happen *chez* Troisgros. Soon the customer laughs himself and goes away happy.

It is nearly impossible to imagine anyone going away from this place other than happy, for among chefs the Troisgros brothers are the greatest dispensers of joy and goodwill. Of all the restaurants in this book, Les Frères Troisgros is the most natural. The other chefs, in their distinct and different ways, have striven to achieve the summit. Jean and Pierre Troisgros appear just to have gone on doing what seemed to them normal and sensible. That this happened to lead to their acquiring three Michelin stars surprises them far more than it surprises anyone else. Yet there is an element of the unexpected. For you do not see here the superb elegance of Thuilier, nor the elaborate simplicity of Alain Chapel, nor the showmanship of Bocuse, nor the sleight of hand of Guérard. Les Frères Troisgros is the epitome of a French restaurant, a meeting place, a home-

The Troisgros brothers inherited a family business and it remains a cheerfully familial establishment. Jean is a widower and Pierre's wife, Olympe, mothers his children as well as her own. Madame Troisgros works at the reception desk where Pierre may be on hand to greet his daughter from school. The hotel is across the street from Roanne station (which is depicted on the cover of their menu) and *haute cuisine* and local bar co-exist comfortably under one roof. Pierre and his wife relax with the regulars before he goes off to cook for gastronomic pilgrims from all over the world—who receive the same amiable welcome.

from-home, a neighbourhood establishment, stamped with the personality of the *patron*, serving excellent food. It just happened that in this case the personalities of the brothers were larger than life, and their ideas of excellence and their talents as cooks so far above the normal that they have created an ordinary French restaurant in the mould of an extraordinary harbour of gastronomy.

This sense of exuberant normality was instilled in the brothers by their father, Jean-Baptiste Troisgros, a simple *cafetier*, the son of a *cafetier*, but a man who believed in doing things well and living life to the full. His café in Chalon was very small and there was no room for his two energetic sons to fight and play. So in 1930 he moved, buying a small commercial hotel in Roanne, Central France, for two reasons. Firstly, it had a large space at the back, where his children could exhaust themselves; secondly, it was well placed, opposite the station, which would ensure good custom.

Soon he had a large number of regulars and travelling salesmen, and he rapidly established a reputation in the town. He was, according to his sons, a considerable innovator. He was the first restaurateur to serve his food already on the plate, as now is general in great restaurants, rather than having waiters dish it out. He was among the first to serve young, red wines cool.

His hotel was essentially a family-run affair. The boys' mother and their aunt, later they themselves and their wives, all worked in the hotel. It was a natural expectation that they would carry on the business, but Père Troisgros also waged a subversive war, as Jean puts it, to make them make the decision to dedicate themselves to something more ambitious. He wanted them to have big restaurants. To this end he sent them, after some initial training, to Lucas-Carton and then to La Pyramide, where the great Fernand Point was transforming French cuisine.

In about 1954, the brothers finally returned to Roanne and started to practise what they had learned from the masters, in the improbable setting opposite the station. In those days they were poor. The dining-room was about one quarter the size it is today. There was no question of putting on the menu salmon imported from Scotland, or, indeed, anything lavish. The fish they served was skate and hake. Yet in 1957 they won their first Michelin star.

In those years their reputation grew in Roanne and their restaurant became for the locals the natural place to meet, to celebrate, to take out a girl for dinner. It remained, however, the commercial hotel it had always been, albeit growing a little in comfort and style. Then Jean-Baptiste Troisgros did two things which confirmed his sons' opinion that he was an exceptional person. He announced his intention to retire and hand over the business entirely to Jean and Pierre, and he advised them to plunge themselves into debt, borrowing as much money as they could in order to expand the business. Even more remarkable, he was as good as his word about retirement. Although, in a familial way, he spent much time in the hotel, he never from that day interfered in any way with the running of the business. He set out to enjoy himself for the last fifteen years of his life, which ended for him rather in the style he had lived, eating oysters in the company of three pretty girls.

Although he never interfered as most would have done, or perhaps because of this admirable restraint, he left both on his sons and on the hotel an indelible stamp of unpretentiousness. It took the brothers ten years to achieve their second star and three more to get their third, and this rather slow progression may, considering their talents, have been due to the rather casual atmosphere of the place. One certainly has no impression here of reverence, in fact planned irreverence might describe it better.

There is no question, for instance, of there being no salt on the table. Some people, particularly smokers, they say, like more salt than others—anyhow how can a large thing be salted inside? When told that Alain Chapel's barman had refused to serve Bloody Marys, they shrug and say, 'Perhaps he doesn't know how to make one.'

With them you can have whatever you want. 'We are not justices. In proving too much, you prove nothing.' Their only rule is that no-one should annoy his neighbours and they laugh at the story of the woman who complained about a man's cigar. He agreed to put it out if she would wash off her perfume. They are completely uncritical of their customers, for theirs is the one three-star restaurant where one feels there might be a connection with eating and survival. They actually think people come to eat in the restaurant because they are hungry and, if they are hungry, what better than to eat the very best food? It is this consideration for the customer which surprises. Jean will ask what kind of wine you like best, red or white? If you prevaricate, saying you have not decided what you are going to eat, he will say, 'Never mind all that, drink what you want to drink. It's your taste that counts.'

It hardly occurred to them that they would ever get three stars and, asked how they achieved it, Pierre says, laughing, 'It has something to do with the cooking, I believe.' Jean, on the other hand, says more seriously, 'It is the family atmosphere. It is the Roannais, the people of the town, who make it. We created an ambience, children are welcome here. We are not sophisticated, opposite the station.' It is Pierre's joke which is the true answer, while Jean's explanation, for all its warmth, probably describes why the stars were slower in coming than their basic talents deserved.

Then, again, there may be something in what Jean has to say—not so much in that the ambience they have created may have earned them anything, but more that that ambience is the result of a solid background of affection on which they have managed to build so much else. Here are two brothers. Jean, a man of fifty-one, thin and tall, handsome in his beard, with a

'Light and digestible, pure and clean' is how the brothers describe their food. In their wood-panelled restaurant they present some specialities. The *mosaïque de légumes truffée* is a terrine of vegetables flavoured with truffles. Pierre serves it on a bed of tomato *purée*.

Fresh salmon is posed with the sorrel leaves that will flavour the sauce in *escalope de saumon à l'oseille Troisgros*, the dish the brothers created for Paul Bocuse's *Légion d'Honneur* lunch for Giscard d'Estaing. Rib of beef from the Charollais cattle bred around Roanne is used in several dishes, such as *côtes de boeuf au Fleurie*. A white Meursault bearing the Troisgros' own label goes well with the salmon, while the house Beaujolais (served, unusually, from a pewter carafe) suits the beef. Awaiting service, while Pierre turns to another task, is a dish of *foie gras de canard poêlé aux épinards*. At other times of the year, the duck liver might be served with tiny turnips.

face which creases easily in smiling. He speaks with a soft rhythmic intonation. He appears the more urbane of the two. Pierre, two years younger, stocky with a face not exactly plain, but not unlike an ox. In every way less polished, yet his wit is that much quicker. Jean is more pessimistic, shy, but he is also precipitate, given to extravagant gestures like throwing not just a glass, but a bottle in the fire. Pierre is as steady as his shape, capable of exhibiting great excitability, but knowing at every moment exactly what he is saying.

You could not take them for two brothers. In the event, it seems that in some mysterious way they complement each other, or perhaps they are really two facets of a similar nature, merely appearing to us so different. Whatever the bond, it spreads over the whole family. Olympe, Pierre's wife, a chic Italian who works behind the desk, treats them both with the same teasing affection. Jean's son and daughter and Pierre's two sons and daughter might all be brothers and sisters, partly, it may be, because Jean is a widower. In any event it is a family, the closeness of which it is pretty to see.

You have only to go into the kitchen for five minutes to feel the sense of family which makes Les Frères Troisgros so different from its peers. This is not a team, schooled and trained to work together, it is a bunch of friends working for the common good. There is chatter, there are jokes. The apprentices play a quick game of football with Pierre's hat. Ted the spaniel wanders in and sniffs at the thrushes waiting to be plucked. The truffle-seller comes and is shown round the wonders of the new kitchen. A Japanese customer arrives to talk to the boy from Japan who is making the *terrine de foie gras*, until Pierre decides he has wasted enough time. The man who comes with the shellfish passes the time of day with the chef who is cutting up the lamb for the staff lunch. The chef pops a few bits in the shellfish man's mouth. Jean plucks a lark or two, each takes him forty seconds. Then he sees the architect and exchanges a couple of thoughts with him. He comes back and passes the news to Pierre, while they shell some *écrevisses*, deftly throwing them into a narrow-necked jar three feet away and never missing. Ted barks and someone gets his lunch, which he eats in the corridor. This isn't a kitchen, it is a home, you think.

Suddenly you realize you have been there for two hours. In that time so many other things have happened. Everyone has known precisely what he has been meant to be doing. The

'To do a good dish for a month is easy. To do it for twenty years, that is hard,' say the Troisgros, suggesting that absolute consistency is the hardest learned part of the chef's art. In the bustle of their old kitchen, the brothers pass on their expertise to youngsters. 'We like teaching because we must continue what was done for us.' They have had foreign trainees—Japanese, Dutch, and the American girl seen at the centre of a technical discussion. Women chefs are still rare in France, but the Troisgros have trained four. Pierre and Jean are interchangeable leaders of their team and one or the other is always in the kitchen. To a degree it can be said that Pierre specializes in the solids and Jean in the liquids; he is the wine-buyer, while it is Pierre who, with pencil poised, asks each chef what is needed from next morning's market.

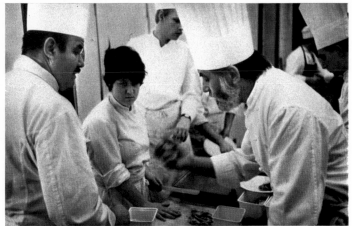

Pierre Troisgros compares cuts of meat at the market in Roanne. (He has his chef's clothes on under his coat, a rare defiance of Escoffier's ruling that the uniform should not be seen outside the kitchen.) Though they mostly buy from the market, the brothers, in common with other *chefs-patron*, like to check on their suppliers' sources to ensure that they are getting the best quality. So they visit the auction yard at St Christophe-en-Brion, near Roanne, to inspect beef on the hoof. The large-boned Charollais cattle are France's favourite breed.

Japanese boy has finished his terrine. The top of each surface has been cleaned half-a-dozen times. Pierre has written the menu on the blackboard and everyone has learned it. The larks have all been plucked. Pierre has shown an apprentice exactly how to cut up a broccoli. Ten minutes later Jean has shown him again. Now he knows. Jean has told a washer-up that you are the health-inspector and that he had better re-do the copper pans he has just hung up. Pierre has blasted to hell a boy who set a pan of boiling water dangerously on the stove. In five seconds he and the boy have forgotten the rage, but the boy has remembered the lesson. The washer-up has hung up the gleaming copper pans. The salmon escalopes have been cut, the salads washed, the vegetables sliced, the sleepier lobsters selected (the friskier ones will still be alive tomorrow), the cheeses taken from the cooler. This is not a home, it is a workshop and a training ground, you think. For two and a half hours the crescendo has mounted, when boom, at 10.59 and fifty seconds, everything stops. It is time for staff lunch.

Jean and Pierre and their aunt and any members of the family who are there all lunch in the kitchen at a special table. The staff eat at the other end of the kitchen. They shout from table to table, asking why England, Scotland, Wales and Northern Ireland can all have teams in the world cup, when France has but one. What about teams for Navarre, Aquitaine and all the others which were countries once? It is a half-hour of fun.

That, in a way, is a key to Les Frères Troisgros. It is fun. For Jean, it is one of the reasons for being a chef. He lives, he says, better than a Rothschild. Who else can sit down at any moment of the day and say, 'Bring me a pot of caviar and a bottle of champagne.' It is the only profession which permits you to *tutoyer* strangers.

The lives of the brothers are well arranged for indulging the comparatively simple pleasures they enjoy. When it comes to buying, they divide their labours, Pierre being in charge of anything solid and Jean of anything liquid. But more than that, there being two of them, they can each take alternate Monday nights off. Pierre goes to play cards; Jean, being unmarried, may look for more frivolous pleasures. They are both keen tennis-players and during the summer Jean plays three hours of tennis a day. In the bar there is the Roanne tennis cup which he has won at least three times. After tennis on Sunday mornings they go to meet with the people of Roanne at the Club des Optimistes.

From their earliest years when they used to bicycle about the countryside searching for produce for their father's larder, depleted by the restrictions of war, they became rooted in the countryside of the region. Pierre in particular is very knowledgeable about the history and architecture of the area.

They also enjoy collecting paintings and sculpture, and every wall of the restaurant and hotel is covered with works of art, mostly local—not necessarily very good, but evidence of their courage in backing their own taste. In the same way, the rather weird decoration of some of the rooms shows a different courage in their acceptance of their architect's advice.

Then, of course, there are jokes. They share with Bocuse and their late teacher, Point, a passion for amiable practical jokes and good-humoured banter. One night in the restaurant Pierre chose my dinner—five exquisite larks. He passed my table as I was eating them, and said in a loud voice, so that the whole restaurant could hear, 'Look, an Englishman eating larks. It's a disgrace.'

On his wine-buying rounds, Jean Troisgros visits the *caves* of Pierre Dezat where a new vintage of Sancerre is ready for 'blind tasting'. Having sampled the wines from different casks, Jean was presented with the same wines from un-labelled bottles; he was challenged to identify not only which casks they were from, but, in one case, from what level of the cask the wine had been taken. He knew.

Staff lunch over. At 12.15 the chefs' hats go on and the waiters' white coats. The service begins. This is indeed serious. The Troisgros cuisine has about it a special character. It is in some ways rich and lavish, but the richness is tempered always by the memory of the days when they could not afford salmon. It is innovative, without ever forgetting the tradition of centuries.

As they put it: 'For forty-five years we were all stuck with Escoffier. Nobody could move. Now there is movement, but one must have a solid technical base. First that base, then reflect—for thinking is everything. It is not just a haphazard affair, a new dish. It is a pondering on a new combination of tastes and then a reconciliation with the technical base.'

As one eats, one remembers not the pranks in the kitchen, not the jokes, but the work. For that old father of theirs imbued in these brothers, along with everything else, a native practicality.

They refuse to talk about money—it isn't their objective. 'If you talk about money, we lose our status as artisans. We are not in the business of making money or of building up something in order to sell it. Anyhow, didn't you know it is bad taste in France to ask about money? I would have thought you would have known that. It is an American thing. Not that we mind, you know.' And they pluck from the air some fictitious figure to show forgiveness.

Nevertheless, they are both canny and at the same time anxious to keep faith with their Roannais customers. While they do not go in for the all-out showmanship of Bocuse, they are linked with him in the public's mind, so that one often hears a departing customer say to either of them, 'Bonsoir, Monsieur Bocuse.' They appear on television. They lend their name to sell wine and truffles and *foie gras* and marmalade. They make flying visits to America and Britain to do special dinners, though they have a rule that they may never both be away from the restaurant. All that has now become a part of the life of the great chefs.

In their case they enjoy it, because they enjoy everything, but it brings with it great problems. Nowadays, they say, there is too much news and publicity. They produce a new dish, their *mosaïque de légumes truffée* for instance, and six months later it is on every menu in France. There is no difference between Paris and the provinces. Their salmon with sorrel, created for Giscard d'Estaing's lunch, now appears on menus in London, New York and Tokyo.

During service, Pierre Troisgros will emerge from the kitchen to talk to the diners. Eating at home, he will likely settle for something simple, such as pasta cooked by his Italian mother-in-law.

Were it not for the need for tourists, much of this would be anathema to them, for their hearts are really in that first image of a neighbourhood restaurant. They worry about protecting the local producers whose wares they have bought for so many years. They worry about the friends who wander in sometimes just for one dish or even only a drink.

They do not worry, as Chapel does, about the rising prices heralding the end of three-star restaurants. They point out that thirty years ago there were only eight three-star restaurants. Today there are eighteen.

They worry about the Roannais and foresee that in their new kitchens they may have to veer towards a more bourgeois cuisine. Otherwise Les Frères Troisgros might cease to be the sort of place where someone may tie a cork to the back of your raincoat.

163

Roger Vergé
Le Moulin de Mougins
Mougins

There is always one in any group who stands out as being different, the nonconformist who seems almost not to belong. In this collection of *chefs-patron*, it is Roger Vergé. Among the others, there are those who may vary from the usual pattern in one particular. Thuilier did not become a professional chef until middle-age; Outhier's parents had nothing to do with restaurants; Barrier learned much of his skill in private houses. On the whole, however, they follow a course which one might conclude was a set curriculum essential for a three-star chef—the childhood dream of being a chef, the training with one of half-a-dozen great chefs, the belonging to a particular region of France with its traditional produce and cuisine, the unwavering slog of dedication, the patient building-up of a reputation, the support of an equally patient wife, the eschewing of all improvisation and then the flair.

None of this really applies to Roger Vergé, except the flair. It may be that in him the flair is greater than in the others, for at times he gives the impression that he is like one of those aggravating, if wonderfully charming, boys at school who appear to do no work and yet always emerge at the top of the class.

His childhood dreams were not of cooking, but of adventure. His hero was the aviator and explorer, Jean Mermoz, who crashed when crossing the Atlantic. The first book he read was about big-game hunting and, when he was seven, he wrote a long story about a hippopotamus. Vergé's father was a blacksmith at Commentry and the boy wanted to become an aviation mechanic. All the same, he was a country boy and his aunt, Célestine, had a small business selling fish and poultry. She was a good cook and Vergé was greedy. He also liked poking his nose into everything. When he was too small to see into the cooking pots, she would stand him on a stool beside her while she cooked. The day which he enjoyed most was Sunday, when the family would sit round the kitchen table for almost ten hours of the day.

In 1948, when he was seventeen, he still wanted to be an aviation mechanic, but he had to take whatever job was going. In Commentry there happened to be an ex-chef from the Tour d'Argent who was prepared to take him on as a *pâtissier* trainee. Food was at least Vergé's hobby, so he was quite happy with this arrangement. He always had considerable energy and great charm, so he did well and, after three years, the chef decided to send him to the kitchens of Tour d'Argent in Paris for further training.

At that time Vergé was a simple country youth, who was terrified by Paris. He couldn't sleep and was afraid to be alone in his small room at night. After three days he ran away, home to Commentry. His old chef promptly sent him back again. It was the last time anyone was to see any timidity in Vergé. He stayed at the Tour d'Argent, but only for seven months. He then moved to the Plaza-Athénée, with its huge team of more than a hundred in the kitchen, where he stayed three years, which was the longest time he ever spent in one place until he bought Le Moulin de Mougins. He had soon adapted himself to the glamour and cosmopolitan atmosphere of Paris, and the ever-changing staff of the hotel's kitchens, who came from all over the world, stimulated the imagination of the boy who had written about hunting in Africa. He wanted to travel. His next job was in Casablanca at the Hotel El Mansour. From then onwards he was never still, taking seasonal jobs—St Moritz in the winter, Monte Carlo in the summer, Jamaica, the South of France and Africa.

Vergé's training was in grand places, often under good chefs, but he never had that steady influence of one of the great masters which the others seemed to need. And Africa was to be a complete break with *haute cuisine*. He got a job in Nairobi, running the kitchens which supplied the airlines for meals in flight. He was highly successful and soon had a contract for sixteen airports all over East and Central Africa. 'So you see, all my childhood dreams came true. There I was involved with aeroplanes, in the land of big game, indulging my hobby of food. I believe we can all do whatever it is we want to do.'

In a way, this view accords with that of Barrier, that vocation is meaningless. All you have to do is to decide what it is that you are going to be. It is strange that these two chefs, whose ways of life, attitudes, interests and methods are the precise opposites of each other, should arrive at similar conclusions by such different routes, Barrier believing that the goal is achieved by work alone and Vergé, seemingly, that what you want falls from the sky like manna.

In June 1969, he opened Le Moulin de Mougins. It was a small mill-house which had failed as a restaurant several times, but it too answered his dream as a young apprentice, when he had planned to end up with a restaurant in the sun with palm trees and mimosa in the garden.

By this time Vergé had left his first wife, who disliked his

Excellence of cuisine must be the criterion of a three-star establishment, but quality of service is also crucial—the chef's skill is wasted if his creation arrives stone cold at the table. At Le Moulin de Mougins, a team of seventeen waiters, as well as two headwaiters, serves ninety covers. The restaurant's Provençal charm provides less than ideal conditions for the waiters, who must negotiate a narrow passage from kitchen to dining-room, bearing loaded trays up a slope, down two steps and round two corners. During service, Vergé is usually by the hatch, where he keeps his eye on the order board and checks the food before it goes to the table, keeping an even-tempered control of this critical crossroads. Within the kitchen, *chef-de-cuisine*, Michel Bering, and second chef, Patrice Braly, preside over feats of co-ordinated activity. An unusual aspect of Vergé's kitchen is that all the saucepans are aluminium-based stainless steel, rather than copper.

The eight-course meal cooked by Vergé and Bocuse at L'Ermitage Restaurant, Los Angeles, was the gastronomic event of the decade for the hundred American celebrities, gourmets and critics who attended. When Bocuse found himself crowded by gastronomic rubbernecks, he smoked them out of the kitchen in seconds with a sprinkle of black pepper on the hotplate. Any discomfort caused was more than compensated by the menu's unique delicacies. The starter, *le gratin*

d'huîtres à la coque, involves a witty transposition: oysters in an eggshell and eggs in the oyster shell. Along with the oysters are spinach and champagne sauce; the scrambled eggs are criss-crossed with toast fingers. This was the prelude to Bocuse's famed truffle soup. An unusually rich follow-up to the meat course (veal) was *le foie gras du Périgord*, served *sans* crust, with peppered jelly and a garnish of *mâche* (lamb's lettuce), and accompanied by a chilled red wine.

restlessness and wanted him to settle near Lyon. With his second wife, Denise, he started to create a place of elegance and good taste. At the beginning they had only five staff and usually only double that number of customers. 'Luckily I am not superstitious, because four times in the first week we did just thirteen covers.'

Ever conscious of the value of publicity, Vergé set out to attract attention. He pitched right in, serving lobster and other expensive dishes, but charged only twenty-eight francs for his menu. Within a month he had lured Gault and Millau, whom he knew well, to visit his restaurant. By the end of the season, the Moulin was packed every day and he was rewarded in the following March by a star in the *Guide Michelin*. Allowing for printing time, he had won the confidence of that conservative institution in a matter of four months. It was a feat that had never been achieved before.

Vergé now makes it all sound easy. His second star came in 1972, but the work involved was prodigious, because it was a period in which he had to consolidate the variety of his experience and, after the improvisations of Africa and Jamaica, reinforce the traditional base from which all three-star chefs must work. To this end, he set about the examinations for the gold medal of a *Meilleur Ouvrier de France*. The judges of this medal are strictly conservative. They demand not so much flair as an ability to adhere absolutely to the precise rules of classic cooking and therein to produce perfection. Needless to say, Vergé won it in 1972, but it was an act of courage, because to have entered and failed would have exposed him to the doubts of those who were rating his restaurant for the Michelin and all the other guides.

At the same time, he had to be creating a characteristic style for his restaurant and it is in imagination, perhaps, that Vergé excels. Louis Outhier has said that Provençal cooking and *haute cuisine* really have nothing in common, and he has responded to the challenge of having a restaurant on the Riviera in his own particular and exquisite fashion. Vergé, with his panache, has taken a riskier course and managed to incorporate more of the region into his cuisine. Outhier's restaurant, from its appearance, could be set in almost any smart holiday resort; Vergé's is essentially Provençal-rustic in its décor. As you go in, it is dark and beamed. There are large, Provençal, wooden cupboards and antiques, tapestry-covered chairs, brass candlesticks on the bar tables. At the entrance to the main restaurant, there is the old stone mill-wheel.

Denise Vergé is a beautifully dressed woman, who is rather shy, but whose Patchouli perfume reveals a certain, unexpected sauciness of character. She is a great collector of antiques and haunter of junk shops (which Vergé does not much care for on account of the dust) and it is she who is largely responsible for the well-judged decoration of the place, striking precisely the right balance between luxury and something which could be a private house. It is an atmosphere which perfectly matches the food. At its best, Vergé's cooking is a triumph of imagination and observation, grafted onto the solid basis of French cuisine, of which his gold medal is the proof. Yet it owes much to that other side of Vergé's character which is half a love of living dangerously and half a love of giving and taking pleasure.

Haute cuisine and Provençal cooking are separate crafts—one the product of bourgeois refinement and the other a peasant tradition—yet Vergé successfully blends the two styles, in proportions which vary from dish to dish. In his lobster salad *(salade de homard)* truffles and artichokes are the accompaniment to the crustacean centre-piece. The Provençal strain emerges strongly in the *daube* (Mediterranean stew). This includes lamb and pork and is cooked with a pastry-sealed lid to concentrate the flavour, which is enhanced by the combination of rosemary, thyme and laurel with tomatoes, orange skin, leeks and garlic. The fish stew may contain gilt-head bream *(daurade)* and red mullet *(rougets)*, or John Dory *(St Pierre)* and hog-fish *(rascasse)*, according to season, which are cooked in a *nage* (fish stock). *Artichauts à la Barigoule* consists of artichokes mixed with 'earthier' vegetables, celery, mushrooms, carrots and leeks and cooked in stock.

Sea-borne chefs meet topless 'gourmette'. Vergé, Bocuse and their cuisine were the star attractions of a three-day 'gastronomic cruise' on the *Danae*, which ferried its passengers from Villefranche to Amalfi and Porto Ferraio and back at up to 5000 francs each.

Bocuse photographed the passengers as they mingled informally with the chefs. To help cope with more than 300 servings at each meal, Gaston le Nôtre, Paris's top *pâtissier* and a specialist in mass catering, was on hand with his team of ten chefs. (Only thus could the Bocuse truffle soup be served without loss of quality.) Le Nôtre surveys one of the cruise's more whimsical creations: a polystyrene, gold foil-wrapped dolphin adorned with thousands of translucent cucumber scales. In the three days 120 kilos of *pâté de foie gras* and 60 kilos of caviar were consumed, along with 1500 bottles of wine and 800 of champagne. As well as food for the body, the cruise provided food for thought in the form of seminars held each afternoon.

'I cannot imagine a pale, thin chef,' he says, puffing out his plump red cheeks. 'I see in the restaurant so many sad people with nothing to worry about. I love every single minute of life— and, of course, if you are lucky, then you must give to others.' It is a question how much with Vergé depends on luck. More probably, it is a matter of his seizing every opportunity. He will plunge into anything, seemingly without any pattern, certainly with none of the calculation which guides, say, Michel Guérard. A couple of kilometres up the road, he runs another restaurant, L'Amandier de Mougins, a simpler, more easygoing place, serving a plainer menu at 110 francs as opposed to 180 francs at the Moulin, but which nevertheless rates one star in the Michelin. He sells pickles, marmalade, jam and wine. In his 'boutique' he has pottery hens and dolls and hats and anything else which takes Denise's fancy. In Japan, a company called Seibu actually makes all these products and markets them under his name. He is consultant to at least seven restaurants around the world. The ones which have a primary claim on his time are the Hotel Plaza in Denmark and the Patin d'Or in Luxembourg. Above all, Vergé enjoys flying to Rio or Florida or Mexico or Scotland or Iran in order to do a special meal. One gets the impression that if two nuns were having a TV supper on St Hilda's Isle, Vergé would be quite unable to refuse an invitation to cook it.

It is the razzamatazz which Vergé enjoys, rather than the commercial advantage of all these enterprises. 'When I was young and I had a girl-friend, I would never tell her that I was a chef. The image of a chef in those days was of a big-mouth and a drinker. Now chefs are stars.' And he admits to

enjoying this status enormously. 'There are many who say they wouldn't enjoy it and who pretend to disapprove, but that is because they cannot achieve it.' He attributes the change in the standing of chefs largely to Paul Bocuse—'He is the leader of the team.'

Every day Vergé talks to Bocuse on the telephone. Partly it is gossip and partly it is the practical co-operation of the team. They may tell one another that they have found that a dry sherry works in a particular sauce better than a white wine. Somebody may be unable to get pigeons for one of his specialities. Somebody else will find them for him. If Vergé needs a *saucier* in Denmark, he can be sure of finding one within twenty-four hours by ringing round his colleagues. There are about a hundred young chefs spinning in orbit round the *bande à Bocuse*, who can be played with like chessmen to fill any seasonal gaps. There is a big exchange in waiters as well. The glamour of the group is extremely useful in keeping up the supply of staff. The three-star restaurants would find it very difficult if unionization were to creep in. Vergé has this problem in Denmark, where there is a forty-hour week. It has meant changing the formula. Already in Paris there are restaurants which are only open for one meal a day, because the alternatives are either prohibitive overtime or two complete teams of chefs, both of which possibilities are uneconomic. By convincing the young chefs that the potential rewards are exciting and glamorous, they can put off such inconveniences. Vergé tells his young staff that one's first passion has to be for one's job, and points out that his father worked eighty hours a week and was happy. Thus indoctrinated, the young cooks, according to

Vergé, complain when they are sent to Denmark because they get bored with not having enough to do.

Le Moulin de Mougins is probably the most suitable place for engendering this belief among the young, for it is undoubtedly the most glamorous of all the restaurants in this book. Vergé's clientele are quite likely to arrive by helicopter, landing in the field behind the mill. The Cannes film festival and Midem music fair bring film stars and singers—the South of France itself brings millionaires from America, potentates from the Middle East and the British aristocracy. All this is very much to Vergé's taste. It is a fantasy world and that is what he has always enjoyed.

Fantasies, alas, have their dangers. Vergé won his third Michelin star in 1974, less than five years after he first opened. Since that time his other commitments have grown at an equally frantic pace. It is interesting to compare Paul Bocuse's reaction to his third star with Vergé's. Bocuse waited several years before launching out on his commercialization and publicity hunting. He was careful to establish his restaurant on an unshakeable foundation. He trained his *chef-de-cuisine*, Roger Jaloux, to a point where it was quite safe to leave him in the certainty that nothing would go wrong. As we have seen, however great the tide of criticism of Bocuse, no-one can ever say he has had a bad meal in his restaurant.

Vergé's nature is different. 'I like to take risks. When I start something, I like to finish it that day. I have a dread of sameness.' So for him, when the third star was won, that was, in a sense, a job finished and done. The result, which is in no way a reflection on his talent, is that his is the only three-star restaurant where it is not impossible for the details of a meal to be less than perfect. You might find the odd piece of oyster shell in the *gratin*, or grit in the asparagus. A sorbet might arrive in a warm glass. In the kitchens, you might see tins of peaches or bottled tomato sauce.

The role of buccaneer has, to some extent, taken Vergé over. His very appearance has something of the Hemingway about it, with sparkling brown eyes and romance-grey hair. His staff admire him as much for his skill as for his physical courage and tell you of the day when he was out in a boat in the Pacific during a storm. Rescue boats arrived to tow him back to port, but he waved them away, determined to get back without help from anyone. If you ask him when it is that he gets his inspiration, he says that it is driving fast in a motor car. 'If I have problems, I go out in my car.' He loves to tell you of all the plane crashes he has been in.

At the same time, he has another picture of himself. 'I like to go down to the shore and talk to the fisher-folk cooking their catch over a wood fire. Or I like to talk to an old lady about her family recipe for jam. For my produce, I like the peasant-farmer who comes with one basket of beans, picked in the evening. Now, for my holidays, I like remote islands untouched by tourism.'

Vergé's is really a constructed character, built up, rather as his fame has been, by a series of campaigns—so that it is hard to tell which part is intrinsic and which adopted.

His instant charm is unquestionable and, among the *bande à Bocuse*, he is the one they love, perhaps because he is the kind

After Bocuse, Vergé is perhaps the most promotion-conscious of the chefs. At Le Moulin de Mougins his wife has organized a 'boutique' with built-in antique show-cases for the various products carrying Vergé's name, such as jams, crockery, wines and glasses. Many of these are exported, particularly to the United States. Vergé signs his menus at the entrance to the boutique and restaurant. The interior of the restaurant combines a busy, lively atmosphere with an elegant rusticity in keeping with the style of cuisine.

of person who gets deeply involved. His marriage to Denise is remarkably happy; by comparison with some of the other chef's marriages it is an idyll. His elder daughter is married to a chef who works in the restaurant in Luxembourg with which he is connected. They have a son who, Vergé hopes, will one day run Le Moulin de Mougins. His younger daughter is only sixteen and is learning to be a hairdresser.

Nevertheless he is really a solitary man, bursting, it is true, with warmth and generosity; but his is the kind of affection which is directed towards life and humanity as a whole, rather than particular individuals.

It may well be that his risk-taking, his wanderlust and his impatience may lead him into trouble. But we may be sure that if this does happen, he will fight his way back through the storm without any help from the rescue boats.

Chez Roger and Denise Vergé. Their home, at the other side of the village of Mougins, is an old house which has been completely refurbished in an elegant style which shows the influence of Denise Vergé. She is a collector of *art nouveau* pieces, which are set among the indoor plants.

175

'. . . reduce the sauce, to which has been added the cooking liquor of the crayfish and cream. Strain . . .'

Edmond Bajulaz, *chef-de-cuisine* at L'Auberge du Père Bise, prepares Sauce Nantua.

THE CHEFS AT WORK:

Menus, Recipes and Advice from the Great Kitchens

In many ways, cooking is an imprecise art. No two pieces of meat, no two ducks or chickens, no two fish are precisely the same. Their age, their size, the weather, the room temperature, the latitude, almost anything will affect them. For this reason there is little talk of weights or timings in real cuisine. It is the tongue, the finger, the eye, the nose or the ear of the chef which tells him whether a thing is right or wrong. To a large extent it is, as Thuilier says, the spirit which counts; and to tell a chef how much butter to use is like telling a painter how much blue to put on his seascape. For if no two ducks are the same, still less are two chefs the same. Indeed, no one chef is the same on two different days. Chapel's *poularde en vessie* is quite different from Pic's. Outhier's *volaille Jacqueline* used to include the wings and legs. Now he uses only the breasts. The dish has the same name, but it is quite different, because if you change one thing you naturally adapt everything else to preserve the balance, as a sailor adjusts his sails to the wind.

So recipes are perverse constructions, trying to express rigidity where there should be none. Chefs produce them, because it is expected of them, but readers of recipes should bear in mind that if a chef were asked to write down how he cooked a dish one day and were then asked to do it again three months later, the two versions would certainly contain many contradictions.

The recipes in this book come from the most inventive chefs in the world. They are put down as nearly as possible as they were told to me by the chefs themselves, at any rate as I understood them. Sometimes there were things so puzzling about them that I consulted other chefs to check. Every so often, a second opinion would be, 'That can't be right,' but then I remembered that the whole point of the great chefs is that they do things others would never dare to do.

Sometimes again, despite all we have said about the new openness of modern chefs, I would detect a flaw in the account. 'Come on, surely you put a little cream in?' A slow smile, 'Ah, yes a little cream at the end, if you like.'

In presenting these recipes, then, we have made various assumptions. First, this is not a cookery book so we have attempted to give only a general idea of each dish and not put in shopping lists. We have imagined a reader who understands the basic rules of cooking. We have ignored cost, the availability of ingredients, and the limitations of home kitchens. We have presumed a world in which you would only buy the best produce. In short, we have used the standards of the subjects of this book. Our hope is that the recipes may amuse those who will never try any of them and inspire those who will enjoy attempting an approximation of what the great chefs produce every day.

THE LANGUAGE OF CUISINE

Chefs are as carefree with their terms as cookery writers. To most people to 'blanch' means to drop into boiling water. To the Troisgros it means to put something into cold water and bring to the boil for three or four minutes.

Similarly, words may be used unexpectedly. The uninitiated might expect Chapel's *foie de lotte* to mean the liver, whereas it means the roe.

It is all a shorthand, but like written shorthand, one person finds another's difficult to read. The glossary is a particular interpretation of the methods of the chefs in this book. The terms are appropriate to the recipes they have given; they do not necessarily apply to techniques from a different range of cuisine.

Acidulé
Acidulated. Made slightly acid, usually by a touch of lemon juice.

Aiguillette
Long thin slice, usually of breast of poultry or game.

Al dente
Stage during cooking where ingredients are still firm. Vegetables when cooked *al dente* are slightly crunchy.

Bain-marie
A pan containing boiling water into which another pan is put—either to keep foods warm or to cook foods which require a gentle heat, such as sauces with an egg base.

Beurre blanc
White butter; made by gently cooking shallots in butter and then adding water, wine or vinegar and seasoning. This is reduced to a syrup and butter is whipped in vigorously over a gentle heat until the sauce becomes white and frothy.

Beurre mousseux
Foaming butter made by squeezing lemon juice into a *beurre noisette*.

Beurre noisette
Butter cooked to a light hazel-nut colour. It often has a drop of vinegar and seasoning added just before serving.

Blanch
Either the immersion of foodstuffs in a boiling liquid or food immersed in cold water, which is then brought to the boil. This is done to reduce the pungency of some vegetables, like onion or garlic, or to make vegetables or fruits easier to peel, like tomatoes or peaches.

Bouillon
The liquid resulting from the simmering of flesh and bones of meat or fish with vegetables, water and seasoning.

Bouquet garni
A flavouring mixture of herbs, usually parsley, thyme and bay leaf. Chefs vary the herbs according to what they are cooking. They might also change the wrapping from the classic muslin bag, perhaps wrapping herbs in leek leaves tied up with string. A *bouquet garni* is always removed from the cooking pot before serving.

Brioche
A bun made from a yeast dough.

Butter
All butter in these recipes is unsalted. Salt is added as required, rather than being unremovable as a basic ingredient, as it would be if salted butter were used.

Chaud-froid
A *velouté* to which gelatine has been added. It is used to coat or glaze cold foods.

Chiffonade
Shredded vegetable. Especially applied to strips of lettuce and sorrel which are cooked in butter and used as a garnish for soups.

Clarify
To make a liquid clear or transparent.

Clarified bouillon
See *consommé*

Clarified butter
Butter which has been melted and skimmed. It keeps better and does not burn as easily as unclarified butter.

Concassée
Roughly chopped foods. Tomato *concassée* refers to blanched, skinned, deseeded, chopped tomatoes cooked with chopped onions and seasoning in butter.

Consommé
A clarified *bouillon*. *Bouillon* is clarified by being brought to the boil with minced meat and whipped egg-white. The *bouillon* is simmered for an hour or so, during which time the egg and meat absorb fats and impurities in the soup and are skimmed off.

Court-bouillon
A liquor for poaching fish, meat or vegetables. It is usually made from wine, vinegar, water and seasoning.

Crème chantilly
Beaten cream with added sugar. Sometimes it also contains vanilla sugar or lemon juice.

Crème fleurette
Single or thin cream.

Crème fraîche •
This slightly sour-tasting cream is not available outside France. However, double or thick cream is a substitute. If available, unpasteurized cream tastes better. A close approximation to the taste of *crème fraîche* can be achieved in one of the following ways: heat thick cream with buttermilk. Leave to cool and thicken for a few hours before refrigeration.

Mix equal proportions of thick cream with sour cream.

Crème fraîche double
Crème fraîche which is too thick to be poured.

Crème patissière
Also known as confectioner's custard. It is used in pastry-making as a filling for various cakes and flans and is made from eggs, sugar, flour, milk and vanilla.

Creole rice
A rice pilaff to which chopped mushrooms, pimentoes and tomatoes have been added.

Deglaze
To loosen and dilute the concentrated cooking juices in a pan in which meat, poultry or game has been cooked to make a sauce. This is done by mixing in water, cream, stock or wine.

Demi-glace
A highly concentrated *espagnole* sauce.

Emulsion
A mixture in which one substance divides into minute particles and completely disperses itself in a second substance. Butter forms an emulsion with a reduced stock.

Escalope
A thin slice of filleted meat or fish cut across the grain.

Espagnole sauce
A fundamental brown sauce from which there are many derivatives, such as *sauce Robert, Genévoise* and *chaud-froid*. It is made from a *mirepoix* sautéed until golden, to which flour is added to make up the basic *roux*. After boiling with water, wine or clear stock, bones, usually of ham, shin of veal or shin of beef, are added with herbs. Onions stuck with cloves make an additional garnish. The stock is then strained, boiled and strained again until it is the required consistency.

Étuver
To cook food gently in butter in a covered pan.

Fines herbes
A mixture of chopped herbs, usually parsley, chervil and tarragon.

Flame
To set light to a liqueur to pour over food for flavour.

Fricassée
Made by cooking meat or poultry first in oil or butter, and then with added wine or stock to form the sauce in which it is served.

Fumet
A well-reduced *court-bouillon*; tends to gell when cool.

Glace de viande
A glaze made from a meat stock which has been strained and reduced to a thick syrup. This solidifies when cold.

Glaze
To pass a dish under the grill or salamander.

Julienne of vegetables
A combination of root vegetables cut into thin strips. Usually the combination is of carrots, onions, celery and leeks, though other vegetables may be added.

Liaison
The process of thickening and binding—with egg-yolks, farinaceous ingredients or blood.

Macerate
To soak an ingredient, usually fruit, in a liqueur or syrup.

Mirepoix of vegetables
A mixture of diced vegetables, usually carrots, onions and celery.

Nage
The cooking of fish and shellfish in a reduced *court-bouillon* flavoured with herbs. It also refers to the cooking liquor.

The great chefs rarely measure as they cook and the *pâtissier* is likely to have the only weighing scales in the kitchen. These conversion tables are for use with the recipes in which the chefs thought that precise measurements were significant.

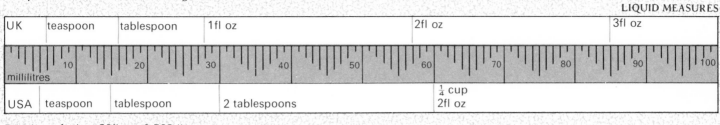

UK	teaspoon	tablespoon	1fl oz	2fl oz	3fl oz
millilitres					
USA	teaspoon	tablespoon	2 tablespoons	$\frac{1}{4}$ cup 2fl oz	

British 1 pint = 20fl oz = 0.568 litre
American 1 pint = 16fl oz = 0.473 litre

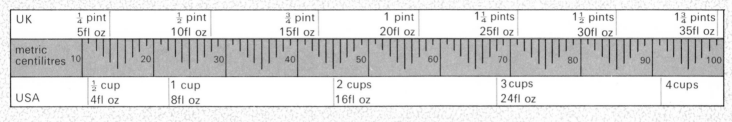

UK	$\frac{1}{4}$ pint 5fl oz	$\frac{1}{2}$ pint 10fl oz	$\frac{3}{4}$ pint 15fl oz	1 pint 20fl oz	$1\frac{1}{4}$ pints 25fl oz	$1\frac{1}{2}$ pints 30fl oz	$1\frac{3}{4}$ pints 35fl oz
metric centilitres							
USA	$\frac{1}{2}$ cup 4fl oz	1 cup 8fl oz		2 cups 16fl oz		3 cups 24fl oz	4 cups

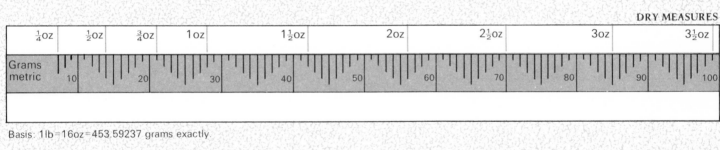

$\frac{1}{4}$oz	$\frac{1}{2}$oz	$\frac{3}{4}$oz	1oz	$1\frac{1}{2}$oz	2oz	$2\frac{1}{2}$oz	3oz	$3\frac{1}{2}$oz
Grams metric								

Basis: 1lb = 16oz = 453.59237 grams exactly.

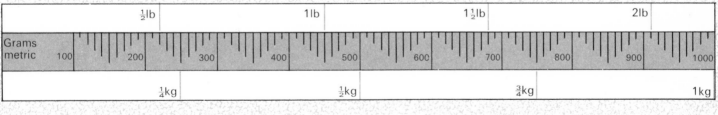

	$\frac{1}{2}$lb	1lb	$1\frac{1}{2}$lb	2lb
Grams metric				
	$\frac{1}{4}$kg	$\frac{1}{2}$kg	$\frac{3}{4}$kg	1kg

Noisette
A round slice cut from a boned piece of meat.

Papillote
A folded envelope of paper in which food is wrapped for cooking.

Purée
The sieved pulp of vegetables, meat or fish. A watercress *purée* is made by blanching watercress leaves and pounding them in a mortar or forcing them through a sieve.

Quenelle
A small dumpling of finely ground fish or meat which has been bound with egg.

Reduce
To evaporate a liquid to a required concentration.

Refresh
To pass quickly under cold running water.

Rice Pilaff
Rice which has been sautéed with onion and butter, then cooked in the oven with chicken or veal stock.

Roux
The *roux* is the thickening element in a sauce, usually made from butter and flour.

Sabayon
Egg-yolks whisked together with a liquid, usually wine, until a light frothy cream.

Sauce à l'américaine
Sauce resulting from the cooking of lobsters *à l'américaine*. Lobsters are cooked in olive oil, chopped onions, garlic, tomato *purée*, herbs, dry white wine, brandy and a fish *fumet*. Then butter is whisked in.

Sauté
A primary cooking technique—to brown or cook food in very hot oil in a shallow pan.

Stock
Stocks are known as *fonds de cuisine*. There are a number of varieties of stocks made from any number of ingredients. A white stock is made from white meat and vegetables boiled in water. Brown stock is made from beef or veal, browned first in butter, to which white stock, water or wine and seasonings are added.

Suprême
The choice parts of a fowl. Usually applied to chicken breast-meat.

Thickening of sauces
The traditional way to thicken sauces is to make an emulsion with butter and concentrated pan juices.

Velouté
A basic sauce made from a *roux* of butter and flour to which white stock is added.

MADAME POINT'S CLASSIC EXAMPLE

RESTAURANT DE LA PYRAMIDE
MADAME POINT
BOULEVARD FERNAND-POINT · 38200 VIENNE FRANCE · TEL. (74) 85-00-96

The menu at La Pyramide seems fresh and modern, though the majority of the dishes are still those created by Fernand Point, many of them forty years ago. Guy Thivard, the present chef, has, it is true, added a few of his own dishes, such as the *assiette de marée, escalope de saumon Pyramide* and *aiguillettes de canard.* But these would not have surprised Point; he would have found them very much in his style.

Many of Point's dishes, for instance the *poularde de Bresse,* either *truffée en vessie* or with *sauce Albuféra,* the *boeuf à la moëlle* or the *jambon cuit madère,* were traditional ones which he simplified or reduced to their essentials, in keeping with his principle that the dominant flavours should be those of perfect ingredients. All these dishes are still prepared with the exactitude which Point brought to them. He would have approved, too, of a traditional dish introduced by Thivard, the *poularde marinière,* done with vinegar.

Point's own inventions, though we have become accustomed to them through imitations, are still striking in their originality. The famous *gratin de queues d'écrevisses* is adventurous in its absolute simplicity: without sauce, and cooked in butter in which other crayfish have been cooked. More unusual is his *truite saumonée farcie braisée au porto*—salmon trout stuffed with very fresh carrots, celery and mushrooms bound with cream and egg-yolk, and braised in a port and white wine stock.

The menu is essentially a country one, aiming at simplicity with its juniper-flavoured thrush *terrine,* the finely cut gratin of potatoes with the *boeuf à la moëlle* and the plain *pièce de boeuf* and *pièce d'agneau.* Yet, with its truffles (a kilo a day, according to Thivard), caviar and fresh *foie gras,* it is lavish as well. Above all, there is the enduring consistency. The legendary *marjolaine* has been on the menu every day, as long as anyone can remember, without varying one iota. That is cuisine.

Menu

Mousse de Foie en Brioche
Délice S.t Jacques

Filet de Sole au Champagne
ou Turbot braisé au Vermouth

Poularde de Bresse Albuféra
ou Pièce de Boeuf à la moëlle
Gratin Dauphinois

Plateau de Fromages

Glace ou Sorbet
Friandises
Gâteaux Succès
Corbeille de fruits

160 Francs

Madame F. Point   23 mars 1978

Nous vous proposons

—

Caviar Extra
Saumon Fumé
Huitres de pleine mer
Pain de Foie gras frais
Salade Délice
Truffe fraiche en Chemise
Terrine de grives au genièvre
Jambon de Parme
Jambon cuit madère
Asperges de Ville laure

—

Gratin de queues d'Ecrevisses
Salade d'Ecrevisses Fernand Point
Cassolette d'Ecrevisses au Viognier
Truite saumonée farcie braisée au Porto
Escalope de Saumon Pyramide
assiette de marée Guy Thivard
Coquille Saint-Jacques

Poularde de Bresse truffée en Vessie
Poularde de Bresse Marinière
Pièce de Boeuf au Poivre vert
Entrecôte à la moutarde
Pièce d'agneau Primeurs
Cassolette de Rognons Pyramide

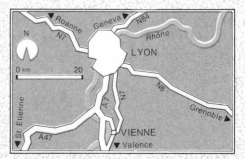

The old Roman town of Vienne, on the Rhône, is thirty kilometres south of Lyon by the A7 autoroute (slightly less by the N7). Following either road to Vienne's southern outskirts, one turns off for the boulevard Fernand-Point to find the Restaurant de la Pyramide.

Point still dominates the kitchen.

'Cuisine is not invariable . . . but one must guard against tampering with the essential bases.'

Madame Point confers with *caviste* and *sommelier*, Louis Thomasi, in the celebrated cellars of La Pyramide. According to Thomasi, her taste in wine is even more discerning than either Fernand Point's or his own.

VIN ROUGE de Moulin-à-Vent

Caves du Restaurant de la Pyramide

VIN ROUGE de Juliénas

Caves du Restaurant de la Pyramide

Bordeaux Rouges

		75 cl.	35 cl.
1974			
*Château Mazeyres	(Pommerol)	70	
1973			
*Château Pape-Clément	(Graves)	70	
*Château Monbousquet	(Saint-Emilion)	50	26
*Château Beau Site	(Saint Julien)	120	
*Château Léoville de Las-Case	(Saint Julien)	75	
*Château Pichon-de-la-Lande	(Pauillac)	230	
1972			
*Château Léoville-Las-Case	(Saint-Julien)	65	
1971			
*Château Trotte Vieille	(Saint Emilion)	90	46
*Château Batailley	(Pauillac)	75	38
*Château Beau Site	(Saint-Estèphe)	60	31
*Château Léoville-Poyferré	(Saint-Julien)	75	
*Château Pape-Clément	(Graves)	110	
*Château Lafite Rothschild	(Pauillac)	200	
*Château Lynch Bages	(Pauillac)	95	
1970			
*Château Pape-Clément	(Graves)	95	48
*Château Ausone	(Saint Emilion)	220	
*Château Beau-Site	(Saint-Estèphe)	70	
*Château Breychevelle	(Saint Julien)	70	
*Château Vieux Certan	(Pommerol)	100	
*Château Cheval Blanc	(Saint Emilion)	190	
*Château Latour	(Pauillac)	180	90
*Château La Tour Blanche	(Médoc)	120	
*Château Brane Cantenac	(Margaux)	120	
1969			
*Château Canon	(Saint Emilion)	100	
*Château Haut Brion	(Graves de Pessac)	200	
*Château Lafite-Rothschild	(Pauillac)	200	
1967			
*Château Cheval-Blanc	(Saint-Emilion)	255	128
*Château Mouton-Rothschild	(Pauillac)	300	150
*Château Latour	(Pauillac)	300	150
*Château Pape Clément	(Graves)	190	
*Château Brane Cantenac	(Margaux)	100	
1966			
*Château Domaine Chevalier	(Graves)	100	
*Château Brane Cantenac	(Margaux)	95	
*Château Ausone	(Saint-Emilion)	280	
*Château Margaux	(Margaux)	350	
*Château Latour	(Pauillac)	360	
*Château Cheval-Blanc	(Saint-Emilion)	350	
*Château Mouton-Rothschild	(Pauillac)	400	
*Château Croque Michotte	(Saint-Emilion)	120	
*Château Pavie	(Saint-Emilion)	155	
1964			
*Château Cheval-Blanc	(Saint-Emilion)	320	
*Château Haut-Brion	(Graves de Pessac)	340	
*Château Mouton Rothschild	(Pauillac)	400	
*Château Lafite Rothschild	(Pauillac)	450	
1962			
*Château Marquis de Saint Estèphe	(Médoc)	100	
1961			
*Château Latour	(Pauillac)	350	
*Château Haut-Brion	(Graves de Pessac)	350	
1953			
*Château Trottevieille	(Saint-Emilion)	250	
*Château Ausone	(Saint-Emilion)	350	
1945			
*Château Teysson	(Néac)	50	
*Pomerol	(Pomerol)	55	
*Château Listrac	(Médoc)	55	
*Château Lafite-Rothschild	(Pauillac)	450	
1943			
*Château Chevalier	(Graves)	120	
*Château Haut-Simard	(Saint-Emilion)	100	
1942			
*Château Gontier	(1re Côtes de Blaye)	45	
*Château Clos-Fourtet	(Saint-Emilion)	120	
*Château Latour	(Pauillac)	300	
1938			
*Château La Mission Haut-Brion	(Graves de Pessac)	250	
1937			
*Château Pavie	(Saint-Emilion)	100	
*Château Croque-Michotte	(Saint-Emilion)	100	
*Château Larcis-Ducasse	(Saint-Emilion)	100	
*Château Clos Fourtet	(Saint-Emilion)	100	
1929			
*Château Poujeaux-Castaing	(Moulis)	85	
1928			
*Château Poujeaux-Castaing	(Moulis)	85	
192.			
*Château Léoville-Poyferré 1920	(Saint-Julien)	120	
*Château Ausone 1921	(Saint-Emilion)	250	
1900			
*Château Latour	(Pauillac)	410	
*Château Lafite-Rothschild	(Pauillac)	410	
*Château Lafite-Rothschild 1898	(Pauillac)	500	
1806			
*Château Lafite-Rothschild	(Pauillac)	1200	

Louis Thomasi has worked at La Pyramide for fifty years. He came as a *plongeur* in 1929, but began to help the *caviste* stack the bottles and soon found himself spending more time in the cellars than washing up. Over the years, he acquired an expert knowledge of wine. Eventually he became both *sommelier* and *caviste*, in charge of what must be one of the world's most distinguished cellars.

The wine list reflects Fernand Point's passion for wines, with not only famous, expensive vintages from Burgundy and Bordeaux, but also local wines, from the Rhône Valley—Côte Rôtie, Condrieu, Gigondas and the southern Côtes du Rhône. Red Burgundies range from 1925 to 1973 and from 500 to 70 francs in price. Perhaps the most impressive selection is of red Bordeaux, going back to Château Lafite-Rothschild 1806 at 1200 francs. For more modest budgets there are five-year-old clarets for about 70 francs.

Three hundred wines are listed on a card two feet across which Thomasi holds as he gives his advice. He wears the traditional green apron of a *sommelier*. His dedication is shared equally between La Pyramide's cellars and the customers he looks after; he is an ally whose recommendations spring from a wealth of experience which he willingly imparts.

'A Beaujolais such as Morgon goes with everything, but it should be drunk cool. Of course red wine can accompany fish: Chateau Batailley 1971, from Bordeaux, would be eminently suitable.' This is characteristic advice, of the kind which Point himself would have given. If a client wants to know more, Louis has an overwhelming fund of information.

There are three cellars. The largest houses all the wines except champagne and young wines still in the cask. Sand on the earthen floor absorbs moisture. Shelves reach up to the arched ceiling. The bins on the shelves are labelled with block-printed wooden slabs. Next to the main cellar is a smaller one where champagnes and liqueurs are kept. It is warmer than the first because 'one drinks these when they are comparatively young.' Even so there are bottles here from 1928 and 1947.

Louis bemoans the fact that these days wines are not being made to keep, but cheers himself with the thought that things may change as younger people seem to be regaining an interest in wine. In the course of his career, he has tasted every wine in the cellar.

He is also in charge of bottling the young cask wines, which are kept in the third cellar. It takes him about four hours to bottle 220 litres. Nowadays, he only does the two house Beaujolais.

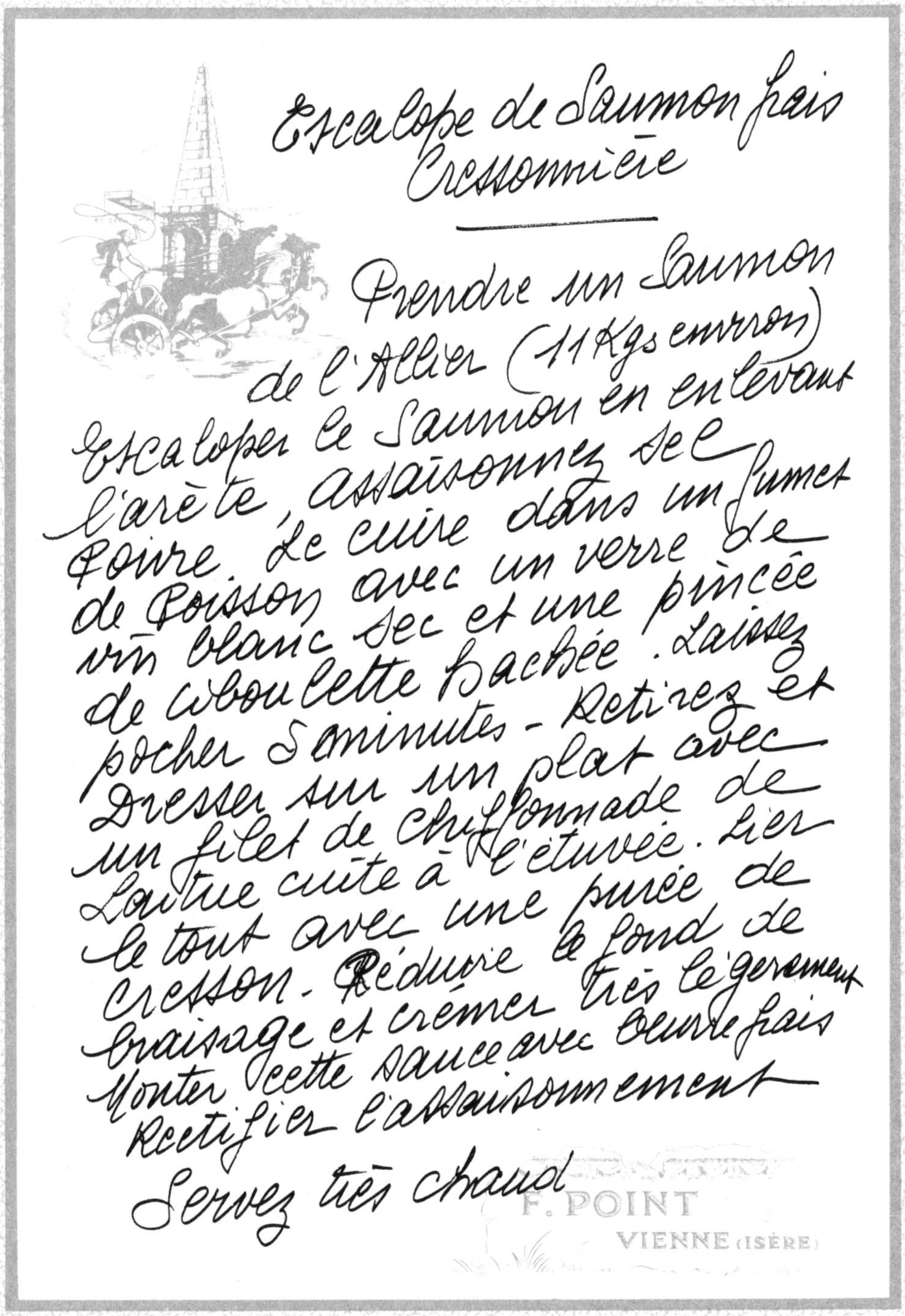

Escalope de Saumon frais Cressonnière

Prendre un Saumon de l'Allier (11 Kgs environ) Escaloper le Saumon en enlevant l'arête, Assaisonnez Sel Poivre. le cuire dans un fumet de Poisson avec un verre de vin blanc Sec et une pincée de Cibboulette hachée. Laissez pocher 5 minutes - Retirez et Dresser sur un plat avec un filet de chiffonnade de Laitue cuite à l'étuvée. Lier le tout avec une purée de cresson. Réduire le fond de braisage et crémer très légèrement Monter cette sauce avec beurre frais Rectifier l'assaisonnement

Servez très chaud

F. POINT
VIENNE (ISÈRE)

The shortlist of Fernand Point's own favourite dishes included several of his own creation, such as the *gratin de queues d'écrevisses* and *truite saumonée farcie braisée au porto*. Such items as the *pâté chaud Rouennaise* and the *terrine de grives au genièvre* showed his preference for traditional and regional cooking.

Escalope de saumon frais cressonière
Take the fillets from a large salmon. Bone and slice them thinly to make escalopes. Season the escalopes with salt and pepper and poach them for about five minutes in a fish *fumet*, with a glass of dry white wine and a few chopped chives. Arrange them on a serving dish with a *chiffonade* of lettuce.

Cover the fish with a watercress *purée*.

Reduce the *fumet* and add a little *crème fraîche*. Thicken the sauce with butter. Check and adjust the seasoning if necessary. Serve hot.

Note: Madame Point's recipe refers to salmon from the Allier region. Canadian or Scotch salmon would be satisfactory for this dish.

A recipe for watercress *purée* is given in the Glossary, under *purée*.

Aiguillette de Caneton glacé Rouennaise

Faire rôtir vert cuit une canette de Bresse 1 Kg 200 environ. Laisser refroidir, lever filets et cuisses. Hacher la carcasse. Faire revenir avec la cuisson du canard une mirepoix de légumes et la carcasse du canard concassée. Mouillez avec un bon vin de Bourgogne. Laisser cuire une heure. Passer le tout à l'étamine en ayant pris soin de mettre un foie de canard finement haché et si possible un peu de sang du canard. Rectifier l'assaisonnement, œuf (?) poivre et 1 verre de cognac.

F. POINT
VIENNE (ISÈRE)

Prendre les cuisses tièdes, les désosser et les reconstituer. Escaloper les filets en forme d'aiguillette. Napper avec le fond du canard dans lequel vous incorporez un peu de gelée. Dresser sur un plat avec des boules de foie gras frais enrobées de brisure de truffes fraîches. Servir avec une salade composée de Haricots verts julienne de Champignons de Paris et céleris et truffes. Sauce moutarde citron Huile d'olive Salez Poivrez

---

Aiguillette de caneton glacé Rouennaise

Roast a duckling until it is just cooked. Remove it from the oven and let it cool. Lift the meat from the carcass. Break up the carcass and the bones. Put these into a large saucepan with a *mirepoix* of vegetables and the juices from the roasted duck.

Mix in some good Burgundy. Simmer this for about an hour. Strain and dispose of the bones. Pass the vegetables, with finely chopped duck's liver and a little of the duck's blood, through a fine sieve. Adjust the seasoning and pour in a glass of cognac.

Bone the legs and reshape them. Cut the breast fillets into long, thin slices. Cover the meat with duck stock to which has been added a little gelatine.

Garnish the serving plate with balls of fresh *foie gras* rolled in chopped, fresh truffles.

Serve at room temperature with a salad of green beans and a julienne of mushrooms, celery and truffles. The dressing for the salad is made from mustard, lemon, olive oil, salt and pepper.

Note: La Pyramide chooses female Bresse duckling for this dish. The everyday vinaigrette is mildly varied by using lemon rather than vinegar.

THE MOST FAMOUS CAKE

The best known of Fernand Point's creations is his *marjolaine*. This extraordinary chocolate layered cake took Point years to perfect. Chefs who trained with him have taken the idea and adapted it; thus Bise has a richer version made with more bitter chocolate.

At La Pyramide, after the *marjolaine*, there is an encore of chocolate truffles.

Marjolaine

On two separate tin sheets roast 900 grams of blanched almonds and 600 grams of hazel-nuts. Then peel the hazel-nuts. Grind the nuts together with 1200 grams of granulated sugar and 100 grams of flour. Beat thirty-two egg-whites until very stiff and fold in the nut mixture without letting the whites collapse. Put into four long, flat buttered and floured moulds and cook in a very hot oven for three or four minutes. A *marjolaine* has to have four layers of cake with three different layers of cream:

Chocolate cream: boil a litre of *crème fraîche*, mix in 1500 grams of bitter chocolate. Leave to cool.

Butter cream: to 125 grams of pounded butter, gradually add *crème chantilly*, until the butter will absorb no more.

Praline butter cream: the same as the butter cream filling with praline powder added.

Build up the cake, with the different creams as the filling between each layer of nut cake. Smooth the sides, cover them with shaved chocolate. Sprinkle icing sugar on the top.

Note: This is a cake for a large party, as it will serve about sixty guests.

Truffes au chocolat

Melt 125 grams of chocolate in a *bain-marie*, add to it a spoonful of water, a spoonful of finely granulated or caster sugar, 100 grams of butter and a yolk of egg (which must not be added until the chocolate has cooled considerably). Leave for five hours, then make balls of the size you like and roll them in powdered chocolate. The truffles should be made the day before they are eaten.

Sorbet Pyramide à l'eau-de-vie de poires William

Peel six William (or other fine eating) pears. Cut them in half and remove the pips. Poach them for fifteen minutes with some lemon juice and a little cinnamon in a syrup of 30° Baumé.

Pass the pears and syrup through a fine sieve. After cooling, check against a saccharometer that the density is at 17° Baumé.

Put the mixture in a *sorbétière* and, at the last moment, add a quarter of a bottle of *eau-de-vie de poire*.

Note: A saccharometer, known also as a syrupometer or sugar thermometer, is a hydrometer which displays the specific gravity of a liquid on a calibrated scale, often measured in degrees Baumé. Distilled water registers zero on Baumé's scale.

A solution of three kilos of sugar to one litre of boiling water produces a syrup of 30° Baumé.

A *sorbétière* (modern ice-cream makers will serve the purpose) keeps the mixture moving evenly and slowly while it freezes.

EXALTED SIMPLICITY AT BARRIER'S

Ch. Barrier

TOURS

Barrier's style belongs very much in the same category as that of Bocuse and Haeberlin. It is based on the region and takes its character from the produce of the region—asparagus, lamb, pigeon, fish from the Loire. The difference lies, perhaps, in its being more austere, there being no grand dishes and scant use of extravagant ingredients like lobster and *foie gras* and truffles. If he does use an expensive mixture, he will present it very plainly, as with his *homard de Bretagne rôti au beurre blanc*, which is simply roasted and served with the sauce apart. This is not to say that his cuisine is uncomplicated. What someone might think was a fish sausage will involve a pike, some sole, scallops, eel, *écrevisses*, truffles, *foie gras*, three kinds of pepper, three herbs, white of egg, cream, brandy and butter.

Barrier sets himself a hard task because his effects lie only in the taste of his food. He aims at simplicity, never clouding the issue with a distracting sauce. His two soups set the pattern. First, *potage crème de faisan*, a pheasant *consommé* thickened with a *purée* of lentils; then *consommé au Xérès*, the standby of every banquet, which only Barrier would put on a three-star menu and be able to justify. His *foie gras* has no truffles but is given a subtle boost by a jelly with port. He uses ingredients that many others would regard as too humble for a restaurant of this calibre—eels in his *matelote d'anguilles au vin de Chinon*, pike-perch for his *sandre grillé au beurre blanc*. His skill lies in elevating the modest and moderating the exalted.

MENU

Potage Crème de Faisan
Consommé au Xérès Chaud ou Froid
Terrine de Légumes au Coulis de Tomates
Mousse de Foies de Canards
Terrine de Canard au Foie Gras
Terrine aux Trois Poissons de Loire
Cœurs d'Artichauts en Salade
Pâté de Perdreau en Croûte, au Foie Gras
Salade de Queues d'Ecrevisses aux Fines Herbes - Suppl. 17,50 F Net
Foie Gras Frais des Landes à la Gelée de Porto - Suppl. 23,00 F Net

Coquilles Saint-Jacques au Naturel
Coquilles Saint-Jacques au Vouvray ou Grillées au Beurre Blanc
Mousseline de Brochet au Coulis d'Ecrevisses
Cervelas de Fruits de Mer, Mousseline de Poireaux
Matelote d'Anguilles au Vin de Chinon
Sandre Grillé au Beurre Blanc
Omelette aux Queues d'Ecrevisses
Sole de Canot Braisée, à la Lie de Vin Rouge - Suppl. 17,50 F Net
Cassolette de Queues d'Ecrevisses, à la Crème - Suppl. 34,50 F Net
Homard de Bretagne Rôti au Beurre Blanc - Suppl. 57,50 F Net

Pigeonneau de Touraine, à la Fleur de Thym
Fricassée de Poulet au Vinaigre de Framboises, aux Nouilles Fraîches
Pied de Cochon Farci aux Truffes
Agneau Grillé ou Rôti, Petits Légumes à la Crème
Suprême de Poularde aux Concombres, Crème d'Estragon
Caille au Ris de Veau et Foie Gras, Céleris Boules
Canard de Challans Saint-Martin de Tours (Pour 2 Pers.) - Suppl. 17,50 F Net P/P

Les Fromages avec Pain aux Noix : 15,00 F

Desserts au Choix : 22,00 F

Gâteau aux Amandes, Crème à l'Anglaise	Ananas Frais au Kirsch
Crème Glacée à la Vanille au Coulis de Fraises	Charlotte aux Poires et son Coulis
Crème Glacée à la Vanille aux Griottes	Poires au Vin de Chinon
Sorbet aux Ananas	Sorbet au Cassis
Sorbet au Citron	Sorbet de Thé au Lotus
Sorbet aux Fraises	Glace au Caramel au Pralin de Noisettes
Pâtisserie du Jour	Petits Fours Frais
Mousse au Chocolat	Œuf à la Neige au Caramel
Compote de Rhubarbe	Compote d'Oranges

A COMMANDER EN DEBUT DE REPAS : Les Desserts Chauds : 25,00 F

Crêpes Gil Blas	Tarte aux Pommes Chaude
Soufflé aux Liqueurs pour 2 Personnes	Sabayon aux Liqueurs pour 2 Personnes
Feuilleté de Poires au Bourgueil	

MENU A 150 F PLUS 15 % DE SERVICE, SOIT : 173 F NET OU

MENU A 120 F PLUS 15 % DE SERVICE, SOIT : 138 F NET EN SUPPRIMANT LE PLAT
DE VIANDE OU DE POISSON

CARTE

TERRINES ET ENTREES

Potage Crème de Faisan	30
Consommé Xérès Chaud ou Froid	20
Cœurs d'Artichauts en Salade	30
Terrine de Légumes au Coulis de Tomates	40
Mousse de Foies de Canard	45
Terrine de Canard au Foie Gras	45
Terrine aux Trois Poissons de Loire	50
Pâté de Perdreau en Croûte au Foie Gras	60
Foie Gras Frais des Landes à la Gelée de Porto	65
Salade de Queues d'Ecrevisses aux Fines Herbes	50
Brioche de Moelle au Beurre Rouge	45

POISSONS ET ŒUFS

Mousseline de Brochet au Coulis d'Ecrevisses	40
Sandre Grillé au Beurre Blanc	45
Matelote d'Anguilles au Vin de Chinon	48
Sole de Canot Braisée, à la Lie de Vin Rouge	55
Cervelas de Fruits de Mer, Mousseline de Poireaux	50
Coquilles Saint-Jacques au Naturel	50
Coquilles Saint-Jacques au Vouvray ou Grillées au Beurre Blanc	50
Omelette aux Queues d'Ecrevisses	45
Ecrevisses au Montlouis, à la Mirepoix	60
Cassolette de Queues d'Ecrevisses, à la Crème	70
Homard de Bretagne Rôti au Beurre Blanc	110

GRILLADES ET ROTIS

Fricassée de Poulet au Vinaigre de Framboises, aux Nouilles Fraîches	48
Suprême de Poularde aux Concombres, Crème d'Estragon	50
Pigeonneau de Touraine, à la Fleur de Thym	50
Agneau. Grillé ou Rôti, Petits Légumes à la Crème	50
Filet Grillé, Sauce Béarnaise, Pommes Soufflées	52
Pied de Cochon Farci aux Truffes	52
Filet au Champigny à la Moelle, Mousseline de Haricots Verts	52
Ris de Veau Bonne Maman	58
Canard de Challans Saint-Martin de Tours (Pour 2 Pers.)	58 P/P
Cailles au Ris de Veau et Foie Gras, Céleris Boules	50
Noisette d'Agneau à la Crème d'Estragon	52
Beuchelle à la Tourangelle - Sur Commande (Pour 2 Pers.)	85 P/P

LES FROMAGES AVEC PAIN AUX NOIX : 15,00 F

TOUS LES DESSERTS : 22,00 F

SERVICE 15 % EN SUS

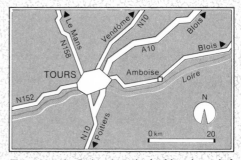

Tours, on the Loire river, is the historic capital of the Touraine region of west-central France, known as 'the garden of France' for its fertile valleys, orchards and vineyards. The restaurant Charles Barrier is just over the Pont Wilson from the city centre, on the Avenue Tranchée.

The wines of the Loire are infinitely varied. Barrier's wine list naturally concentrates on the vineyards nearest to him—Vouvray and Chinon.

VINS DES COTEAUX ET DE LA VALLÉE DE LA LOIRE

Blancs

		Bt	1/2 Bt	Magnum
1974	Vouvray Pétillant brut	60,00	30,00	
1976	Sauvignon de Touraine Domaine du Bouc	50,00	25,00	
	Groupement des Vignerons Oisly-Thésée			
1976	Sancerre Clos du Chêne-Marchand	50,00	25,00	
	Bailly-Reverdy, Bué			
»	Vouvray sec	50,00	25,00	
	Bertrand, Rochecorbon			
1976	Blanc Fumé de Pouilly-sur-Loire	50,00		
	Jolivet Fils, Coane-sur-Loire			
1973	Montlouis sec	50,00		
	Chauveau René, Saint-Martin-le-Beau			
1974	Vouvray sec	25,00		
	Bertrand, Rochecorbon			
»	Montlouis sec	50,00	25,00	
	Chauveau René, Saint-Martin-le-Beau			
1975	Muscadet sur Lie	50,00	25,00	
	Chauveau René, Saint-Martin-le-Beau			
1975	Montlouis sec	50,00	25,00	
	Chauveau René, Saint-Martin-le-Beau			
1970	Vouvray moelleux	50,00		
	Bertrand, Rochecorbon			
»	Montlouis sec	50,00		
	Chauveau René, Saint-Martin-le-Beau			
»	Montlouis moelleux	60,00		
	Chauveau René, Saint-Martin-le-Beau			
1969	Montlouis sec	60,00		
	Jean Bertrand, Rochecorbon			
1961	Vouvray demi-sec	60,00	30,00	120,00
	Robert Allet			
»	Vouvray demi-sec	60,00	30,00	
	Bertrand, Rochecorbon			
1959	Vouvray demi-sec	60,00		
	Jean Bertrand, Rochecorbon			
1955	Vouvray demi-sec		30,00	
1953	Vouvray moelleux	60,00		
1947	Vouvray moelleux		30,00	
»	Saumur moelleux Château Pas de Loup	60,00		
1937	Vouvray moelleux	80,00		
	Marc Brédif, Rochecorbon			

Rouges

		Bt	1/2 Bt	Magnum
1976	Chinon Domaine de la Perrière	50,00	25,00	
	Jean Baudry			
»	Bourgueil	50,00	25,00	
»	Chinon Sélection Charles Barrier	50,00	25,00	
	Couly-Dutheil			
»	Bourgueil rosé	40,00	20,00	
»	Champigny • Domaine Filliatreau •	50,00		
1975	Chinon Sélection Charles Barrier	50,00	25,00	
	Couly-Dutheil, Chinon			
»	Champigny • Domaine Filliatreau •	50,00		
1974	Bourgueil A.C. • Domaine du Grand Clos •	70,00		
	Georges Audebert			
»	Bourgueil Sélection Charles Barrier		25,00	
»	Bourgueil A.C. Les Marquises	70,00		
	Georges Audebert			
1974	Saumur Champigny	50,00	25,00	
1972	Saumur Champigny	60,00	30,00	
»	Chinon Sélection Charles Barrier			130,00
1971	Chinon Sélection Charles Barrier	60,00		130,00
»	Chinon Sélection Charles Barrier	60,00		
	Couly-Dutheil, Chinon			
1964	Chinon	90,00		
	Couly Père et Fils, Chinon			

Consommé aux ailerons

Remove the wings from a chicken and work the rest of the flesh into a paste with salt and nutmeg. Chill the paste. When cool, work in, over a bowl of ice, a couple of egg-whites. Then slowly add a small amount of *crème fraîche*. Shape the mixture with two teaspoons into small *quenelles* and poach these in barely simmering water. Drain after a few minutes and dry the *quenelles*.

Poach the chicken wings in unclarified chicken stock and chop up the meat.

Clarify the chicken stock and add chopped truffles that have soaked in cognac. This is now the basic *consommé*.

Make a julienne of carrots, leeks and celery. Cook this in butter until the vegetables are tender and drain the liquid.

Add the chicken-wing meat, poached *quenelles* and the julienne of vegetables to the *consommé* and serve the soup hot.

Note: Salt added to raw flesh when making a paste helps with the consistency of the *quenelle* mixture.

Bar grillé au beurre blanc Nantais

Clean and descale a large bass. Lay the fish down with its head to the left and flour the top side. Oil the fish and grill it slowly, about eight minutes a side.

While the fish is on the grill, prepare this *beurre blanc*. Take six shallots of medium size and slice them thinly. Put them in an enamelled or, better still, a china pot. Add a wine glass of white wine vinegar and two-thirds of a glass of dry white wine. Reduce this liquid until it is a syrup. Remove the pot from the heat and let it cool slightly. Add small pieces of butter which should be whisked in vigorously. When the mixture takes on the consistency of a sauce, add a pinch of salt. Pour the sauce into a sauceboat and, just before serving, grind in white pepper.

Lay the bass on a bed of parsley decorated with carrots and turnip roses.

Note: Fish should be served with the head to the left; thus the floured side, which will be more attractively marked by the grill, will be on top.

Barrier recommends a Sancerre or a dry Vouvray to accompany this dish.

Filet de brochet à la lie de vin rouge

Season a skinned and filleted pike with salt and pepper.

Lightly sauté chopped shallots and lay the pike fillets on top. Pour a glass of Chinon wine over the fish and simmer for about five minutes.

Place the fish on a serving dish and keep warm.

Add more wine and a cupful of wine lees to the pan and reduce the liquid contents by two-thirds. Take the pan from the heat and blend in butter and *crème fraîche* by gently swirling the liquid around in the pan. Check the seasoning and pour the sauce over the fillets. Serve with a sprinkling of chopped chervil.

Note: Barrier would obtain his lees from the vats of wine-cellars; at home, the sediment from good wine can be stored in a well-sealed bottle with a little brandy to halt fermentation.

Pigeonneau de Tourraine à la fleur du thym

Cook baby pigeons in butter (one per person) in a casserole just large enough to hold them. Leave for fifteen minutes in a very hot oven, basting from time to time; the flesh must remain pink.

Blanch separately in boiling, salted water, broad (shell) beans or turnips, coarsely chopped cabbage and peeled cloves of garlic. Then sauté them gently in butter.

Sear chicken livers and the pigeons' livers in butter.

Cut the pigeons in half and remove the main bones. Lay the pigeons, skin-side up, on a plate and decorate with the vegetables and the garlic. Place the livers on the birds and garnish with a sprig of flowering thyme. Pour sherry vinegar into the pan in which the livers were seared. Reduce this liquid right down and remove from the heat. Whisk in small lumps of butter. Correct the seasoning and pour this sauce over the pigeons and serve.

Note: Pigeons less than five weeks old are used by Barrier. The birds have not yet flown and their meat is very tender.

Noisettes d'agneau à l'estragon

Prepare filleted noisettes of lamb about an inch thick. Salt and pepper both sides and cook in a pan with very hot ground-nut oil to which a lump of butter has been added. The lamb should be pink inside. Take it out of the pan, set aside and keep warm.

Drain off the oil and melt some more butter in the pan; pour in a little madeira. Add roughly chopped fresh tarragon and a little *crème fraîche*. Reduce the sauce slightly and pour it over the meat through a fine sieve.

Serve with buttered noodles, cooked *al dente*.

Note: Barrier uses lamb which has grazed on land rich in thyme and rosemary and this gives it an aromatic flavour.

A MORNING BONUS

One reason for the varied ingenuity of French cooking is the tradition of peasant frugality — everything used, no opportunities wasted. This applies to the many kinds of edible wild mushrooms, each of which lends its own subtlety to dozens of recipes.

Fresh wild mushrooms are a seasonal commodity, but cultivated ones can be obtained the year round. The French pioneered mushroom cultivation in the late seventeenth century, in disused quarry caves near Paris. Today they are still grown in these caves and in others in such regions as the Bas-Vendômois. Cultivated mushrooms *(Agaricus bisporus)* grow in warm darkness on compost in slatted oak trays and come in three sizes: button (small), cup (medium) and, with the best flavour, flat (large).

The three most favoured wild mushrooms in *haute cuisine* are the *girolle* or *chanterelle (Cantharellus cibarius)*, *cèpe (Boletus edulis)* and *morille (Morchella esculenta)*.

Delicately ribbed, a striking yellow and shaped like an old gramophone horn, the *girolle* has such a fine flavour that it is often cooked as simply as possible: lightly sautéed in butter with chopped shallots and parsley, with scrambled eggs or in a simple omelette. The fat-stemmed *cèpe*, when available, is preferable to cultivated mushrooms. With its firm, succulent texture it can be cooked in many ways and dries and pickles well. The springtime *morille*, with its convoluted cap, is particularly good with poultry *(poulet aux morilles)* or *à la crème*. The field mushroom or *mousseron de prés (Agaricus campestris)* is the cultivated mushroom's wild and tastier cousin.

Perhaps the most famous mushroom dish is *champignons Duxelles*, believed to have been named by La Varenne in honour of the Marquis d'Uxelles. Onions are sautéed with shallots, nutmeg and seasoning and fine strips of the mushrooms are added at the end. The result is often used as a basis for sauces and stuffings.

A typical dish of Barrier's region is *quenelles de brochet à la Vouvrillone* which uses not only the local mushrooms, but the light, fragrant wine of Vouvray.

In the same street as his restaurant, the pharmacies have mushroom identification charts on their walls; the ingenious, thrifty French sometimes need reminding of the Dumas story of the family whose walk in the woods ended, 'They brought back a dish of mushrooms, which they had for dinner. In the morning, husband and wife were dead of poisoning and no hope was held out for the daughter.'

Chanterelle or girolle

Cèpe

Morille

BISE: TRADITION WITH VITALITY

François Bise's is one of the shortest three-star menus. This is partly because he would rather cook for fewer customers than he does. Perhaps, too, it reflects the diffidence which he has always felt as a result of his parents' fame. One senses a reluctance to stray too far from their celebrated standards. The *poularde braisée à la crème d'estragon*, which appears as soon as fresh tarragon comes into season, and the *gratin de queues d'écrevisses* were two of his mother's most famous dishes. These, and several others of the formidable Marguerite Bise's recipes, are still the foundation of the menu at L'Auberge du Père Bise.

The other great influence on François Bise's cooking is, of course, that of Fernand Point, under whom the young Bise studied for three years. The basic recipe for Bise's superb *marjolaine* chocolate cake comes from Point, but Bise has managed to make it even richer and quite unforgettable—as is the unbelievable quality of the chocolates and *friandises* which appear with the coffee.

It is Bise's belief that it would be wrong to abandon the old cuisine when so much of it was perfect. Indeed, some critics have been tempted to dismiss him as an echo of the past. The charge is unjust on two counts.

Firstly, he brings to traditional dishes an individuality and variety which make it possible for them to be served over and again without losing their vitality. Thus, Bise's *poularde aux truffes* is, for some, a livelier version of a traditional dish than any of those highly praised, somewhat similar *poulets en vessie* one may find in the Lyon area.

Secondly, Bise has of late branched out with several lighter dishes in a more modern style. This has resulted in such delicacies as the *salade riche* with virtually raw *coquilles St Jacques* marinated in lemon juice, the *escalope de foie gras Richelieu* with

artichokes, and lobsters sautéed with herbs.

Perhaps Bise's most distinctive characteristic is his willingness or rather his positive anxiety to discuss beforehand with his clients exactly how they would like a dish cooked especially to their taste. *Sur commande* he delights in producing *poulet à la Marengo*, based on the dish said to be served to Napoleon after the Battle of Marengo (1800), when his cooks combined the only available ingredients: chickens, crayfish and eggs.

L'Auberge d

Hors-d'oeuvre

Mousse de foie de volaille au Xérès 35
Pâté de caneton aux pistaches 35
Parfait de foie gras 70
Jardinière du lac sauce vermeille _____
Salade riche 40
Pâté chaud sauce poivrade 70
Consommé en tasse 20
Jambon fumé du pays 30

Poissons et Crustacés

Gratin de queues d'écrevisses 80
1/2 homard grillé au feu d'enfer sauce vendéenne 90
Soufflé de truite aux queues d'écrevisses 70
Omble chevalier ou truite du lac meunière 80
ou sauce mousseline 80
Blanquette de homard 90

SERVICE C

190

Père Bise

Grillades et Rots

Poularde aux truffes 80
Poulet de Bresse grillé (2 pers.) sauce diable 120
Pintadeau rôti Albufera 75
Carré (2 pers.) ou selle (4 pers.) d'agneau 70 par personne
Tournedos du Quercy 85
Chateaubriand (2 pers.) sauce béarnaise 140

Plateau de fromages 25

Desserts

Entremets petits fours
et pâtisseries 35

Hors menu ou sur commande

Caviar d'Iran
Petite salade de homard ou d'écrevisses
Chausson de queues d'écrevisses
Omble chevalier braisé au Porto
Omble chevalier à la Nantua
Bisque d'écrevisses
Escalope de foie gras Richelieu
Poulet sauté Marengo
Volaille Souvaroff

❦

A prévoir en début de repas pour 2 personnes :

Soufflés au choix : chocolat, noisette, café, citron,
Grand-Marnier, Rothschild 55
Vacherin glacé 50

15 %

Nous cuisinons avec des denrées fraîches et
naturelles. Si un jour un arrivage ne se fait pas,
ne nous en veuillez pas, nous faisons tout pour
vous satisfaire.

MENU 225

composé

d'un hors-d'œuvre

d'une entrée

d'un rôti ou grillade

avec légumes

à choisir dans la carte chiffrée

suivi

des fromages du pays

et d'un plateau de fruits

accompagné de petits fours

et des pâtisseries

Suggestion du jour

Gelée de bar perceau 30
Cassolette de ris de veau 50
Asperges du Vaucluse 70

Ravis de vous avoir présenté Talloires sous la neige
Talloires 16/3/78
P. et Ch.

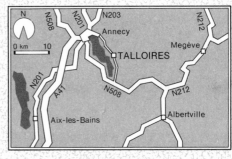

Talloires, on the eastern side of Lake Annecy,
Haute-Savoie, is within easy driving distance of
Geneva. This made L'Auberge du Père Bise a
favourite dining place of the League of Nations'
diplomats in the years before World War II.

THE CRAYFISH

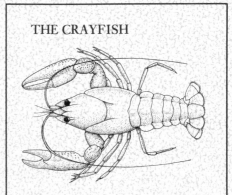

With its delicate flavour, the *écrevisse* or
crayfish has long found favour in French
cuisine. These freshwater crustaceans,
shaped like miniature lobsters, scavenge
on the bottoms of streams, ponds and
lakes. Nowadays they are often 'farmed'.
Three main kinds are eaten in France:
the red-clawed (*pattes rouge*), which has
the best flavour, the smaller white-
clawed and, imported from central
Europe, the slender-clawed crayfish.

Écrevisses must be kept alive until
cooked, so many restaurants have a *vivier*
or fish tank. Kept in a cool place, they
can survive out of water for up to two
days.

Only the tail-meat (a fifth of the total
weight) is eaten, though the shell may
be pounded and made into a *purée* to add
to a *bisque*. *Écrevisses* are often cooked
à la nage—in a *court-bouillon* of water,
white wine, vegetables, herbs and
seasoning. Another method is with a
mirepoix of vegetables cooked in butter.
The tails are gutted before cooking.

Bise's menu may offer four *écrevisse*
dishes. The *gratin de queues d'écrevisses*
is a *ragoût* of crayfish tails browned in
the oven. Then there is a *soufflé* of trout
with crayfish tails. On request Bise will
serve a *petite salade d'écrevisses* and a
bisque d'écrevisses.

Menu de Printemps

Cassolette de ris de veau

Gratin de queues d'écrevisses

Pâté chaud sauce poivrade

Soufflé Rothschild

Sweetbread casserole
Gratin of crayfish
Pâté with pepper sauce
Fruit soufflé

Cassolette de ris de veau

Gently heat the *noix* of veal sweetbreads in butter. Add thinly sliced onions, a clove of garlic, carrot, thyme, bay leaf, salt, pepper and nutmeg.

After a few minutes pour on some dry white wine, a couple of tablespoons of madeira and some truffle juice. Let this simmer on a low heat for about forty-five minutes.

Remove the sweetbreads and keep them warm. Make a sauce from the cooking juices to which *crème fraîche* has been added. Reduce the sauce.

Poach mushrooms in lemon juice, butter and water for about ten minutes. Cut the sweetbreads into quarters and mix them with the mushrooms into the sauce.

Serve the sweetbreads and sauce in a small silver casserole dish.

A good accompaniment to this dish is a little fresh tomato *concassée*.
Note: Sweetbread is the thymus gland of the calf, divided into the *noix* and the *gorge*. It is found at the top of the breast. The *noix* is round in shape, while the *gorge* is elongated.

Pâté chaud poivrade

The following will make four good helpings:

Make two stuffings: the first from 150 grams of minced lean pork and an equal amount of finely chopped veal; the second from 200 grams of lean minced pork and the same amount of pork fat.

Blend the two together, adding thinly sliced truffles. Season with salt and pepper and sprinkle with cognac. Let the mixture stand for several hours.

Fill flaky pastry shells with the stuffing and seal, allowing one per person. Glaze them with egg-yolk and cook in a moderate oven.

Make a *sauce poivrade* by reducing veal stock, red wine and shallots. Add crushed black peppercorns.

Serve the *pâté* straight from the oven with the pepper sauce.

Soufflé Rothschild

Thoroughly mix together three egg-yolks and seventy-five grams of sugar. Sprinkle about forty grams of flour into the mix and stir well.

Heat a quarter of a litre of milk and pour this onto the egg and sugar, stirring vigorously. When this is well blended, pour it into a clean pan and stir continuously over a gentle heat until it thickens.

Remove from the heat and, in an oven-proof dish, stir in fruits macerated in Grand Marnier. Leave to cool.

Taking five well-beaten egg-whites, mix in a small amount and then fold in the rest.

Place in a very hot oven for fifteen minutes and serve immediately.

Gratin de queues d'écrevisses

Heat a couple of tablespoons of olive oil in a thick-bottomed saucepan. Drop in onion rings, shallots, a clove of garlic, a couple of tomatoes, a *bouquet garni* and a little crushed white pepper.

When all this is cooked but not glazed, turn the heat full on and drop in gutted live crayfish. (Bise recommends eighty crayfish for four people.) Flame the crayfish with half a glass of liqueur brandy and douse the flames with three-quarters of a glass of white wine. Slightly season with salt. Cook in a covered saucepan for about fifteen minutes.

Take the crayfish from the saucepan and extract the tails whole. Pound some of the crayfish shells and add them to the sauce. Let this reduce for twenty minutes, then pass it through a fine sieve, crushing the vegetables against the side of the sieve with a wooden spoon.

Pour in a jug of heavy cream. Reduce the sauce until it is thick. Check the seasoning.

Put the crayfish tails into ovenproof bowls and cover them in the sauce. Grate Gruyère cheese on top and brown lightly under the grill.

The *gratin de queues d'écrevisses* may be served with Creole rice.

Truite du lac sauce mousseline

Prepare a very large trout.

Make a *court-bouillon* from two bottles of fine white wine, a half-litre of water, sliced carrots, onions, shallots, an unpeeled clove of garlic, *bouquet garni*, freshly ground pepper and a bay leaf. Simmer for about half an hour and then cool.

Pour the *court-bouillon* into an oval fish-kettle, bring to the boil and lower the heat. Poach the fish for twelve minutes on each side, taking care not to damage the skin when it is turned over. Do not let it boil.

While the fish is cooking, prepare a *mousseline* sauce by putting a quarter-litre of cream, four egg-yolks and two soupspoons of water in a deep saucepan. Whip the sauce vigorously as it begins to heat up over a low flame. When the sauce has doubled in volume, pass it quickly through a fine sieve and stir with a large spoon. Season with salt and lemon juice.

Dry the fish on a napkin and set on a plate garnished with parsley. Serve the sauce separately.

Filet de perche Marguerite

Cook thinly sliced carrot, onion and shallot for a few minutes in butter in a covered pan with thyme and a bay leaf. Lay perch fillets on top (one per person), pour over the fillets two glasses of white wine and simmer for ten minutes.

Lightly sauté julienne strips of carrots, celery and the white of leek with *petits pois* and sliced green beans. Then add most of the cooking juices from the fish, leaving enough to keep the fish moist in a warming pan. Simmer the vegetables in the *bouillon* for about twenty minutes. Remove the vegetables and put them on a buttered plate.

Reduce the stock, remove the pan from the heat and whisk in butter. Fold in a liaison of *crème fraîche* and beaten egg-yolk. Add finely chopped chives, parsley and chervil.

Lay the perch fillets on the vegetable julienne and cover them with the sauce.

Decorate the plate with slices of lemon and sprinkle with *fines herbes*. Serve hot.

Poularde braisée à la crème d'estragon

Stuff a large pullet with fresh tarragon.

Salt and pepper the bird. Put it, with the giblets, in a heavy casserole with butter. Seal tightly and cook for forty minutes on a low heat so the juices remain light in colour.

Set the chicken on a warm serving plate. Remove the tarragon stuffing and cook it alone in the casserole juices. Add a few tablespoons of thick *crème fraîche*.

Put the sauce through a sieve and serve it with the chicken in a side dish.
Note: Use a casserole dish only a little larger than the bird to maintain the maximum flavour.

Gratin Savoyard

Build up three or four layers of thinly sliced potatoes in a well-buttered oval dish and cover with boiling, salted unpasteurized milk.

Grate Gruyère on top of the potatoes and simmer on the top of the stove for about fifteen minutes. Then put the dish in a hot oven until the cheese has browned.
Note: If unpasteurized milk is unavailable, add heavy cream to pasteurized milk.

Gâteau aux fraises des bois

In a pan over a low heat mix eight whole eggs and 250 grams of sugar. Add 250 grams of sieved flour and turn the mixture out into a floured and buttered baking dish. Cook in a low oven for about twenty-five minutes.

Turn the sponge out onto a cloth or a baking grid and let it cool. Slice the cake into three layers. Sprinkle each with kirsch and set *fraises des bois* and *crème chantilly* onto two of them as a filling. Rebuild the cake, ice the top and decorate it with cream and strawberries.

Menu d'Été

Filet de perche Marguerite

Poularde braisée à la crème d'estragon

Gratin Savoyard

Gâteau aux fraises des bois

Perch fillets with a julienne of vegetables
Chicken in tarragon sauce
Potatoes with cheese
Wild strawberry cake

Faisan Souvaroff

Remove the liver, gizzard and wings from a pheasant. Salt and pepper the inside of the bird and slide slices of truffle underneath the skin of the breast, legs and wings.

Colour six chicken livers in butter.

Deglaze the pan with sherry, brandy and white wine.

Stuff the pheasant with roughly chopped chicken livers, truffles and *foie gras*.

Truss the pheasant and put it in a roasting pan with its giblets, two or three nuts of butter and a drop of water. Colour it in the oven for fifteen minutes, basting frequently and adding a little water from time to time to prevent the butter burning.

Once browned, put the pheasant in an enamelled casserole together with one whole truffle per person, the juices from the roasting pan, brandy, sherry, a drop of port and a little water. Cover the pan and cook for thirty minutes.

Marinate four escalopes of fresh *foie gras* in sherry for a few minutes, dry them, add salt and pepper and cook them quickly over a high flame in butter.

When serving, slip these escalopes under the truffles cooked with the pheasant.

Le Négus

Whisk twelve egg-yolks with 450 grams of sugar. Add 180 grams of flour and 120 grams of cocoa. When well mixed, fold in eighteen well-beaten egg-whites. Pour this mixture into a buttered, floured tin and cook in a low oven.

When cooked, turn out of the tin and let the cake cool.

Make a cream by putting twelve whole eggs in a saucepan with 600 grams of sugar. Set this on a low flame and whisk continuously until it is of a thick, creamy consistency. Then add 450 grams of bitter, dark chocolate which has been melted in a cup of strong black coffee. Mix well, allow to cool, then add 350 grams of well-beaten butter.

When the cake is cold, cut across it twice to make three sponges. Put the cold cream between the slices and decorate the top with chocolate granules.

Menu d'Automne

Truite du lac sauce mousseline

Faisan Souvaroff

Le Négus

Lake trout with cream sauce
Pheasant and foie gras
Chocolate cream cake

THE LIVING KITCHEN OF BOCUSE

The Bocuse menu cover shows the restaurant from the neatly kept courtyard. Save for the name emblazoned in huge letters along the roof, it is an unassuming building, dedicated to comfort and good food rather than grandeur.

Paul Bocuse comes from a long line of restaurateurs. The family has lived for two centuries or more only a few kilometres from the centre of Lyon and the Bocuse menu reflects the tradition of Lyonnais cooking. The countryside round Lyon is some of the most abundant in Europe and the great markets of Lyon are the best in the world.

The variety of locally grown produce colours the choice and style of Bocuse's dishes. On his menu there will always be several recipes based on the remarkable chickens from Bresse. There will be the almost peasant dishes for which Lyon is famous: eel stew, pike, knuckle of veal, casserole of thrush and perhaps a woodcock or wild boar. The *amuse-gueule* is *cervelas*, the Lyonnais sausage normally seen on much lesser menus than this one.

While Bocuse can produce the most elaborate dishes, his own taste is for these essentially country ingredients, simply cooked. His less expensive menu of the day is never settled until Bocuse returns from the market, bringing back some perfect mussels for his *soupe de moules au safran* or a ferociously fresh pike for his *mousse de brochet au coulis d'écrevisses*.

Presentation is not one of the most important aspects of Bocuse's cooking—though the *poulet de Bresse au feu de bois* appears, theatrically, with embers from the fire on which it was cooked. He is concerned with taste rather than appearance, striving always to preserve the essence of an ingredient. This emphasis may make his cuisine seem a little rougher than that of, say, Outhier or Haeberlin.

Bocuse's unselfish camaraderie with his fellow professionals is shown by the in-

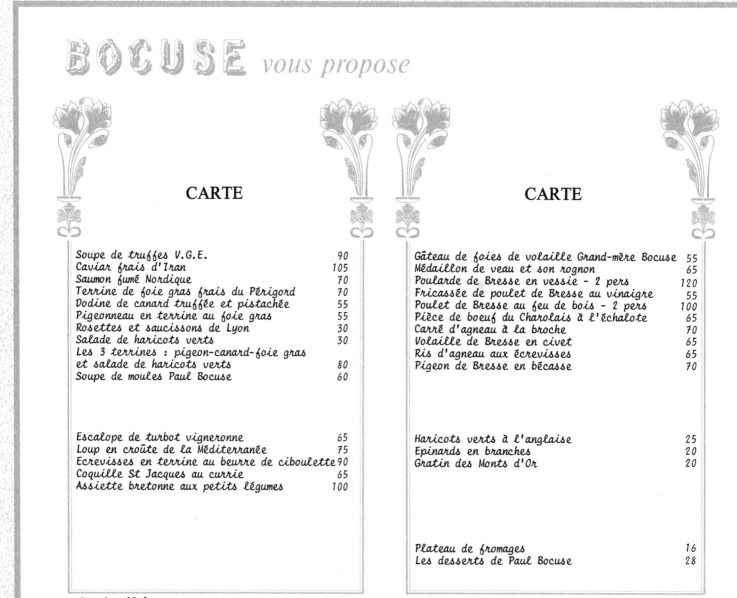

BOCUSE *vous propose*

CARTE

Soupe de truffes V.G.E.	90
Caviar frais d'Iran	105
Saumon fumé Nordique	70
Terrine de foie gras frais du Périgord	70
Dodine de canard truffée et pistachée	55
Pigeonneau en terrine au foie gras	55
Rosettes et saucissons de Lyon	30
Salade de haricots verts	30
Les 3 terrines : pigeon-canard-foie gras et salade de haricots verts	80
Soupe de moules Paul Bocuse	60

Escalope de turbot vigneronne	65
Loup en croûte de la Méditerranée	75
Ecrevisses en terrine au beurre de ciboulette	90
Coquille St Jacques au currie	65
Assiette bretonne aux petits légumes	100

CARTE

Gâteau de foies de volaille Grand-mère Bocuse	55
Médaillon de veau et son rognon	65
Poularde de Bresse en vessie - 2 pers	120
Fricassée de poulet de Bresse au vinaigre	55
Poulet de Bresse au feu de bois - 2 pers	100
Pièce de boeuf du Charolais à l'échalote	65
Carré d'agneau à la broche	70
Volaille de Bresse en civet	65
Ris d'agneau aux écrevisses	65
Pigeon de Bresse en bécasse	70

Haricots verts à l'anglaise	25
Epinards en branches	20
Gratin des Monts d'Or	20

Plateau de fromages	16
Les desserts de Paul Bocuse	28

+ Service 15 %

clusion on his menu of dishes invented by the other chefs of the *bande à Bocuse: pâté d'anguille chaud Roger Vergé, chapon farci de la Mediterranée Louis Outhier, cassolette d'écrevisses marinière Charles Barrier.* In the same spirit, his *chef-de-cuisine,* Roger Jaloux, receives an individual credit on the menu.

The Bocuse kitchen is a living one. He is forever trying out new dishes, never using them until he has perfected them. Mostly it is a question of new combinations, as for instance his recently devised *soufflé d'artichauts et truffes.* It is not quite right yet, for the tiny *soufflé* on top of the chopped artichokes and truffles is too small to have a real fluffiness. 'But the marriage is perfect, isn't it?'

The phrase sums up the simple excellence of everything which comes from his remarkable kitchen.

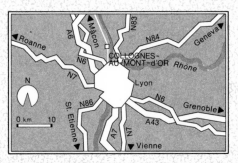

Collonges-au-Mont-d'Or, originally a small village outside Lyon, has become part of the city's northern suburbs. The restaurant is on the bank of the Saône by the bridge of Collonges-au-Mont-d'Or; it is reached by roads D433 and D51.

Dimanche 19 Mars 1978

Paul Bocuse

MENU

Terrine de foie gras frais du Périgord
Salade de haricots verts

————

Loup en croûte de la Méditerranée
Sauce choron

————

Poularde de Bresse en vessie Renaissance

————

Plateau de fromages

————

Les desserts de Paul Bocuse
Petits fours

————

190 F.

MENU

Soupe de truffes V.G.E.
(plat créé pour l'Elysée)

————

Assiette bretonne aux petits légumes
ou
Ecrevisses en terrine au beurre de ciboulette

————

Pigeon de Bresse en bécasse

————

Plateau de fromages

————

Les desserts de Paul Bocuse
Petits fours

————

200 F.

Chef des cuisines : Roger JALOUX - Meilleur Ouvrier de France - Paris 1976

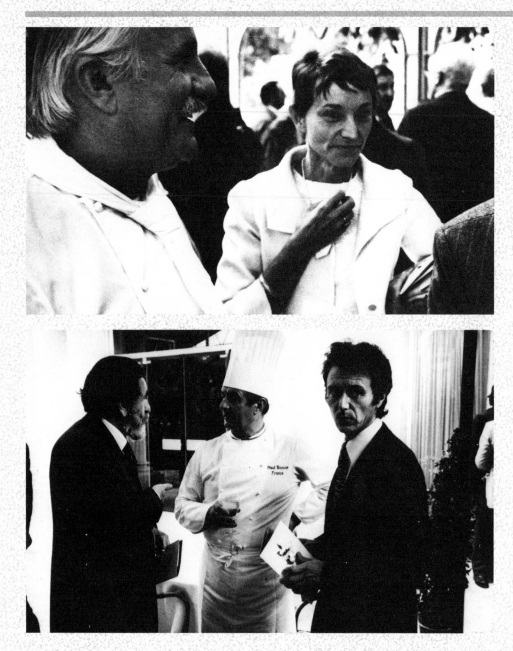

Wine makers for the great chefs: Madame Bize-Leroy with Roger Vergé; Georges Duboeuf (right) with Paul Bocuse.

the venerable cellars, dating from 1622, of the Boyau family at Auxey-Duresses. In 1942 her father, Henri Leroy, added to the business a half-share in the Domaine de la Romanée-Conti, which produces the most expensive wine in the world. Madame Bize-Leroy now controls the entire business.

The wines from the Domaine de la Romanée-Conti include all of Romanée-Conti itself (just 8500 bottles a year) and La Tâche, and some of Grands-Echézeaux, Échézeaux, Richebourg and Montrachet. These are the greatest Burgundies produced and every three-star restaurant has to have some on its wine list. But it is the other Burgundies produced by Bize-Leroy which may appeal more to the chefs.

The one area in which the revolutionary chefs prefer the old-fashioned product is wine. Modern-style wine is mellow, quick to mature and facile. Madame Bize-Leroy produces classic wines whose high tannin content makes them taste harsh in their youth. But in time her wines develop an excellence that no modern wine can match. In her devotion to her product the chefs recognize a dedication equal to their own.

Every year Lalou Bize-Leroy gives a wine party which is one of the great occasions of the chefs' calendar. At the blind tastings, a prize is won, more often than not, by Georges Duboeuf, whose palate is reputed to be one of the best in France.

Duboeuf, whose father has a small vineyard in Pouilly-Fuissé, has built up a business which sells several million bottles a year, mainly Beaujolais. This success comes largely from his close attention to wine as an adjunct to cuisine. He will study a restaurant's cuisine and tailor his wines to suit the chef's cooking and palate. Duboeuf's closest links are with Bocuse, who has no wines in his cellar which Duboeuf has not tasted. The wines sold in the United States under Bocuse's name (about 20,000 cases a year) are all supplied by Duboeuf, as are those exported by the Troisgros brothers. He selects the regional wines for the Saveur Club, presided over by Jean Troisgros.

Duboeuf has been closely involved with the chefs' growing fame. It was he who organized the wines for President Giscard d'Estaing's famous *Légion d'Honneur* lunch. He often instigates the promotional trips undertaken by the chefs in all parts of the world. In Duboeuf's cellars at Romanèche-Thorins one may run into Jean Troisgros, who holds about four tastings there between November and January, Alain Chapel, Thuilier's representative, who comes for the Morgon and Beaujolais-Villages, and Jean-Pierre Haeberlin, who takes six different *appellations*. Others may merely trust Duboeuf to provide them with his own selection for, as he says, 'Being trusted means one must give one's best.'

'One can make a very good lunch drinking water,' says Bocuse. He is, of course, exaggerating, to make the point that it is possible to be too fussy and pretentious about wine. On the other hand, no-one is more aware that cuisine and wine are inseparable: 'Good cuisine goes with places where there are vineyards.'

Some of the best wines on every great *chef-patron's* list are supplied by two of France's most outstanding producers—Madame Lalou Bize-Leroy and Georges Duboeuf. Their association with the members of the *bande à Bocuse* has been especially close.

Madame Bize-Leroy is probably the most important woman in any section of the wine business. Her family have been shippers since 1868, when her grandfather acquired

Pot-au-feu

The *pot-au-feu* is a traditional dish consisting of a variety of meats cooked with vegetables and water. It originates from the days of cooking over an open hearth. Bocuse, with his love of cooking on an open fire, has given us the following recipe for *pot-au-feu*, suitable for twelve people for at least two meals.

Put rib bones in the bottom of a *marmite* (a large, heavy cooking-pot) so that the other meats will not touch or stick to the bottom of the pot. Set on top of the bones 1500 grams of shin of beef and then 500 grams of each of the following meats: beef shank, beef chuck, oxtail, knuckle of veal and neck of lamb. Fill the *marmite* with cold water, making sure that all the meat is covered. Do not add salt at this point. Bring to the boil over a very high flame (otherwise the broth will become cloudy) and cook for twenty minutes.

Prepare 300 grams of carrots and an equal weight of turnips, onions and leeks, one head of fennel, two celery heads and a parsnip.

Cut the leaves from the whites of leeks. Tie the whites together. Wrap the green leaves around parsley, thyme and bay leaves to make a *bouquet garni* and tie.

Tie round slices of carrot onto the ends of marrow bones to seal in the marrow.

Tilt the *marmite* and skim off the fat with a ladle. Continue to cook over a gentle heat for twenty minutes. Skim again, add salt and black peppercorns wrapped in muslin.

Slide slices of truffle under the skin of a chicken, truss and put it into the *marmite*.

Stick a few cloves into each onion and drop these into the *marmite* along with a whole head of garlic, and all the vegetables. Simmer for about forty minutes, skimming occasionally. Lift out the parsnip after fifteen minutes and extract the other vegetables as they become cooked. (They can be pierced with a needle to check that they are ready.) Keep vegetables warm in a covered saucepan with a little *bouillon*. The chicken should also be removed when cooked and kept warm in the same way.

Continue cooking the other meats for another thirty minutes, skimming from time to time. Remove the knuckle of veal and the neck of lamb. Cook the rest of the meats for about an hour and then add a lean piece of beefsteak (with a piece of string round it, so that it may be removed easily), the marrow bones and three tomatoes. Cook for fifteen minutes.

Remove the meat and marrow bones and reheat the chicken and the vegetables in the *bouillon*.

Put the shin of beef in the middle of a serving dish and set around it all the other meats, chicken and vegetables. Strain, skin and season some *bouillon* and serve in a tureen on the side.
Note: The meat and vegetables may be served with a sauce such as a horseradish or tomato sauce, or a herb butter. Bocuse suggests a sauce made from one part wine vinegar to four parts walnut oil, seasoned with salt, pepper and chervil.

Soupe aux truffes Élysées

Stew small-diced carrots, onion, celery and mushrooms in butter. Put two tablespoons of the mixture into deep, individual, ovenproof soup bowls. To each add sliced truffles, sliced *foie gras* and half a cup of chicken *consommé*.

Roll out a thin layer of flaky pastry and brush the edges of it with beaten egg-yolk. Cover the soup bowls with pastry, tightly sealing each dish.

Put the bowls into a very hot oven. When the pastry has risen and turned golden, remove from the oven.

When you set the dish on the table, break open the pastry with a soupspoon, allowing the pastry topping to sink into the soup.

Every year, Paul Bocuse sends his friends a New Year card, usually of a lighthearted kind. Nearly twenty years ago, he printed four recipes of an unexpected nature, which reveal the rougher, rustic aspects of cooking which appeal to him.

Dinde de Crémieu truffée

Here is a family recipe for winter. Take a two to three kilo turkey (preferably from Crémieu). Stuff it with 400 grams of sausage meat and an equivalent amount of chopped truffles. Slide several truffles under the bird's skin before trussing it. Wrap the turkey in wax or grease-proof paper and tie it up in a jute sack. Dig a hole in your garden, not too deep, and bury the turkey. The damp and chill of the earth will encourage the truffles to give off their richest scent. Two days later prepare a *court-bouillon* with carrots, celery, onions, leeks, cloves, salt, pepper, knuckle of veal and pieces of ox-tail. Dig up your turkey and poach it for one and a half hours. Serve with a rice pilaff.

Soupe de courge à la crème

The pumpkin is a vegetable which it is wrong to neglect. One can make *gratins* and soup with it. Here is a delicious recipe. Cut the top off a four to five kilo pumpkin so that it looks like a soup-bowl. Scoop out the seeds and three-quarters fill the pumpkin with alternate layers of grilled *croûtons* and grated Gruyère. Add salt and pepper and fill up the pumpkin with cream. Put in a hot oven for two hours and then put it on the table. There detach the flesh of the pumpkin with a spoon. Then stir with a ladle to mix the flesh with the soup and serve.

Cervelas truffé sous la cendre

For dinner in the garden or a picnic, the barbecue encourages a return to a delicious, but frugal, form of cooking. Here is a recipe for sausage which provides a variation on recipes for grilled meat. Take a truffled Lyon *cervelas* and wrap it in foil. Roll the foil in such a way that it is shaped like a cornet, with one end pointed and sealed. Fill it up with a good Beaujolais at the other end and then seal that as well. Round this, put damp newspaper. Bury it in the embers of the fire and let it cook for forty-five minutes. Take off all the paper and foil. The *cervelas* will be lightly roasted and will have taken on a delicious taste of caramel of wine. Serve with potatoes cooked in the ashes.

Chapon de Bresse gros sel

Ten kilos of rough sea-salt are needed for this unexpected recipe. Take a fine capon, preferably from Bresse, clean it and slide slices of truffle under the skin of its wings and legs. In a large cast-iron pot put a bed of about three kilos of sea-salt. Lay the capon on the salt and fill the whole pot with the remaining seven kilos. Put the pot, with no lid, in a very hot oven for one and three-quarter hours. The salt will form a solid block; turn it out and break it. The capon will be beautifully roasted and deliciously scented with iodine. Serve it with vegetables, like a roast.

CHAPEL'S SUPREME INVENTIVENESS

There is no other menu like it. Here is a chef who is deeply rooted in his region, strictly schooled in the tradition of classic cuisine—yet there is not a dish on Alain Chapel's menu which does not reveal an inventiveness and imagination which lift him into the rare class of supreme chefs. There is no dish which does not surprise. No-one else cooks a calf's ear, let alone stuff it with sweetbreads and truffles and sprinkle it with fried parsley. Who but Chapel would add the subtle flavours of the *morille* and *écrevisse* to the classic combination of cockerels' crests and kidneys? His salads, too, are extraordinarily inventive; for instance pigeon's breast and lobster with a mustardy green sauce, or warm *foie de canard* with purple artichokes.

Even Chapel's conventional dishes have unexpected touches—the tiny macaroni with the lamb, or the *sauce choron* with beef and bone marrow. The more elaborate dishes pile on the astonishment, as with the salmon made into a *millefeuille* with chervil and peas, which then has a *champagne sabayon* to go with it. Such touches might not in themselves be distinguished—there are many pretentious experimenters—but each ingredient of every dish is so beautifully cared for. Long after eating, say, Chapel's *poulette de Bresse en vessie*, one remembers not only the perfection of the chicken, but also the superb quality of the carrots which went with it. Chapel's real distinction is that each item, however simple, is faultless, down to his little *amuse-gueule* of gudgeon.

Not the least enjoyable part of the menu is that when you think you have finished there is always another sorbet, another gem of *pâtisserie*, another irresistible chocolate. The only thing anybody could complain about is that Chapel has given up making his own unique crystallized fruits, which came in hand-made boxes and surpassed anything else of the kind.

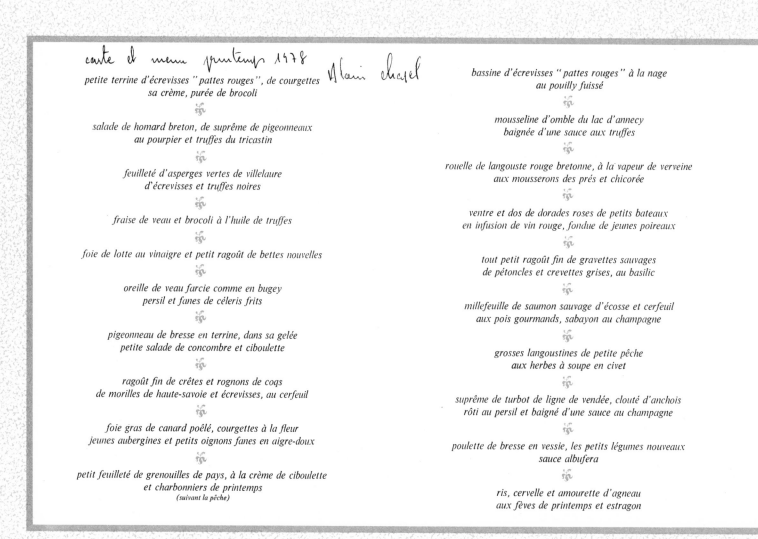

carte et menu printemps 1978

Alain Chapel

petite terrine d'écrevisses "pattes rouges", de courgettes
sa crème, purée de brocoli

salade de homard breton, de suprême de pigeonneaux
au pourpier et truffes du tricastin

feuilleté d'asperges vertes de villelaure
d'écrevisses et truffes noires

fraise de veau et brocoli à l'huile de truffes

foie de lotte au vinaigre et petit ragoût de bettes nouvelles

oreille de veau farcie comme en bugey
persil et fanes de céleris frits

pigeonneau de bresse en terrine, dans sa gelée
petite salade de concombre et ciboulette

ragoût fin de crêtes et rognons de coqs
de morilles de haute-savoie et écrevisses, au cerfeuil

foie gras de canard poêlé, courgettes à la fleur
jeunes aubergines et petits oignons fanes en aigre-doux

petit feuilleté de grenouilles de pays, à la crème de ciboulette
et charbonniers de printemps
(suivant la pêche)

bassine d'écrevisses "pattes rouges" à la nage
au pouilly fuissé

mousseline d'omble du lac d'annecy
baignée d'une sauce aux truffes

rouelle de langouste rouge bretonne, à la vapeur de verveine
aux mousserons des prés et chicorée

ventre et dos de dorades roses de petits bateaux
en infusion de vin rouge, fondue de jeunes poireaux

tout petit ragoût fin de gravettes sauvages
de pétoncles et crevettes grises, au basilic

millefeuille de saumon sauvage d'écosse et cerfeuil
aux pois gourmands, sabayon au champagne

grosses langoustines de petite pêche
aux herbes à soupe en civet

suprême de turbot de ligne de vendée, clouté d'anchois
rôti au persil et baigné d'une sauce au champagne

poulette de bresse en vessie, les petits légumes nouveaux
sauce albufera

ris, cervelle et amourette d'agneau
aux fèves de printemps et estragon

198

Terrine d'écrevisses 'pattes rouges' et légumes verts sauce sabayon au champagne
Pound crayfish meat into a fine *purée*.

Prepare and cut into small dice equal amounts of carrots, unpeeled courgettes, young leeks and green beans. Also shell a couple of handfuls of fresh peas. Cook all these vegetables separately in covered saucepans and pass them, again separately, through a *chinois*.

Butter small individual moulds and line them with blanched spinach leaves. Add salt and pepper.

Fill the moulds in layers starting with the carrot and alternating the other vegetable *purées* and the crayfish *purée*. Cover the moulds and poach, covered, in a *bain-marie* for twenty minutes.

Make a *concassée* of tomatoes using one underripe and one very ripe tomato. Cook gently in butter, lemon juice and fresh chervil. Add some trout *fumet* and bring to the boil. When this mixture is fully reduced, remove from the heat and cool. Gently blend in two parts *hollandaise* with one part champagne; mix in one part whipped cream to make a *sabayon* sauce.

Turn the terrines out from the moulds and serve with the *sabayon* sauce.

Note: Chapel is using the term '*sabayon* sauce' very loosely here; there is no such sauce. But it is common terminology in a kitchen if the sauce is in fact made by adding a *sabayon*.

Poule faisane à la crème et aux chicons
Cut a hen pheasant into pieces: legs, wings, back and breast. Season with freshly milled salt and pepper. Put the pieces into a heavy saucepan with a large knob of butter and lightly sauté the meat. When the meat has a good colour and aroma, remove it from the pan. Deglaze the pan with a couple of tablespoons of madeira and add three or four endives or whole chicory. When the chicory has cooked a little, add a couple of cups of *crème fraîche*. Correct the seasoning and add the juice of one lemon.

Pour the sauce over the pheasant and serve with mushrooms.

Note: *Chicons* or whole chicory should be cooked soon after buying as they go brown when removed from their packing paper.

A mix of black and white peppercorns is favoured by some chefs for meat and game.

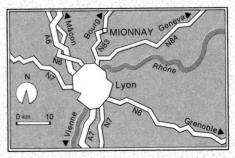

Mionnay, a small village in the most fertile area of France, lies on the N83 just twenty kilometres north-east of Lyon.

---

*pot-au-feu de pigeons ramiers et ravioli d'herbes
à l'anis étoilé*

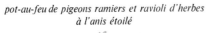

*côte de bœuf de normandie à la moëlle, sauce choron
et fondue de tomates, poêlée d'aubergines, sa garniture
de petits légumes nouveaux*   (pour 3 personnes)

*agneau de lait de sisteron, sa parure
timbale de petits macaroni de naples
et ragoût d'artichauts violets*

*caneton nantais grillé, à la vinaigrette d'herbes
étuvée de laitues nouvelles
petit paillasson aux courgettes et cerfeuil*

*salade de roquette, reine des glaces
feuilles de chêne et éclergeons, de pintadons de bresse
aux chapons et huile de noix*

quelques fromages fermiers

*desserts glacés, mignardises, pralines, candis et chocolats
pâtisserie maison*

*friands au miel, délicate gelée d'oranges sanguines
et mousse glacée de citrons verts*

pommes chaudes caramélisées, aux pignons

melons en sorbet, sauce aux fraises, gros palmiers chauds

*foie gras de canard poêlé, courgettes à la fleur
jeunes aubergines et petits oignons fanes, en aigre-doux*

*feuilleté d'asperges vertes de villelaure
d'écrevisses "pattes rouges" et truffes noires*

*ou ris, cervelle et amourette d'agneau
aux fèves de printemps et estragon*

*ou ventre et dos de dorades roses de petits bateaux
en infusion de vin rouge, fondue de jeunes poireaux*

*poulette de bresse en vessie, les petits légumes nouveaux
sauce albufera*

*ou salade de roquette, reine des glaces
feuilles de chêne et éclergeons, de pintadons de bresse
aux chapons et huile de noix*

*ou suprême de turbot de ligne clouté d'anchois
rôti au persil et baigné d'une sauce au champagne*

quelques fromages fermiers

*desserts glacés, mignardises, pralines
candis et chocolats*

pâtisserie maison

TANGLES OF TASTE BY GUÉRARD

Michel Guérard

Michel Guérard's *carte gourmande* is the most untraditional of all the three-star menus, and the least fixed. Dishes appear and disappear in restless fashion, reflecting the chef's volatile nature. The consistent theme is one of lightness and, to some extent, fantasy.

Among the *hors d'oeuvres*, two of Guérard's flights of fancy are the *deux oeufs poule au caviar*—lightly scrambled eggs mixed with chopped onion, chives and cream, put back in their shells and topped with caviar—and the *trois feuilletés legers de saison*—pastry leaves which, depending on the season, may contain asparagus, cocks' crests and kidneys, artichokes, oysters, *foie gras*, truffles or duck.

The *soup aux écrevisses de rivière* exemplifies Guérard's talent for producing the lightest of creations from a complicated tangle of tastes: besides crayfish, this amazing soup includes olive and ground-nut oil, carrot, onion, tomato, shallot, garlic, a small *bouquet garni*, armagnac, port, white wine and, to complete it, a *sauce nage* and chervil, tarragon, cream, butter and chives. His claim that it 'blossoms in the mouth' is no exaggeration.

It is in the main courses of the *carte gourmande* that one sees the *cuisine minceur* influence, for instance in the combination of duck liver and turnip *purée* in the *foie de canard poêlé à l'émincée de navets*.

There is the *minceur* tendency to undercook food and rely for tenderness on the youth of the produce, as with the *baron de lapereau mangetout aux nouilles fraîches*. Guérard cooks the baby rabbit for less than ten minutes (the thighs get a bit more) and presents it beautifully, in thin slices on a bed of spinach leaves with little turnips 'prettily disposed all around it' (as he puts it).

The profusion of *pâtisseries*, sorbets, sweets and *gâteaux* is evidence of Guérard's early training. They are quite different from anyone else's, and he concentrates less on flans and cakes and more on such surprising combinations as his *pêche blanche de Castel-jaloux au granité de Pomerol*—a poached peach sitting on a bed of wine sorbet.

At each meal there is also a *cuisine minceur* menu, no doubt excellent for slimmers and cooked with the same care as the *carte gourmande*—but who would want costume jewellery when the cave of Ali Baba beckons?

LA CARTE GOURMANDE

Le Foie Gras Frais Préparé à la Maison tout Naturellement
Le Pâté de Pigeon Musqué à la Marmelade d'Oignons Doux
Les Trois Feuilletés Légers de Saison :
(Asperges, Crêtes de Coq, Foie Gras, Huîtres, Langoustines, Ecrevisses, Grenouilles, Artichaut...)
Les Trois Salades Impromptues :
(Mousserons, Cerfeuil, Ecrevisses, Poissons Fumés, Truffes, Foie Gras, Aile de Canard...)
Les Deux Œufs Poule au Caviar
La Soupe Crémeuse aux Ecrevisses de Rivière
La Galette de Truffes au Vin de Graves

Le Saumon Frais au Beurre Blanc de Laitue
La Sole Grillée aux Huîtres et à la Ciboulette
Le Homard en Vessie à la Compote de Légumes et à l'Huile d'Herbes Fines
Les Ecrevisses à la Nage Sauce Fleurette

Les Aiguillettes Rosées de Caneton au Poivre
Le Petit Pigeon Tendre sur un lit de Choux Verts Frais
La Charlotte d'Agneau de Lait à l'Aubergine
Le Baron de Lapereau Mangetout aux Nouilles Fraîches
Le Pintadeau à la Marinade, Farci et Cuit en Coque d'Argile
Le Foie de Canard poêlé à l'émincée de Navets
Le Bœuf de Chalosse Cuit à la Braise de la Cheminée

Quelques Fromages de Terroir
La Feuillantine de Poires Caramélisées
Les Crêpes pralinées à l'Eau-de-Vie d'Abricot
La Tarte Chaude aux Pommes Acidulées
Le Granité de Chocolat Amer et sa Salade d'Oranges
La Grande Assiette de Fruits et Sorbets du Temps
La Pêche Blanche de Casteljaloux au Granité de Pomerol
Le Soufflé Léger à la Poire et au Fruit de la Passion
La Marquise au Chocolat et sa Sauce aux Grains de Café
Les Tartelettes "d'une Bouchée"

Service en sus 15 %

Michel
le 4 avril

LA DINETTE D'EUGENIE

L'Œuf Poule au Caviar

~

Le Feuilleté Léger de Saison
ou
La Salade Impromptue

~

Le Saumon Frais au Beurre Blanc de Laitue

~

L'Aile de Pigeonneau sur son Lit de Choux Verts Frais
ou
La Charlotte d'Agneau de Lait à l'Aubergine

Pommes à la Peau

~

Dessert et Douceurs Candies

~

En Guise d'Apéritif :
Le Badinguet et ses Petits Croûtons

~

La Richesse des marchés de Saison nous fera souvent aussi
vous conseiller, des mets du jour,
"de Bouche à Oreille"

Eugénie-les-Bains, in the hilly, evergreen area of the Landes, is fifty-three kilometres north of Pau and twelve kilometres south of the intersection of the N649 and the N124.

Michel Guérard

Guérard's menu covers are reproductions of paintings that hang on the dining-room walls. This one is offered to the host at a table: it contains the prices.

THE POTS TO WATCH

Most chefs choose copper pots and pans because copper conducts heat better than any other metal except silver. Good heat conduction gives *even* cooking, with heat coming in from all sides as well as the bottom, and a quick response to variation in temperature when needed. Thus copper is ideal for consistent and controlled cooking, above all for *sauciers* who need absolute control over thickening liquids. As Fernand Point said, 'Take your eyes off a *sauce béarnaise* for an instant and it will be unusable.'

The one disadvantage of copper is that, from contact with acid foods, it easily forms a surface film of green-blue verdigris, which is poisonous. For this reason, copper pans must be lined with tin. The lining wears thin with use and, in a busy kitchen, copper pots and pans must be relined frequently. In France, this is often done by visiting tinkers who trundle their tinning equipment into the kitchen and do the job on the spot.

Frying-pans are the exception to the rule that copper is best; for these, most chefs favour black iron, the thicker the better. Thick iron frying-pans give a gentle, constant heat; as the metal is a relatively poor conductor, it is easy to prevent fat from reaching smoking point and deteriorating. However, tin-lined copper is used for high-sided omelette pans, because it is important for the sides of the omelette to be cooked evenly.

Traditional earthenware pots are still used for certain styles of cooking, particularly of regional dishes, *pâtés* and terrines. The properties of pottery are almost exactly opposite to copper in that it heats only slowly but, once hot, retains its heat for a long time (that is, it is a poor conductor). Thus pottery vessels give little control but are well suited to slow, prolonged cooking— of stews, for instance. Earthenware pots are usually glazed inside to limit moisture absorption, but unglazed outside to help the absorption of heat. The general term for cooking done in earthenware pots is *potée*.

The shapes of pots and pans are largely dictated by common sense. *Sauciers* need to reduce liquids quickly so they use wide, shallow pans with a maximum of surface area for fast evaporation. Tall, narrow pots are used for long, slow boiling; the small surface area minimizes evaporation and skin formation. Professional pans tend to have loop handles rather than long handles so that they can fit into ovens several at a time. Long pans, called fish-kettles, are used for cooking delicate, whole fish.

In describing the utensils used by French cooks, French terms as used in English do not always mean the same thing in France. What is called a saucepan in English is a *casserole* in French, and in France the word *cocotte* is used for the vessel described as a casserole in English. One French word, *marmite*, describes both a stewpot (*marmite à ragoût*) and a stockpot (*grande marmite*).

There is a subtle difference between a sauté pan (*sautoir* or *plat à sauter*), which is shallow but straight-sided, and a frying-pan (*sauteuse*), which is also shallow but has angled sides. To sauté (*sauter*) is to fry lightly in a little fat or oil, making the contents 'jump' (*sauter*) in the pan to prevent sticking. However, a *sauté* is meat or fish cut into pieces and sautéed *and then* simmered in the oven with a sauce. A sauté pan is used for the entire process. For deep frying potatoes, a *friture* is used—a deep pan with a wire basket which enables the contents to be gently immersed and quickly removed.

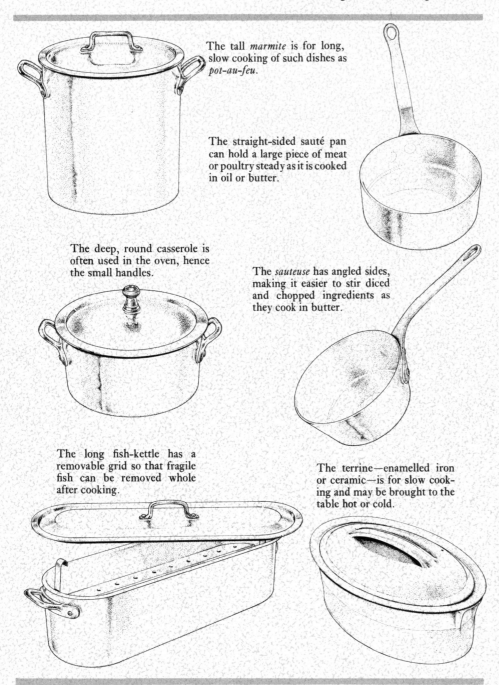

The tall *marmite* is for long, slow cooking of such dishes as *pot-au-feu*.

The straight-sided sauté pan can hold a large piece of meat or poultry steady as it is cooked in oil or butter.

The deep, round casserole is often used in the oven, hence the small handles.

The *sauteuse* has angled sides, making it easier to stir diced and chopped ingredients as they cook in butter.

The long fish-kettle has a removable grid so that fragile fish can be removed whole after cooking.

The terrine—enamelled iron or ceramic—is for slow cooking and may be brought to the table hot or cold.

A DELICACY BY FORCE

The question of the balance between cruelty and flavour is a vexing one. Michel Guérard, for instance, says that lobsters should be killed before cooking to spare them needless suffering. But Roger Vergé maintains that lobsters must come to the fire alive and kicking. *Foie gras*, one of the world's great delicacies, has been produced since Roman times by stuffing geese full of food in order to distend their livers.

There have been stories about geese with their feet nailed to the floor in front of a fire, to soften their livers. These are untrue today. The *gavage*, or force-feeding of geese, is hardly natural, but it does not cause great suffering and only lasts for the last few weeks of their lives.

A large producer of *foie gras* has about thirty acres of land and raises some 700 geese a year. The birds are ordinary grey geese; no particular breed is used. For their first eight months they roam about in fields, being shut up only at night to protect them from foxes. In this period they eat what they can grub up, together with ordinary amounts of maize. The greater part of their lives, then, is much more natural than that of a battery hen or a broiler calf.

The *gavage* begins about halfway through the eighth month, when the birds are kept in indoor pens with about twenty geese to a pen. Over a four to six week period they are fed three times a day on maize mixed with water and fat which is warmed in a large pan. The quantity is gradually built up to more than a kilo a day. The warm maize is fed into a hopper which hangs from the ceiling and tapers to a tube about half an inch in diameter. This is pushed into the bird's beak and about half-way down its neck. A small electric motor forces the maize into the bird; the goose-girl helps it down by massaging the goose's lower neck or *jabot*. Bizarre as this seems, the geese accept it after the first few days when the *jabot* grows larger. They are killed at ten months, when the average weight of their livers is about one kilo.

The price of a good, fattened goose ranges from 200 to 250 francs, depending on the weight and quality of the liver. A good-quality liver is one which retains the indentation of a finger pushed into it. Its colour should be creamy-white, tinged with pink. The farmers usually sell their geese to a factory, and most of the livers are made into *pâtés* for sale to retailers. But the best restaurants buy their *foie gras* raw and unprepared, making their *pâté* fresh every day.

The cooking has to be very gentle, in a terrine in a *bain-marie*. The *foie gras* is first marinated, generally in port, brandy and spices, then it is put in the oven for about one and a half hours. Some chefs cook it in an oven which is cooling from being very hot.

The goose head symbol identifies the products of Jean Rougié, seen here with Vergé and Bocuse among the geese that, later in their lives, will be force-fed to make *foie gras*.

Seasonal salad with poached eggs
Frogs' legs with watercress and mushrooms
Salmon baked with vegetables
Breast of duck with herb butter
Fresh fruits and sorbets

Salade du jardin de curé

Cover the bottom of a saucepan with olive oil and add a thick layer of carrots and celeriac in julienne strips. Add garlic and about half-a-dozen peppercorns. Gently cook the julienne for ten minutes. Let the mixture cool and drain the julienne, keeping the oil for later.

Prepare equal proportions of cress, *trevise* (red batavia) lettuce, lamb's lettuce and purslane. Lightly boil soya leaves and green peas separately. Cool these for a minute or two in a bowl of iced water.

Mix all the prepared vegetables in a large salad bowl and put to one side. Break quails' eggs into a plate (about six per person). Bring an eight-inch shallow saucepan half-filled with equal amounts of water and red wine to simmering point. Do not add salt to this liquid. Put the eggs gently into the saucepan and let them poach for a minute. Remove the pan from the heat.

Season the salad and add a *vinaigrette gourmande* with thin slices of smoked pork breast. Toss the salad. Gently place the

warm quails' eggs on top of the salad. Sprinkle with chopped chives and chervil and serve.
Note: Quails' eggs may be replaced by hens' eggs, allowing one per person; poach them for three minutes.

A *vinaigrette gourmande* should be mixed in the following order and in the following proportions: one spoon lemon juice, two spoons ground-nut oil, two spoons olive oil, one spoon Xérès vinegar, one spoon chopped chervil and one spoon chopped tarragon.

A slice of hot toast is ideal with this salad.

Feuilleté de grenouilles au cresson et aux mousserons

On a lightly floured working surface roll out puff pastry into a rectangle the size of this page and a quarter of an inch thick. Cut into four equal parts (one per person) and place on a baking tray. Brush the tops with beaten egg-yolk, not allowing the yolk to trickle down the sides as this will prevent the pastry from rising. Cook the pastry in a moderately hot oven for fifteen minutes, remove and keep warm.

Sauté a handful of mushrooms in butter for two minutes. Pour on *crème fleurette* and bring to the boil. Add the frogs' legs, cover the pan and simmer for five minutes. Extract the frogs' legs with a perforated spoon and put them on a plate to cool. Continue simmering the cream and mushrooms, this time uncovered, for just under ten minutes. Add a teaspoon of watercress *purée* and lemon juice. Reduce the mixture.

Take the meat from the frogs' legs and put it into the mushroom sauce. After a few moments, remove from the heat and add a couple of soupspoons of dry white wine and chopped shallot. Mix everything well with a fork and cover to keep warm. Slice the pastry in half. Arrange the bottom halves on individual plates or on a serving dish. Place an equal number of frogs' legs on each pastry, letting the sauce slide over the edges. Sprinkle with chopped watercress leaves, cover with pastry tops and serve immediately.
Note: A recipe for watercress *purée* is given in the Glossary, under *purée*.

Papillotes de saumon à l'étuvée de légumes

Cut carrots, mushrooms and onions into thin strips. Sauté the carrots and the onions in butter for five minutes. Add the mushrooms and further cook the vegetables for three minutes. Stir constantly with a wooden spoon to prevent the vegetables from browning or sticking to the pan. Add salt, pepper and a few tarragon leaves. Cover the saucepan and braise the contents for two minutes. Allow to cool.

Brush large circular sheets of grease-proof paper with ground-nut oil. On one side of each circle put enough of the julienne of vegetables for one person.

Take out all the little bones from the salmon with tweezers. Then slice the salmon very thinly. Place three slices of salmon on each julienne. Season with salt, pepper and a little chopped shallot. Then put a few tarragon leaves, some small pieces of butter, two soupspoons of white wine and a soupspoon of chicken *bouillon* on the fish. Close the *papillote* by folding the empty half of the circle over, then pinching the edges together tightly, ensuring that the *papillote* is sealed. Grease a roasting tray with ground-nut oil and slip it into a pre-heated medium oven for five minutes. Put the *papillotes* on the heated tray, not touching each other, and cook briefly. Serve immediately.
Note: An advantage of using *papillotes* is that there is little smell of cooking. The *papillotes* may perfectly well be made from baking foil which can be sealed more readily and will not burn or tear as easily as other paper.

Grillade de canard de Chalosse au beurre d'herbes fines

Score diamond shapes on the skin side of boned breasts of duck and put them in a marinade of olive oil, ground-nut oil and red wine. Leave for twenty-four hours in the refrigerator, turning them over and remixing the marinade after twelve hours.

The duck-breasts can be cooked either by grilling them over embers or in a cast-iron pot. Cook skin-side down, for about ten minutes. The duck produces its own fat when cooking. After ten minutes turn the duck-breasts over and cook for a further three minutes.

Remove them from the heat and keep warm between two plates in a pre-heated oven. In this way the duck flesh becomes tender.

Make a sauce by reducing wine vinegar with a chopped shallot over a low heat until it reaches the consistency of a syrup. Add Xérès vinegar and bring to the boil. Lower the heat and add butter in small pieces, whisking the contents until the sauce becomes creamy. Season with salt and freshly milled pepper. Add chives, chervil, parsley and tarragon. Keep the sauce warm in a *bain-marie* if it is not served immediately.

Cut the duck-breasts lengthwise in thin slices. Arrange in a fan shape around the individual warmed plates. In the centre of the plate, put potatoes which have been fried in duck fat. Cover the duck slices with herb butter and serve.

Soupe aux écrevisses de rivière

Gently sauté cleaned live crayfish in equal proportions of olive oil and ground-nut oil. When the crayfish have turned red, remove them from the pan with a perforated spoon. Take the meat out of the tails and keep to one side.

Pound the shells of the crayfish in a mortar or grind in a mixer. Melt butter in a sauté pan and drop in the pounded crayfish shells with a *mirepoix* of carrots, onion, shallot, *bouquet garni*, salt and pepper, stirring regularly with a wooden spoon.

Add armagnac and port, half cover the pan and allow the mixture to reduce. Add a third of a bottle of dry white wine and twice as much water. Also mix in peeled tomatoes and concentrated tomato *purée*. Again reduce the liquid.

Finely sieve this sauce into a bowl. To a reduced fish *fumet* add *crème fraîche double* and small amounts of chervil and tarragon. Reduce again. Remove from the heat and whisk in small pieces of butter. When this has been built up to a thick consistency, add the sieved crayfish shell mixture. Drop in the crayfish shells and heat the soup. Pour the soup into individual dishes and sprinkle with chopped chives and serve.
Note: To prepare live crayfish, twist the middle fin at the end of the tail and bring this towards the fish's head. The intestines should come away.

Feuilleté de truffes au vin de Graves
Cook four small pastry shells in a moderately hot oven for fifteen minutes and keep warm.

Cut truffles into small thin slices, allowing one large fresh truffle per person. Heat a small amount of butter in a pan and put in the truffles with salt and pepper, cooking lightly for a few minutes. Pour in equal quantities of Graves and sherry, bring to the boil and reduce by a third. Add a couple of cups of *crème fleurette* to the reduced liquid and again bring the ingredients to the boil and simmer for fifteen minutes.

Thinly slice fresh *foie gras*.

Use a serrated knife to slice the puff pastry shells in half. Arrange the bottom halves on individual plates or on the serving dish. Cover these with a slice of *foie gras*, then spoon the truffles onto the liver. Add lemon juice and seasoning to the sauce and pour it over the truffles. Cap with the pastry top and serve.

Coquilles St Jacques à la coque de Didier Oudill
Prepare two live scallops per person, keeping some cleaned, empty shells. Cut the white of each scallop in two.

Prepare and cut equal amounts of carrots, onions and mushrooms into a julienne. Sauté the carrots and the onions in butter for five minutes. Add the mushrooms and further cook the

vegetables for three minutes. Stir constantly with a wooden spoon to prevent the vegetables from browning or sticking to the pan. Add salt, pepper and a few tarragon leaves. Cover the saucepan and let the contents braise for two minutes. Allow to cool.

Put a thick layer of cooking salt in a roasting pan and in this firmly embed the scallop shells to prevent movement while cooking.

Use half the vegetables to garnish the shells, sprinkle them with chopped shallots and put a coral and three rounds of halved whites on top. Season with salt and pepper and cover with the rest of the vegetables. Put a knob of butter on each filled shell.

Cover each shell with its corresponding flat shell and seal with a strip of pastry moistened with egg. Put into a very hot pre-heated oven for about ten minutes.

When the roasting pan comes from the oven, the cooking salt can be used to garnish the individual plates or the serving dish.
Note: To prepare live scallops prise them open and slice off the round part which clings to the flat upper shell. Using a soupspoon, loosen the white and the coral from the concave bottom.

Didier Oudill is the *chef-de-cuisine* at Guérard's restaurant.

Navarin de faisan aux pieds de cochon
Press down on the breastbone of a plucked hen pheasant to loosen the meat from the bone. Cut along both sides of the backbone and remove it. Cut the pheasant into four pieces and season. Gently sauté these pieces in a saucepan. When they are a golden colour, add equal amounts of chopped mushrooms, carrots and baby turnips. Cook together for five minutes.

Pour away the juice from the pan and then pour a couple of measures of armagnac over the pheasant. Return the pan to the heat. When the armagnac has reduced a little, add a cup of chicken *bouillon*, a cup of red wine, a *bouquet garni* and a large pig's trotter (which has had the central bone removed, and been cut into quarters). Cover the pan and cook in a hot oven for about twenty minutes.

Take six rashers of bacon and a dozen small onions and brown them in a sauté pan. Add to the pheasant, with diced potatoes, and cook for twenty minutes.

Make a tomato sauce by blending a few tomatoes, a clove of garlic, olive oil and seasoning.

When the pheasant is cooked, place it on a low heat and gently stir in the tomato sauce. Just before serving, scatter cooked peas over the dish.
Note: To prepare the pig's trotter, first singe, scrape and salt it, then put it in a saucepan with white wine, a little vinegar and water, bring to the boil and simmer for at least six hours.

Crayfish soup
Truffles in pastry with a wine sauce
Scallops baked in their shells
Pheasant with pig's trotter
Apple tart

Tarte fine chaude aux pommes acidulées
Peel and core some reinette or other eating apples. Cut each apple into thin sections. Put these in a bowl and sprinkle with lemon juice.

Put thinly rolled rounds (about the size of a dessert plate) of puff pastry on a baking sheet.

Scribe a circle around the edge of each pastry round with a kitchen knife. This should be about half the depth of the pastry and its purpose is to cause the edge to rise and form a rim round the tart. Cover the area inside with overlapping rings of apple sections. Paint the apples with melted butter and dust with sugar. Bake for fifteen minutes in a hot oven. Then repaint and redust the tarts with butter and sugar and put them back in the oven for another fifteen minutes. Serve at once on hot plates with *crème chantilly*.
Note: The sprinkle of lemon juice over the apples prevents them from going brown. At the end of baking the tarts should be a golden colour and the apples have a caramelized sheen.

The circle on which the apples will sit can be pricked with a fork, which prevents the centre from rising when in the oven.

HAEBERLIN: SAFE AND SUPERB

L'AUBERGE DE L'ILL
des
Frères Haeberlin

Paul Haeberlin's cuisine is a safe one, reflecting his strict principles, and yet enlivened with the bursts of imagination which distinguish this otherwise relaxed man. Many of his dishes are based on the simpler materials which you can find, rather ordinarily done, in any respectable French restaurant, but in his hands they are elevated to a status which they rarely acquire elsewhere.

Several dishes would have been greeted as old friends by Escoffier, such as *la fameuse truffe sous la cendre* and the *noisettes de chevreuil aux champignons des bois*. Some, like the *blanc de turbot au champagne rosé*, are basically plain, but coloured by his own originality.

The *homard 'Prince Wladimir'* is typical of Haeberlin's regard for tradition; he learned the recipe from his teacher, Weber, who brought it back from the Russian court.

Alsace is, of course, traditionally game country and a variety of game dishes appear on the menu. According to season, Haeberlin will prepare on request *côtelette de perdreau 'Romanoff'*, *lièvre à la Royale*, *canard sauvage au sang* and *petit pâté chaud de pigeonneau*.

But in addition to such superb but traditional fare, there are Paul Haeberlin's own creations, his bursts of imagination: the spectacular *saumon soufflé 'Auberge de l'Ill'*, his famous *pêche Haeberlin* and the *mousseline* and *gâteau* of frogs' legs.

With the return of Haeberlin's son, Marc, from his training, some of the influence of the Point-Bocuse style is appearing in the cooking. The fish is more lightly cooked, pink near the bone. Vegetables have assumed a new importance and may, some hope, gradually oust the Germanic noodles which from Alsatian custom go with many of the elder Haeberlin's dishes. The son's *salade de lapereau*, served with a vinaigrette and truffles, uses the liver as well as the meat of tender young rabbit, and is a promise of the kind of cuisine that may come from this kitchen in the future.

L'AUBERGE DE L'ILL

MENU

Le saumon soufflé "Auberge de l'Ill"
ou
Le gratin de lotte et de langouste aux pistils de safran (supp. 10, frs.)
ou
Le délice de truite saumonée à la mousse de cresson
–:–
Le tournedos à la moëlle et au pinot noir
ou
L'aiguillette de canard aux pleurottes fraîches et aux petits oignons
ou
Le feuilleté de ris de veau aux 3 légumes (supp. 10,– frs.)
–:–
Les fromages
–:–
Le sorbet champagne
ou
Les fraises à la glace au lait d'amande
Les petits fours

Le 16 mai 1977
95,– frs. boissons et service en sus

Paul Haeberlin's menu of the day; sketch by Jean-Pierre. This is the menu that reflects the morning market's best buys.

ENTRÉES

Le potage du jour	15
Le potage aux grenouilles	25
Le jambon de parme	30
Le caviar frais d'Iran	80
Les œufs brouillés aux truffes	45
La salade de langouste et d'artichauts	75
La ballotine de sole aux anguilles, sauce caviar	35
La salade de lapereau, vinaigrette aux truffes	45
La brioche ou la terrine de foie gras frais	45
La fameuse truffe sous la cendre	75
Le pâté de canard au foie gras	35
Le boudin de caille et de ris de veau·au foie gras frais	40

CRUSTACÉS ET POISSONS

Le saumon soufflé "Auberge de l'Ill" (Création P. Hæberlin)	45
Le homard "Prince Wladimir"	85
La mousseline de grenouille "Paul Hæberlin"	45
Le blanc de turbot au champagne rosé	50
Les goujonnettes de sole et de homard à la nage	60
Le gratin de lotte et de langouste aux pistils de safran	60

Sur commande, suivant la saison, nous vous proposons :

Le gâteau de grenouilles au Pinot Noir (Création P. Haeberlin) · Les hors-d'oeuvre de l'Auberge
Le soufflé aux truffes · Le turbot à la nage aux écrevisses · La truffe "Souvaroff" · La côtelette
de perdreau "Romanoff" · Le lièvre à la Royale · Le canard sauvage au sang · Le petit pâté chaud
de pigeonneau · Le foie de veau entier poêlé aux truffes · Les pêches soufflées "Cardinal de Rohan".

Service 12% en sus.

THE MOST FRENCH TREAT

Frogs' legs have been a delicacy in France at least since the sixteenth century. However, as Alexandre Dumas observed in his *Grand Dictionnaire de Cuisine*, 'In Italy and Germany, great quantities of these batrachians are eaten. The markets are full of them.' He went on to take a swipe at the British for caricaturing the French as frog-eaters, pointing out that many British in the West Indies preferred frogs to chickens.

The stereotype takes another knock as far as France's three-star provincial menus are concerned, for frogs' legs appear on few of them. It is in German-influenced Alsace, at the Haeberlins', that as many as three different batrachian specialities are served, a *potage aux grenouilles* and, as we have seen, a *mousse* and *gâteau* of frogs' legs.

These days, many frogs eaten in France are imported from Central Europe because they are plumper than French ones. The native varieties, such as the green frog and the rusty or mute frog, have a more delicate flavour. The best and most expensive come from the Dombes, north of Lyon.

Only the frog's back legs are eaten. Sometimes they are marinated in white wine and herbs. There are many ways of cooking frogs: dipping in batter and deep frying in oil; casseroling in butter, wine and cream; frying in butter and serving with cream and *béchamel* sauce; and *à la poulette* with egg yolks and cream, or simply *à la meunière*.

L'Auberge de l'Ill is on the east bank of the river Ill at Illhaeusern, about seventeen kilometres north-east of Colmar and a short distance from the main N83 road from Colmar to Strasbourg, capital of Alsace.

VOLAILLES

La volaille truffée et rôtie à la broche (2 pers.)	90
Gratin de nouilles au foie gras	
L'aiguillette de canard aux pleurottes fraîches et aux petits oignons (2 pers.)	90
Le pigeonneau de Bresse en salmis	55
et son gâteau de foie blond	

VIANDES

L'entrecôte double aux échalotes (2 pers.)	90
Le tournedos à la moelle et au Pinot Noir	45
Le rognon de veau à la moutarde	50
Le filet de bœuf au poivre vert et aux concombres	45
Le médaillon de veau aux truffes et aux pointes d'asperges fraîches	60
Le filet d'agneau au basilic et aux petits légumes du marché (2 pers.)	120
La cassolette de ris de veau aux légumes frais	60

LES FROMAGES   15

DESSERTS

La pêche Hæberlin (pêche pochée, glace pistache, sabayon au Champagne)	20
Les fraises à la glace au lait d'amandes	20
Le sorbet au Champagne ou aux fruits	20
La barque de l'Ill glacée au croquant, sauce caramel	20
Les profiteroles glacés au chocolat	20
Le vacherin glacé aux fruits de saison	20
* Le gratin de framboises "Laetitia"	25
* Les crêpes fourrées de pommes au miel et flambées	25
Nos gâteaux et pâtisserie	15

* A commander au début du repas.

le 14.3.78

WILD DELICACIES

'The term "game" includes all animals which enjoy a state of natural liberty in the fields and woods and are fit to be eaten.' So begins Brillat-Savarin on game in his *Physiologie du Goût*, and he goes on to sub-divide game, birds and animals into three groups. The first includes song birds; the second 'the snipe, the beccafico, the corncrake, the partridge, the pheasant and the hare; this is game in the proper sense of the term—ground game and marsh game, feathered game and furry game. The third is more generally known by the name of venison and includes the wild boar, the roe deer and the other hoofed animals.' However, we now apply the term 'venison' only to deer.

Wild birds and animals have more flavour than most domesticated ones; they are also tougher, so they must be prepared accordingly. In Britain, game birds are hung for as long as two weeks. In France, they are rarely hung for more than two to three days; consequently they are likely to be cooked by long, slow simmering rather than by roasting. Game birds are much used for *pâtés* and terrines.

Meat from the roe deer or *chevreuil* (the buck is better than the doe) is the most common French venison. It is usually marinated to tenderize it and develop the gamey flavour. Hares are either cooked fresh, as soon as they are shot, or after being drawn and hung for three days at the most; they are never eaten high. Wild boar appears on menus as *sanglier* or under different names, depending on its age, ranging from *marcassin* (under six months; the most delicate) to *solitaire* (over five years).

Pâté of crayfish and young vegetables

Salmon soufflé

Breast of duck with mushrooms and baby onions

Cheese

Wild strawberries in pastry

Terrine d'écrevisses aux petits légumes
Prepare live crayfish and boil them for
five minutes in a spicy crayfish *fumet*.
Take them out and shell.

Strain the *fumet* and reduce it. Check
the seasoning, add gelatine and allow it to
stand for a while.

Poach separately the spinach, carrots,
celery and green beans in salted water.
Plunge into cold water—so that they keep
their fresh, natural colours—then cut
into small dice.

Line a terrine with successive layers of
crayfish tails, each of the vegetables and
poached truffles. Cover with the crayfish
fumet and chill.

Before serving the terrine, prepare a
tomato *concassée* which is reduced until it
takes on the consistency of a sauce. Add
fines herbes. Slice the terrine and serve it
with this tomato sauce.
Note: Fresh truffles should be poached in
champagne or dry white wine for this
dish (canned truffles will already have
been poached).

Saumon Soufflé 'Auberge de l'Ill'
Fillet fresh salmon and cut into thin slices.

Make a fine mousse from 500 grams of
pike flesh, four egg-whites and a
half-litre of *crème fraîche*. In a buttered
ovenproof dish, put chopped shallots,
white wine and some fish *fumet*. Put the
salmon fillets in the dish and cover them
with the mousse. Poach for about fifteen
minutes in a moderate oven.

Take out the cooked salmon slices and
reduce the liquid. Add *crème fraîche* and
reduce again, finally adding butter, a thin
slice of lemon and seasoning.

Place the salmon fillets in individual
dishes and cover with the sauce. Heat in a
moderate oven and serve.
Note: Salmon from the Rhine was once a
speciality in Alsace. Scotch or Canadian
salmon serves perfectly well for this dish.

**Aiguillettes de canard aux pleurottes
et aux petits oignons nouveaux.**
Fillet breasts of duck by lifting the meat
off the breastbone with a filleting knife.
Roast the duck-breasts in a hot oven for
about fifteen minutes so that they are a
good rosy colour.

Cook mushrooms and baby onions in
butter, glazing the onions.

Make a sauce from duck stock, red wine,
shallots, *crème fraîche* and cognac. Thicken
the sauce by whisking in nuggets of butter.

Cut the breasts into long thin slices
(*aiguillettes*), cover with the sauce and
serve garnished with the onions and
mushrooms.
Note: *Pleurottes* are a genus of edible
fungi which grow on wood, of which the
Oyster Mushroom is the most common.
However, cultivated mushrooms may be
used for this dish.

Feuilleté tiède aux fraises des bois
Make small rectangular cases of puff
pastry. Brush with melted butter and bake.
Line them with a *crème patissière* to which
crème chantilly and wild strawberry
liqueur have been added. Fill the pastry
cases with wild strawberries soaked in
strawberry juice.
Note: A dessert of this kind can be made
with strawberries or raspberries.

ALTERNATIVE BRANDIES

When brandy is mentioned, people tend to
think of grape brandies—cognac or armagnac. But these are far from being the only
finale to a good meal with wine. France
offers an entire range of delicate and
delicious brandies distilled from stone and
berry fruits. These fruit brandies are called
alcools blancs (white spirits) because, unlike
grape brandies which are aged in oak, they
are matured in glass jars or glass-lined vats,
which keeps them colourless and does not
affect the fragrance of the particular fruit.

No region of France is more famous for
its fruit brandies than Alsace, with its
abundance of wild and cultivated fruits and
berries, slowly ripened to maximum flavour
and sweetness by the late, dryish summers of
eastern France. As one might expect, some
of the brandies of polyglot Alsace have
German and others have French names.
Among them are *kirsch* (cherry), *quetsche*
(plum), *mirabelle* (golden plum), *poire* (pear),
framboise (wild raspberry), *fraise* (wild and
cultivated strawberries), *myrtille* (wild bil-
berry), *sorbes* (mountain ash or rowan berries)
and *mures des forêts* (blackberry).

Brioche de foie gras

Prepare the *foie gras* as in Point's recipe for *parfait de foie gras Fernand*.

Then place the *foie gras* in a buttered metal mould which has been lined with unsweetened *brioche* dough and cover it with a sheet of the same dough. Wrap the mould in buttered paper to prevent the dough from rising over the edges. Leave the dough to rise and then bake for forty minutes in a moderate oven. Unmould it. It may be served either hot or cold.

Mousseline de grenouille 'Paul Haeberlin'

Trim the feet off the frogs' legs and put the legs into very cold water. Change the water every two hours until the legs are whitened and swollen. Dry them before cooking in a fish *fumet* with Riesling and shallots. Save the *fumet* and bone the frogs' legs.

Make a fine fish mousse of sole and pike. Line buttered ramekins with some of the mousse.

Then make a Riesling sauce with the *fumet*. Warm the filleted frogs' legs in the Riesling sauce. Ladle the frogs' legs and some of the sauce into the ramekins and cover with the rest of the fish mousse. Poach in a *bain-marie* in the oven for about fifteen minutes.

Turn the ramekins out onto plates and add extra Riesling sauce to which finely chopped chives have been added.
Note: Frogs' legs, the only edible part of the creature, have a mild flavour. In France they are bought fresh by the dozen, on skewers; six would be enough for one person.

Noisettes de chevreuil Saint-Hubert

Take a saddle of venison, bone the fillets (keeping the bones for stock) and cut the meat into thick steaks (noisettes) of about 100 grams each. Leave overnight in a marinade of Alsatian white wine, juniper berries, thyme and bay leaves, carrots and onions.

Make a game stock with the venison bones.

Lightly cook the noisettes in a shallow frying-pan with clarified butter. Place them on a serving plate and make a sauce with the pan juices by adding cognac, game stock, *crème fraîche double* and a teaspoonful or redcurrant jelly.

Correct the seasoning and pour the sauce over the noisettes. Garnish each plate with poached apples filled with bilberries (huckleberries) and pastry shells containing *chanterelle* mushrooms in a cream sauce.
Note: The male roebuck is more delicate than the doe. The noisettes of venison may also come from the loin and upper end of the haunch.

Pêche Haeberlin

Poach skinned white peaches in a syrup.

Make a *sabayon* by whisking egg-yolks, sugar and champagne in a *bain-marie* until it thickens to form a ribbon. Remove the pan from the heat and whisk the mixture until it cools, adding, towards the end, a little *crème fleurette*.

Make a pistachio ice-cream. Pound pistachios to a fine paste in a mortar or use a blender. Add a little milk to prevent oiling. Heat equal proportions of milk and *crème fleurette*. Let these scald and pour onto sugar beaten with egg-yolks (one yolk to twenty-five grams of sugar). Beat quickly and continuously. When a rose forms, it is ready. Immediately plunge the saucepan into a bowl of cold water to prevent further cooking. Strain the mixture before freezing.

Serve the peach and the ice-cream together, covering the peach with the *sabayon*. One bottle of champagne makes enough sabayon to cover thirty-five peaches.

Menu d'Hiver

Brioche de foie gras

Mousseline de grenouille 'Paul Haeberlin'

Noisettes de chevreuil Saint-Hubert

Pêche Haeberlin

Foie gras in pastry

Frogs' legs in a fish mousse

Venison steaks in sauce

Peach with champagne and ice-cream

Not surprisingly a fruit brandy is an appropriate *digestif* at L'Auberge de l'Ill. In contrast to grape brandy, which achieves its full *bouquet* when the glass has been warmed by the hand, fruit brandies are served in glasses which have been chilled. This brings out the full flavour of the fruit, enhances the brandy's smoothness and moderates the fierceness of the alcohol. When your brandy has been poured, you gently turn the glass around until it is misted over, breathe in the full fragrance of the fruit—and sip slowly. The Haeberlins particularly encourage their guests to try the *eau-de-vie de poire*, with a pear that has actually been grown in the bottle by placing the bottle over a branch in bud.

The rough spirit known as *marc* is distilled from the residue of grapes after they have been pressed for wine-making. Many French people, and not only peasants, persist in believing in the virtues of *marc au vipère*, which is *marc* with a viper or adder pickled in it. Even a fine restaurant may keep a bottle in the cellar. If a customer asks for some, the waiter often wraps the bottle in a cloth so as not to alarm more squeamish diners.

VISUAL ENCHANTMENT BY OUTHIER

A LA CUISINE

L'Oasis La Napoule

Louis Outhier's menu is singular for two reasons. Firstly, he has created it almost without regard for the region in which he is situated. Secondly, in terms of what is called *nouvelle cuisine*, it is quite conservative. Outhier's response to Roger Vergé's culinary fireworks, up the coast at Mougins, is to entrench himself in his craft, rather than to compete by trying to astonish.

Several of Outhier's dishes originated with his mentor, Fernand Point: the *brioche de foie gras frais*, the *filet de Saint-Pierre au noilly* and what is now perhaps Outhier's most famous dish, the *loup en croûte Fernand Point*—sea bass in pastry with *sauce choron* and tomato *concassée*.

There is also ample evidence of Outhier's own imagination and individuality. He creates supreme salads from the freshest of ingredients: wild asparagus, lamb's lettuce and red batavia lettuce, enlivened with *foie de canard*, truffles and lobster or whatever else he can find that is fresh and perfect at that moment.

The main courses are usually quite simple: turbot with champagne sauce, plain lobster, whole kidneys in a Xérès sauce and lamb with port. They are beautifully done, but Outhier's special touch is in the dishes, such as a *cassolette* of scallops and Belon oysters, which he writes on the menu by hand. These he creates from ingredients he happens upon from day to day; they vary through the year but are always light, ingenious—and superb. The *pâtisseries*, mostly cakes and flans, are exquisite, the *marjolaine à l'orange* and *tourte au fromage blanc* being quite exceptional.

The conservative, or rather, classic aspect of the menu is in its attention to detail and presentation. No-one can make a dish look more interesting than Outhier—and the taste always fulfils the promise of the appearance.

Such is his craftsmanship. Combined with the talent revealed in such dishes as the *millefeuille de saumon au cerfeuil*, the result is enchantment.

Restaurant

Menu à 120 f

Brioche de Foie Gras frais
Turbot braisé au Champagne (à partir de 2 pers.)
Les Fromages de la Ferme
Timbale Cardinal
Mignardises

Menu à 140 f

Soupe de Poissons
Filet de St-Pierre au Noilly (à partir de 2 pers.)
Sorbet William
Suprêmes de Pigeon Marie-Louise
Salade de Mesclun
Les Fromages de la Ferme
Coupe Oasis
Mignardises

Menu à 160 f

Foie Gras de Canard frais
Saumon Frais Alexandra (à partir de 2 pers.)
Sorbet William
Selle d'Agneau en noisette au vieux Porto
Salade de Mesclun
Les Fromages de la Ferme
Caravane de Desserts
Mignardises

...asis, La Napoule

Saláde d'Automne 50 f

Salade Oasis 55 f

Soupe de Poissons de Roche 30 f

Saumon fumé 60 f

Salade de Truffes 65 f

Truffe Surprise 60 f

Brioche de Foie Gras 50 f

Foie Gras de Canard frais 55 f

Cocktail de Langoustes 55 f

Caviar Beluga 125 grs pour 2 pers. 250 f

———◆———

Mousseline de Rascasse 35 f

Loup en Croûte Fernand Point (à partir de 3 pers.) 60 f p.pers.

Turbot braisé au Champagne (à part.de 2 pers.) 55 f p.pers.

Turbot Soufflé Lagrenée (à partir de 2 pers.) 55 f p.pers.

Filet de St-Pierre au Noilly (à part.de 2 pers.) 50 f p.pers.

Saumon Frais Alexandra (à partir de 2 pers.) 60 f p.pers.

Mille-Feuille de Saumon au Cerfeuil (à partir de 2 pers.) 55 f p.pers.

Langouste Belle Aurore (à part.de 2 pers.) 150f p.pers.

Homard à la Courte Nage (à partir de 2 pers.) 150 f p.pers.

———◆———

Truffe Fraîche en Paupiette (à part.de 2 pers.) 90 f p.pers.

Suprêmes de Pigeon Marie-Louise 55 f

Selle d'Agneau en noisette au vieux Porto 60 f

Suprême de Volaille Jacqueline (à partir de 2 pers.) 50 f p.pers.

Rognon de Veau Entier dans son Fond de Xérès 60 f

Escalope de Foie Gras aux Reinettes 70 f

Délice de Poularde Vendémiaire 60 f

Aiguillettes de Canard à l'Armagnac 60 f

———◆———

Marjolaine à l'Orange

Alhambra Chocolat

Charlotte Bavaroise

Tourte au Fromage blanc

Mousse Chocolat

Tarte au Citron meringuée

Savarin au Rhum

Glaces et Sorbets

(handwritten in margin:) Asperges Nouvelles 50 f

(handwritten in margin:) Cassolette de St Jacques et Bellons 60 f

(handwritten signature:) ...thier 30.3.76

...% en sus

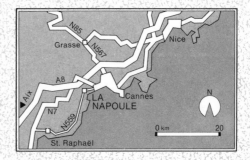

La Napoule-Plage, on the Golfe de la Napoule, is the first of a string of resorts linked by the N559 road along the Côte d'Azur from Cannes to St Raphaël. The road was built in 1903 at the instigation of the Touring Club de France.

FROZEN REFRESHERS

Among the delights offered by three-star restaurants are the deliciously refreshing sorbets, or sherberts—first cousins to the water ices of Italy, which were first introduced from China by Marco Polo. Imported into France along with other Renaissance influences, sorbets became so fashionable that the great estates had specially constructed ice stores. The ice was collected from the Alps and later imported from as far afield as Norway.

Sorbets were, and still are, eaten between courses as entremets. The reason for this was the (erroneous) belief that ice, like alcohol, is an aid to the digestion. Sorbets now take the place of the liqueurs which used to be served between courses, such as the nip of calvados known as the *trou normand*.

Basic sorbets are made with fruit, syrup, water and wine. The mixture is churned in a *sorbetière* as it freezes, then stiff egg-white is added.

The chefs constantly seek new sorbet flavours: Outhier has used *eau-de-vie de poire*, Vergé, grapefruit and vermouth and Pic, passion fruit and honey.

Peach of foie gras
Seasonal salad
John Dory in red wine
Pear sorbet
(see Point's recipe for *sorbet Pyramide*)
Lamb with port

Foie gras hedgehog
Seasonal salad
Scallops with a vegetable julienne
Pear sorbet
Breast of chicken with apples

Note: *Salade d'automne* consists of the freshest vegetables and salads of the season based on those ingredients that grow wild in the surrounding hills.

Pêche de foie gras

Make a perfectly rounded stone from a mixture of chopped almonds, butter and truffle. Mould duck *foie gras* around the stone to the shape and size of a peach. Coat the *foie gras* with a green pepper sauce followed by another coat of *chaud-froid*—very thinly so the green shows through.

Colour half the peach in pink with cochineal and then dip it quickly in an amber aspic to make it glisten.

Serve with a real peach leaf placed on top of the ball of *foie gras*.

Salade de printemps

Prepare a seasonal *salade de mesclün*. Add finely sliced avocado pear and fresh mushrooms. Toss in a mild vinaigrette dressing and top with asparagus tips dipped in *hollandaise* sauce.

Note: *Salade de mesclün* is a Provençal term for a mixed salad of mostly wild ingredients, which vary with the time of year. It might include, for instance, dandelion leaves, oak leaves, and red batavia lettuce.

For this salad, vinaigrette must not be too acid. Place a little thyme, rosemary, chives, a bay leaf and unpeeled garlic cloves in a large bottle with olive oil and wine vinegar (or lemon juice) in a ratio of 5:1; add sea-salt, freshly milled pepper and Dijon mustard and shake well to blend.

Hérisson de foie gras

Mould a ball of fresh duck *foie gras* into the shape of a mouse. Make the eyes out of two fragments of fresh truffle.

Grill some almonds and slice them finely. Push these into the back of the mouse so that they become the spines of a hedgehog.

Noix de St Jacques à la nage

Bring a *court-bouillon* of wine, water, thinly sliced onions, leeks, a *bouquet garni*, salt and black peppercorns to the boil. After fifteen minutes, add the whites of scallops cut horizontally in half.

Remove the scallops and place them on a julienne of vegetables cut very finely and sautéed in butter for a few moments.

Saint-Pierre au vin rouge

Make a *fumet* with the head and bones of a John Dory and equal quantities of red wine and water. Reduce.

Marinate fillets of the John Dory in red wine for fifteen minutes, drain them and cook lightly in butter. Keep the fish fillets warm on a serving plate.

Mix the marinade with the pan juices and reduce until very thick, then add the fish *fumet* and reduce to a consistency suitable for coating. Add butter to the sauce, then incorporate a julienne of mushrooms. Reduce the acidity of the sauce with a little sugar and add crushed parsley.

Pour the sauce over the fish fillets and serve.

Note: John Dory is a flat, oval fish and is sometimes called *poule de mer*. The flesh is white and solid, delicate in flavour. Each side produces a large, triangular fillet which can be cut in two.

Selle d'agneau au porto

Cut noisettes from a saddle of lamb and cook them quickly on a high flame so that they are pink inside and keep all their juices.

In another pan, gently heat a glass of light brown stock with a little *foie gras* and *crème fraîche*. Do not let it boil.

Deglaze the pan in which the noisettes have cooked with a glass of vintage port. Boil vigorously and then pour in the cream sauce. Mix with a whisk, correct the seasoning and heat almost to boiling point. Pour over the noisettes and garnish each one with a slice of truffle.

Suprême de volaille Jacqueline

Lightly season and flour some breasts of chicken and brown them in hot butter. When the chicken has browned, pour in a glass of port and the same amount of meat stock. Cover the pan and cook gently for about fifteen minutes.

For each serving, soften in butter a quartered dessert apple. Arrange the *suprêmes* on a round plate and decorate with the apple quarters.

Add *crème fraîche double* to the pan in which the chicken was cooked and reduce to a syrup. Remove the pan from the heat and produce a sauce by mixing in pieces of butter. Add finely chopped almonds to the sauce and pour over the chicken.

Garnish the dish with lemon slices.

Note: Outhier dedicated this dish to his wife, Jacqueline.

Outhier used to cook this dish also using the legs and wings of a chicken. Now he cooks only with the *suprême*, the best part; in this case, the breasts of chicken served skinned and boned.

THE SEMANTICS OF THE SEA

'Fish, in the hands of a skilful cook, can become an inexhaustible source of gustatory delight,' wrote Brillat-Savarin; nowhere is this more true than in French cuisine. The *matelote*, or fish stew, to which he gives the highest praise, describing it as 'the staple diet of bargemen . . . brought to perfection in riverside taverns,' is served today by such chefs as Paul Haeberlin and Roger Vergé, who does a Mediterranean version with gilt-head bream and red mullet.

Nothing edible in the way of fish and shellfish escapes the French, who, unlike the British, are not deterred by the alarming looks of such species as the angler-fish. Consequently, the culinary repertoire in this area is immense. Here, however, is a guide to some of the species which most often appear on three-star restaurant menus.

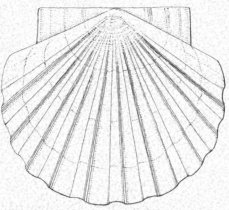

The scallop or *coquille Saint-Jacques* runs the oyster close as the most succulent of edible shellfish. Both the white and orange-yellow parts are eaten; some of the many ways of cooking are *en brochette*, sautéed, *à la meunière* or baked with herbs. The shells are often used as dishes for small helpings of other delicacies; in the Middle Ages they were the emblem of pilgrims to the church of St James (St Jacques) of Compostela.

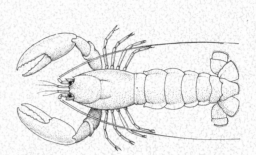

The lobster or *homard*, the largest marine crustacean, is a classic ingredient of *haute cuisine*. It can be simply boiled (which changes the natural dark blue of its shell to bright red) and served with a mayonnaise or oil and lemon dressing, or in a variety of elaborate presentations. Michel Guérard serves lobster with truffles, fresh tomatoes and basil.

The John Dory or *Saint-Pierre* is caught in Mediterranean and Atlantic waters. It is a primitive, spiny fish with two dark spots, one on each side, which are supposed to be Saint Peter's finger-marks. It is highly rated for its delicately flavoured flesh, which separates into boneless fillets. It is expensive because two-thirds of the weight are taken up by the inedible head and gut.

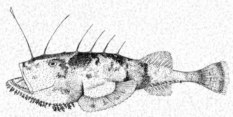

The grotesque angler-fish, *lotte* or *baudroie*, is found in northern European as well as Mediterranean waters. Lying camouflaged on the sea-bed, it attracts smaller fish to its huge mouth by waving its 'fishing-rod'. The firm tail meat tastes very like lobster. Alain Chapel cooks the roe, which, confusingly, is served as *foie de lotte*.

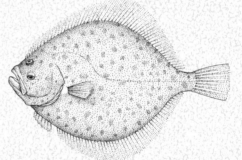

The turbot, of the flat-fish variety, is one of the best flavoured of all sea fish; to cook it whole the French have a turbot-shaped fish-kettle, the *turbotière*. Turbot is best in winter and may be cooked in dozens of ways, some quite simple: simmered in water, sliced and fried, poached in white wine or filleted and cooked like sole.

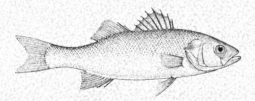

The sea bass, *loup de mer* or *bar*, is an estuarine as well as Mediterranean and Atlantic fish. Its firm flesh, with few bones, is much favoured. Large ones are cooked in a *court-bouillon* and served with sauce, or braised in white wine; small ones may be done *en papillote* or grilled. Outhier's speciality is *loup en croûte*, Pic's *loup au caviar*.

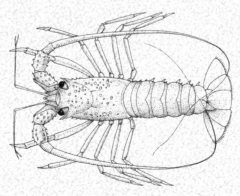

The spiny lobster or *langouste* is considered by some gourmets to be even better eating than the larger, regular lobster. Spiny lobsters are generally cooked in the same way as lobsters, but the flesh is so delicately flavoured that it should not be masked.

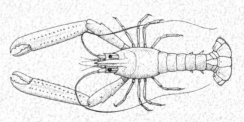

The Italian name *scampi* is loosely applied to several species of large prawn (known as jumbo shrimp in the USA); strictly it belongs to the Dublin Bay prawn, shown here, which the French call *langoustine*.

THE INDEPENDENT CUISINE OF PIC

Jacques Pic's menu is a rich one, and stands apart from the others in its complete lack of self-consciousness. There is a measure of homage to his father: the *boudin de brochet aux écrevisses* is basically one of André Pic's recipes, as are the *poularde de Bresse en vessie* and the *truffe de grignan en chausson*. Jacques Pic has, however, invented dozens of intriguing dishes. Some, like the *homard de camaret au safran*, are in a traditional style. Others are extremely modern, such as the *salade de pêcheurs au Xérès*, which includes scallops, shrimps, sole, lobster, and crayfish tails with truffles and Xérès vinegar.

The range of Pic's menu is possibly wider than anyone else's (except for that of Paul Bocuse). It is fascinating that one man can bring so much creative originality to fish, meat, poultry and game and yet have energy

Jacques P

Emincé de Foie de Canard aux Truffes 75
Salade de Pêcheurs au Xérès 80
St-Jacques Sultane 60
Terrine de Foie Gras Frais 60
Queues d'Ecrevisses Aïda 65
Suprême de Bécasse en Feuilleté 70
Huitres Gratinées Favorite 40
Truffe de Grignan en Chausson 120

Le Menu "Rabelais" à la Valentinoise à partir de 2 personnes 320

Filet de Loup au Caviar 85
Escalope de Turbot aux Morilles 70
Noix de St-Jacques Arlequin 70
Médaillon de Loup aux Huitres 65
Julienne de Sole aux Légumes 50
Filet de Barbue aux Poireaux 50
Homard de Camaret au Safran 120
Langouste au Champagne 100
Gratin de Queues d'Ecrevisses 70
Safari de Poisson aux Oursins 75
Boudin de Brochet
aux Ecrevisses 45

Jacques Pic
le 10 Janvier 1978

SERV

left to produce such incomparable delights as his *soufflé glacé d'orange*—to mention just one of Pic's wonderful *desserts de saison*. Perhaps the dominant note of Pic's cuisine is its independence, in that he is neither bound by tradition nor does he struggle to make a splash of trendiness. His manner is unassuming, but his generosity is limitless. He quietly takes the best of everything and gives the best of all.

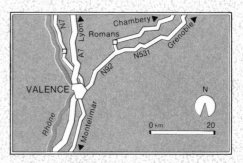

Valence-sur-Rhône is on the N7, one hundred kilometres south of Lyon. This cathedral town of the Drôme is renowned for its vineyards and has a fine Roman theatre. Montelimar, the nougat town, is forty-four kilometres to the south.

vous propose

Fricassée d'Agneau au Basilic 60
Foie de Canard Sauce Cresson 80
Côte de Bœuf à la Gousse d'Ail 140
Ris de Veau au Pistil 50
Pigeon de Bresse Fourré Florentine 55
Rognon de Veau à la Menthe 50
Tournedos à l'Hermitage 50

Noisettes de Chevreuil aux Petits Oignons 70
Bécasse Flambée deux personnes 140
Canard Sauvage aux Pruneaux deux personnes 80

Choix de Fromages
Dessert de Saison

✦ Sur Commande
Ragoût Princesse
Poularde de Bresse en Vessie "André Pic"

Notre Champagne Brut illustré par Peynet

COMPRIS

Menu « Rabelais »

Huitres à la Ciboulette

Cassolette d'Ecrevisses aux Morilles

Feuilleté de Bécasses

Suprême de Saumon Frais
aux Poireaux

Aiguillettes de Caneton en Salade

Rognon de Veau à l'Oseille

Loup et Langouste Sauce Oursin

Filet de Pigeon Bohémienne

If you have a gargantuan appetite, it follows that the best way to eat *chez* Pic is to have the Menu 'Rabelais', made up of eight small dishes which give a fair idea of every aspect of Jacques Pic's cuisine. The oysters reveal the extra touch he adds to simplicity, the *écrevisses* his love of mushrooms, the *feuilleté* his skill with game, the salmon his idea of modern cooking, the duck his lightness, the kidneys his sense of combining tastes, the *loup* his ingenuity and the pigeon his impeccable use of produce. After all that, there are Pic's sorbets, ices and *gâteaux*. And then you understand what is meant by the generosity of chefs. In fact, many of the great chefs, particularly Bocuse and the Troisgros, will provide a selection of small dishes for guests who want to sample a cross-section of the menu.

Menu d'Hiver

Salade des pêcheurs au Xérès

Chausson aux truffes

Filet de loup au caviar

Poularde de Bresse en vessie 'André Pic'

Soufflé glacé d'orange

Seafood salad

Truffles in pastry

Sea bass with caviar

Chicken cooked in a pig's bladder

Cold orange soufflé

The *chausson aux truffes* is similar to Guérard's *feuilleté de truffes.* The *soufflé glacé,* one of Pic's most delicious creations, is missing from our recipes because it is the one secret which he would never impart.

Salade des pêcheurs au Xérès

Make a vegetable julienne (carrots, leeks, celery and onion). Sauté lightly in butter before marinating in a sherry vinegar dressing for about an hour.

Poach two live lobsters and extract the meat whole from the tail. Poach large red shrimp and whole scallops in a good fish *fumet* for a few minutes.

Decoratively arrange the tepid, shelled fish on a bed of lamb's lettuce with the vegetable julienne. Sprinkle with the Xérès vinegar dressing and serve.
Note: Shellfish for cooking should be bought alive. They deteriorate very quickly and, if cooked when dead, can cause food-poisoning.

Filet de loup au caviar

Lightly poach fillets of sea bass in a fish *fumet*. Set the fillets on a warm serving plate.

Reduce the fish *fumet*. Add *crème fraîche* and reduce until it is a thick consistency. Remove from the heat and whisk in small pieces of butter. At the last minute, add a little lemon juice.

Top the fish with a thick layer of caviar, pour sauce round the fish on the serving plate and serve.

Poularde de Bresse en vessie 'Andre Pic'

Slice truffles and slide them under the skin of a large chicken. Stuff the chicken with seasoned *foie gras.*

Scrape a pig's bladder and clean it with salt and vinegar. Turn the bladder inside out and put the chicken inside. Tie the end with string. Prick the bladder in several places and put it in a pot of boiling chicken *consommé.*

Simmer for two and a half hours, then put on a warm serving plate. The bladder is removed and the chicken is then ready to eat.

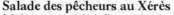

Menu d'Été

Salade bohemienne

Escalope de turbot Arlequin

Fricassée d'agneau au basilic

Duckling salad

Turbot and salmon with foie gras

Lamb with kidneys and brains

Soufflé of fruit

Salade bohemienne

Carve a cold roast duckling into *aiguillettes.* Lay these slices on a bed of lamb's lettuce and garnish with poached asparagus tips and finely sliced truffle. Serve with a light vinaigrette; not too vinegary and with only a hint of garlic.
Note: Roast the duckling so that it is slightly pink. Leave it to cool for an hour before carving so that the meat settles and the duck does not lose its juices.

Escalope de turbot Arlequin

Cut the white of leeks into matchstick strips and stew them gently in butter in a heavy covered pan.

In another pan, cook turbot and salmon fillets together in butter with herbs. Sit the turbot on a warm serving plate, cover with the *chiffonade* of leeks, then a layer of fresh *foie gras* and cover with the salmon fillets. Keep in a warm place for a minute to allow the *foie gras* to heat. Coat with a *sauce américaine* to which a touch of saffron has been added, and serve.

Fricassée d'agneau au basilic

Sauté noisettes of lamb in a little clarified butter. After a few minutes, add cleaned halves of lamb kidney and blanched brains. Continue to sauté until the lamb is tender.

Serve the *fricassée* with a light brown sauce made from veal stock to which a touch of basil has been added.

BLACK DIAMOND OF CUISINE

The truffle has always exerted a mysterious, almost hypnotic force on epicures. The Romans imported it from Greece and parts of North Africa. Plutarch believed that truffles were produced by lightning. 'Since during thunderstorms flames come from moist vapours and deafening noises from soft clouds, there need be no surprise that when lightning strikes the ground, truffles, which do not resemble plants, should spring into existence.'

Truffles belong to the subterranean fungoid family of *Tuberaceae*. Of the many varieties, the most famous is the Perigord or black warted truffle *(Tuber melanosporum)*, the 'black diamond of cuisine.' When ripe, the flesh is, in fact, a very dark brown, grained with white.

Perigord truffles grow under oak trees, beeches and hazels—and never beyond the spread of the branches.

They are found at depths of up to a foot, which is why dogs and pigs are used to sniff out their whereabouts. Young sows have the keenest nose for truffles, but dogs are preferred because they are less inclined to eat the fruits of their labours. Once a truffle is located, the farmer carefully exposes it with a hoe and takes it away if it is ripe and of a suitable size. Otherwise it is reburied for later harvesting. A prematurely exposed truffle must not be touched by hand or it will rot. In one day a *trufficulteur* may gather nine kilos of truffles, which he will sell for around 5400 francs.

During the *cavage*—the truffle-digging season, which lasts from mid-December until February—there is a daily market in many towns and villages of the Perigord. Buyers from all over France rely on personal contacts with the farmers, who are reluctant to sell to anyone they do not know. It is a time-honoured trade, carried on with mysterious rituals and careful weighings on old-fashioned scales.

It is because they cannot be cultivated that truffles are so expensive. At best, their diffusion can be encouraged by planting acorns collected under oak trees where truffles have been found. The acorns may carry microscopic truffle spores, increasing the chance that truffles may grow around the seedlings which spring from the acorns.

On the whole, truffles grow where they choose, not where man chooses—although the French National Institute for Agronomic Research has recently announced that, after twenty years' work, they have produced truffles associated with specially treated trees.

When the first truffles of the season arrive in a grand restaurant there is great excitement. Monsieur Laroche, the late *patron* of La Reserve at Beaulieu, would

descend to the kitchen, where the chefs had laid out the new truffles on a crisp, white cloth, with a clean pan and a bottle of champagne. Removing his coat, *le patron* poured champagne into the pan and cooked the truffles gently. When they were done, he put his coat on again and went to the restaurant, to eat the truffles with hot, buttered toast.

Perhaps the main role of the truffle is its effect on other ingredients; its scent permeates anything with which it comes into contact, even penetrating the shell of an egg. Truffles under the skin of a bird not only perfume the bird, but mysteriously strengthen the bird's flavour. Pre-war chefs, as Jacques Pic says, 'went mad' with truffles. Even today, a fine restaurant may use a kilo—sixteen to eighteen—truffles a day, at a cost of 200,000 francs a year.

The last word on truffles rests with Monselet who, as he lay dying, said, 'I would like to be buried *aux truffes.*'

Wet springs, hot summers and frosty winters—the time of the harvest—suit the Perigord truffle. The scent improves as the season goes on.

THUILIER'S GRAND DELIGHTS

Raymond Thuilier's is a grand menu. There is something of Provence about it, with the dishes of *rouget*, *loup de mer*, and *grives*, and perhaps a slight emphasis on the olive oil of the region, but otherwise it is a menu which would serve perfectly well elsewhere. Even if it is grand, there is something pleasingly straightforward about the dishes. Out of the sixteen first courses, there are only two which are elaborate—the *mousseline de rouget*, which is mullet cooked in the oven with wine and vermouth and then enlivened with anchovy, cream and fish stock and served cold as mousse with a tarragon sauce, and the *feuilleté de ris de veau*, which is somewhat like a *vol-au-vent*. The other dishes are plainly what they say, although they do not lack ingenuity. For instance when scrambling the eggs for the *oeufs brouillés aux truffes*, he slips in a spoonful of *hollandaise*.

Many of Thuilier's effects in his other dishes are achieved by stuffings, the brill with a slice of smoked salmon, *loup à la mousseline de poissons*, *gigot d'agneau en croûte*, *pigeon farci aux pointes d'asperges*. At the same time he can achieve wonders of simplicity, as with his *rouget à la nage au basilic*, or even his curious *caneton aux citrons verts*, which is duck (strangled to keep in the blood) covered with a light creamy sauce of limes and white wine, which is amazingly bitter. He is also extremely fond of *soufflés*, making a lobster one as first course and two among the desserts; even his *crêpes* are *soufflés*.

There is nothing in this menu which could remotely be thought of as *nouvelle cuisine*, but it belongs, nevertheless, very much in the tradition of cooking established by Fernand Point, Thuilier's friend and adviser.

---

bisque d'écrevisses 40

consommé "Baumanière" 30

salade "Baumanière" 25

asperges de Provence sauce mousseline 65

œufs Bénédictine 35

œufs brouillés aux truffes 45

foie gras en surprise 60

foie gras frais truffé 60

saumon fumé 60

salade de queues d'écrevisses 50

mousse de grives 40

terrine aux quatre poissons 40

terrine de canard à l'orange 35

mousseline de rouget et sa sauce 45

feuilleté de ris de veau 55

soufflé de homard 45

rouget à la nage au basilic 50

loup à la mousseline de poissons 60

sole aux nouilles fraîches 50

barbue au saumon fumé 60

ragoût de crustacés aux petits légumes 90

saumon au cresson 65

gigot d'agneau en croûte 120
(pour 2 personnes)

côtelettes d'agneau farcies "Baumanière" 55

caneton à l'orange 50

caneton aux citrons verts 50

poularde de Bresse aux écrevisses 55

ris de veau au foie de canard 65

côte de bœuf à la moelle 120
(pour 2 personnes)

carré d'agneau sur le grill 120
(pour 2 personnes)

rognons de veau à la moutarde 50

pigeon farci aux pointes d'asperges 65

gratin d'aubergines 18

gratin dauphinois 18

mousse d'artichants 18

Taxes comprises - Service 15 % en sus

ALOUETTE, MAUVIETTE

'Small game birds start with the thrush and include in a descending scale all lesser birds.' And Brillat-Savarin continues with his opinion that among the smaller birds, the first in order of excellence is beyond all question the beccafico or fig-pecker. . . Nature has endowed it with a unique and wholly exquisite bitterness, quite irresistible and ravishing to the organ of taste.'

Small birds have lent themselves all too easily to the capricious predations of chefs and gourmets and there is consequently as much fantasy as fact attached to them. We hear of Aesop spending a small fortune on a pie made only from birds which could imitate the human voice; that in Toulouse they knew how to fatten ortolans better than anywhere else. To kill them they asphyxiated them by plunging their heads into very strong vinegar—a way of death thought to improve their flesh. The advantage of the ortolan is that, unlike other wild birds, it does not sulk in captivity and very quickly gets fat on oats and millet.

The lark too has a delicate tasting flesh, from which lark pie is often made. When talking of the lark as a song bird, the French call it *alouette*. When it is eaten, it is properly called *mauviette*.

The thrush, the brown song bird welcomed in any garden, is turned by culinary hands into a *pâté* of rough and gamey flavour. The thrushes of Provence are favoured because they eat juniper and myrtle berries. On Thuilier's menu they appear in a *mousse de grives*.

Les-Baux-de-Provence is in the picturesque mountain landscape of the Alpille. It is a steep drive up a small road off the N99, just outside of St-Rémy-de-Provence. The Roman city of Nîmes is forty-four kilometres west of Les Baux; Arles is nineteen kilometres to the southwest.

---

et voici nos desserts...

toutes les pâtisseries

soufflé chaud au grand marnier

soufflé froid aux fraises avec la liqueur de cassis

soufflé chaud aux pruneaux

soufflé glacé au chocolat

crêpes soufflées "Baumanière"

avec les friandises de "Baumanière"

25 f

PLANNING THE MENU

'*Un menu! . . . C'est le plus adorable poême*,' said Saulnier. For it to be a poem, the menu must be planned with care and this, as Escoffier said, 'is among the most difficult aspects of our art.' The ingenuity of Thuilier's menu is that although it is not long, one could compose from it ten perfectly balanced meals without repeating a dish. To some extent a menu plans itself naturally, according to the availability of produce. 'One must fight with the weapons one has,' as Louis Outhier puts it. 'After that it is a question of doing what one likes.'

There are no set rules, but a menu must have an equilibrium, avoiding repetitions and similarity in sauces. Outhier maintains that when cooking for strangers, the menu must be fairly standard. Indeed the restaurant critics, Gault and Millau, censure Outhier for his caution in this respect, but even the adventurous Roger Vergé includes some reassuring dishes for foreign tourists. To match his clients to the menu, Alain Chapel likes to meet them before they eat.

There must be dishes for people who like copious meals and dishes for those who do not like too full a plate. A restaurateur must make allowances for people's budgets. Some dine out twice a year and do not mind spending a fortune; others prefer to spend less more often. There must be plain dishes and elaborately cooked ones. The menu must change but clients expect old favourites on it.

Perhaps the only rule which can be firmly stated is that there should be no dish on the menu in which the chef is not absolutely confident. This is why chefs often spend months (in Fernand Point's case, years) experimenting with a new dish before including it in their menu.

Scrambled eggs in brioche

Sea bass with a fish mousse

Chicken with crayfish

Leg of lamb in pastry

Artichoke mousse

Strawberry cake

Oeuf en surprise

Slice the tops off several *brioches* (allowing one per person). Scoop out and discard the insides and keep both parts warm.

Brush and clean fresh truffles, chop them into small pieces and braise in butter.

Scramble eggs in a *bain-marie* (about three per person per *brioche*) in plenty of butter. The eggs should be worked with a spatula or whisk, so that they become creamy and do not coagulate. As the cream begins to form, add a little salt and pepper, some tiny pieces of butter and a *soupçon* of nutmeg.

Just before serving, remove from the heat, add the truffles and when the egg has taken the form of a well-blended mousse, pour into the warm *brioche* case. Put back the tops, with a slice of truffle on each.
Note: Eggs will continue to cook when removed from the heat. To prevent further cooking, many cooks add a splash of cream.

Loup à la mousseline de poisson

Cut along the back of a sea bass and lift out its backbone without detaching the head or tail of the fish. Open the fish, season the inside with salt and pepper and lay it on its stomach in an ovenproof dish with shallots, white wine, vermouth, fish *fumet* and a few mussels.

Make a *mousseline* by chopping the flesh of pike or trout finely before passing it through a sieve. Slowly incorporate *crème fraîche* and whole eggs over a bowl of ice. Season to taste.

Fill the fish with the *mousseline*, put the dish in a hot oven and poach for about twenty-five minutes under baking foil.

Remove the fish from the pan and keep it hot. Add some *crème fraîche* to the cooking juices and reduce slightly. Whisk in small pieces of butter to make a light sauce. Check the seasoning.

Lay the bass on a serving dish and garnish with poached crayfish, slivers of fresh truffles and small crescents of puff pastry. Cover the fish in the cream sauce and serve hot.

Poularde aux écrevisses

On a low heat, poach a plump Bresse pullet for about an hour in a *bouillon* of white wine, water, onions, cloves, carrots, tarragon and a *bouquet garni*.

While this is cooking, drop live prepared crayfish into very hot butter. Let the crayfish redden, then flame with armagnac. Add plenty of *crème fraîche* and reduce. Remove the crayfish, peel the tails and put to one side. Pound the shells and put them back into the sauce; cook until the sauce is a smooth, rich cream.

Cut the chicken into four pieces and arrange on a plate with a few poached mushrooms, thin strips of truffle and the crayfish tails. Generously cover the chicken pieces with the sieved sauce and serve hot.

Gigot d'agneau en croûte

Bone a leg of lamb.

Sauté a couple of diced lamb kidneys in butter. Deglaze the pan with madeira and add thickly sliced mushrooms, thyme, rosemary and tarragon. Press this mixture into the space left by the bone. Reconstruct the joint by tying thin string around it.

Season and rub the lamb with softened butter and put in a very hot oven. After fifteen minutes remove the lamb from the oven and let it stand for a while.

Entirely cover the lamb with finely rolled puff pastry, brush with egg-yolk and return to the oven for fifteen minutes.

Serve with a *gratin Dauphinois*.
Note: For the *gratin Dauphinois*, Bise's recipe for *gratin Savoyard* may be used.

Mousseline d'artichauts

Poach artichoke hearts in a *bouillon* made from salted water, a little lemon juice and a tablespoon of flour which should be well mixed with the liquid. When well cooked, remove from the heat, drain and sieve. Discard the *bouillon*.

Put the sieved artichoke hearts back in the warm pan on the edge of the heat and mix in vigorously with a wooden spoon some *crème fraîche*, a couple of nuggets of butter, a glass of madeira and truffle juice. Season with freshly milled salt and pepper. Reduce the liquid until it has the consistency of a thick sauce.

This is the perfect accompaniment to roasted meats like beef, lamb or chicken.
Note: The artichoke heart is the fleshiest part of the artichoke which remains once the stalk, leaves and choke have been removed.

Le fraisier

Beat three eggs and ninety grams of sugar together in a *bain-marie* until the mixture doubles its volume. Remove the bowl from the *bain-marie* and continue whisking until cool. Slowly fold in ninety grams of flour.

Pour the mixture in a *génoise* mould and bake in a medium oven for half an hour. Turn the cake out onto a cloth or a grid.

Make a butter cream from a sugar syrup poured onto stiffly beaten egg-whites. Add softened butter and mix well.

When the *génoise* sponge is cool, divide into two rounds. Sprinkle each with kirsch and spread half the butter cream onto one round. Add a layer of strawberries, being sure to arrange them neatly round the edge, and cover these with the rest of the butter cream. Place the second cake round on top of the covered one. Cut the crust off the sides of the cake to make an octagonal shape showing the half-strawberries.

Sprinkle the top of the cake with icing sugar and roasted, flaked almonds.
Note: The sugar syrup is ready to mix with the egg-whites when a drop of syrup solidifies into a ball in a bowl of water.

TRUE BLADES

A chef's knives are like a musician's violin—very personal to him—and are used with the same dexterity. The weight, balance and feel are therefore critical. The chosen metal is usually carbon steel, which takes and keeps a better edge than stainless steel. Although some chefs use unorthodox knives (like Bocuse's jack-knife) the group shown here is a professional set, the contents of a fitted attaché case.

Vide-pommes
apple-corer

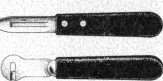

Moule à pommes
potato scoop

Éplucheur
potato-peeler

Canneleur
lemon-dresser

Couteau d'office
cook's knife

Couteau filet de poisson
fish-filleting knife

Couteau de cuisine
chopping knife

Forchette chef
carving fork

Couteau spatule
palette knife

Grande couteau de cuisine
carving knife

Couperet de cuisine
meat cleaver

Couteau d'office
all-purpose knife

Couteau de saigner
boning knife

Couteau de chevalin
meat knife

Couteau du tranchelard
slicing knife

Fusil
sharpening steel

CLOSER TO THE LAND AT TROISGROS

The Troisgros brothers have managed to keep an earthy simplicity in their menu, at the same time elevating it to the highest level of *haute cuisine*. Their guiding principles are still those laid down by their father. No all-purpose bases for sauces and no starch for the liaisons. No complicated presentations, but everything served on a large plate, and certainly nothing cooked or finished in the dining-room. Everything must have a purpose; there must be no irrelevant, traditional garnishings, such as boiled potatoes, tomatoes, watercress or *croûtons*.

In essence it is family cooking which the Troisgros most admire. The *escalope de saumon à l'oseille*, their most famous dish, which was served at President Giscard d'Estaing's *Légion d'Honneur* lunch, was based on an improvisation by Pierre Troisgros' mother-in-law when she had some left-over sorrel after making sorrel soup. The *mosaïque de légumes truffée*, their next most famous dish, is simply carrots, artichokes, peas, beans, truffles and vine leaves bound in a mosaic by a stuffing of ham, white of egg and lemon.

As with all the chefs who trained with Fernand Point, the emphasis is on quality of produce, but the Troisgros (together with Alain Chapel) are perhaps the closest to the land. Many of their childhood friends are farmers or market gardeners. They send out schoolchildren to hunt for snails. Much of the menu is inspired by peasant cooking, for instance the *pigeonneau à la gousse d'ail en chemise*—pigeon roasted with whole garlic cloves (which are marvellous when well cooked). To this simple recipe they add a sauce with *foie gras* and brandy, but that is merely refinement.

In the opposite manner, the Troisgros also reduce grandeur to an unexpected matter-of-factness, as with the *huîtres chaudes 'Julia'*—hot oysters with finely shredded vegetables, a surprising but successful combination. At the same time, their *salade riche* of *foie gras*, lobsters and truffles is pure grandeur. All in all, the Troisgros menu achieves a perfect blend of tradition and modernity, down-to-earth but constantly surprising.

Customers apparently resist the temptation to fill in the missing features of the Troisgros brothers' faces on their menu cover. Roanne station in the background symbolizes their lack of pretension. The original painting for the menu cover hangs in the bar among their contemporary art collection

A KEY TO THE APPETITE

In France, especially, the pre-dinner or pre-luncheon aperitif is an important ritual because many people are firmly convinced that one, or more, is necessary as a kind of skeleton key to unlock the appetite. Probably, though, the aperitif's real function is social rather than alimentary, enhancing a pleasant prelude during which diners can settle into the restaurant's ambience. Equally to the point, the menu may be studied and orders taken over a leisurely aperitif.

In bygone days the term 'aperitif' referred to alcoholic infusions or decoctions of 'stimulating bitters', such as wormwood, peel of bitter oranges, gentian roots or germander. Nowadays the word is applied to any alcoholic drink taken before a meal—that is, wines, fortified wines or spirits.

Though whisky, gin and vodka are popular aperitifs elsewhere, the three-star restaurants are inclined to discourage spirits before a meal because they tend to dull the palate for the food and wine to follow. The house aperitif at a three-star establishment is most likely to be a dry, fruity wine, chilled and often mixed with a fruit syrup, such as *fraise*, *framboise*, *grenadine* or *cassis*. (White wine and *cassis* is known as Kir, after Canon Felix Kir, a Mayor of Dijon who is said to

have added blackcurrant syrup to a wine he didn't care for.) *Champagne framboise*, mixed at the table or at the bar, is especially popular. Pic serves it from an elegant glass jug, adding a splash of Dubonnet to cut the sweetness of the *framboise*.

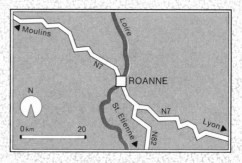

The Lyonnais textile town of Roanne is on the Loire, a rich area for produce. It is eighty kilometres north west of Lyon, along the infamous N7. To the south-east is Clermont-Ferrand.

On literature from the restaurant, the T for Troisgros has as its background a foetus, the symbol of life

> **'One must have a solid technical base, then reflect—for thinking is everything.'**

1978

Fritot de Poulet au Vinaigre de Vin 30
Aiguillettes de Canard aux Charbonniers 50
Pigeonneau à la Gousse d'Ail en Chemise 48
Pilons de Canette en Civet 38
Emincé de Rognons de Veau Côte d'Or 44
Trois Côtes d'Agneau Poêlées aux Feuilles de Thym 48
Côte de Veau à la Graine de Moutarde 40
Les Gibiers

Château au Fleurie à la Moelle 42
Côtes de Bœuf Saint-Christophe (2 personnes) 90
Pièce de Bœuf au Poivre Blanc 42
Filet Mignon aux Câpres Capucine 37
Entrecôte Poêlée aux Echalotes 40

Gratin Forézien 18
Légumes de Saison 26
Salade Verte à l'Huile de Noix et de Colza 18
Tous nos Fromages 18

Le Grand Dessert et les Pâtisseries 32
Crêpes Flambées à l'Orange (2 personnes) 44
Coffret de Poires au Caramel 26

Champagne Brut Blanc de Blancs Sélection Troisgros 60   Service 15 % en sus.

A new kitchen is a rarity. Because of the need for continuity, most kitchens are improved piecemeal—new ovens one year, cold stores another, air-conditioning another. The Troisgros brothers were lucky enough to have space to create an entirely new kitchen on a new site. While the work was being done, they continued in the old one. As soon as the new kitchen was finished, in February 1978, they converted the old kitchen to enlarge the dining-room.

The planning had taken three years. The Troisgros employed Hubert Cormier, an architect they have known and worked with for fifteen years. 'We know each other well enough to understand when we really mean no.' Chefs, being traditionalists, see nothing wrong with old ways. Architects have little experience of cooking, but understand how to design a working environment. A good combination can produce wonders.

Chefs believe that all equipment stands on legs. Cormier has put the ovens on tiled pedestals, which makes for cleanliness. Chefs are accustomed to hot kitchens, which they then make draughty by opening windows—which also wastes heat. Cormier has devised an ingenious and economical solution. Over the stoves he has fitted two glass screens coming down two feet from the ceiling. As the heat rises it is caught and then used to run the air-conditioning system for the restaurant. The air in the kitchen is changed every five minutes; in the dining-room four times an hour.

Chefs know that if they leave a sauce for fifteen seconds it can be ruined. So that a chef may constantly watch his pots, the Troisgros now have chilled drawers at each work point, with enough supplies for one service. Sinks run the whole length of the kitchen under the window, so that no-one is more than three paces from running water.

After long consideration, both architect and chefs were agreed on conversion to electricity. By nature chefs like a flame, but this means gas, which increases the heat of kitchens and is more dangerous than electricity. The Troisgros and Cormier visited Jacques Pic and saw his new electric ovens and hotplates. This convinced them that while gas can be regulated quickly, electricity allows for more accurate adjustment of heat. So the Troisgros installed electric hotplates, thermostatically controlled and close in effect to the graded coal ranges on which they trained.

In most kitchens the ceiling has to be painted once a year. The Troisgros brothers now have a purplish glass ceiling which can be wiped down as often as necessary. There are three separate boilers, so that there can never be a complete failure of the hot water and heating systems.

'It has been an extended exchange of ideas, a marriage of our two crafts,' says Cormier. The result is a kitchen which is elegant to look at and supremely functional.

1. Chefs' changing room.

2. Cold storage for meat and poultry.

3. Chilled drawers for fish.

4. Cold storage for vegetables.

5. Work-top for cutting and preparing ingredients.

6. The *garde-manger* area is raised (there is a cold store underneath) and Pierre Troisgros finds the step here the best vantage point for checking all the kitchen's activities.

7. The larder area of the kitchen is the province of the *chefs garde-manger*, who prepare all the produce. The *brigade* lunch at a table in this area.

8. Work-top for cutting and preparing ingredients, with sinks for washing vegetables.

9. Stairs and a service elevator for bringing produce from the delivery area.

10. The *saucier* works here, with his built-in stockpots simmering against the wall.

11. The *poissonnier*'s area, with chilled drawers and work-tops, where the fish is prepared for each service.

12. The salamander is a very hot grill used to finish off a dish that needs browning or glazing.

13. The 'piano'—the main cooking range—has four groups of three graded hotplates with ovens underneath.

14. Glasses are washed here.

15. The Troisgros brothers' dining table. Orders are posted on the glass screen which separates this area from the kitchen.

16. A plate warmer and more cold drawers are beneath the work-top from which all dishes leave for the dining-room.

17. The broken lines mark the extent of the heat trap to the kitchen's main extractor-fan system.

18. The kitchen's electric blender.

19. The waiters' routes to and from the dining-rooms. The open line is the path for those bringing back dirty dishes.

20. *Plongeurs* work here, washing the dishes, cutlery, pots and pans.

21. Cash desk.

22. The *pâtissier*'s area, with sinks, hotplate, cold drawers and an oven.

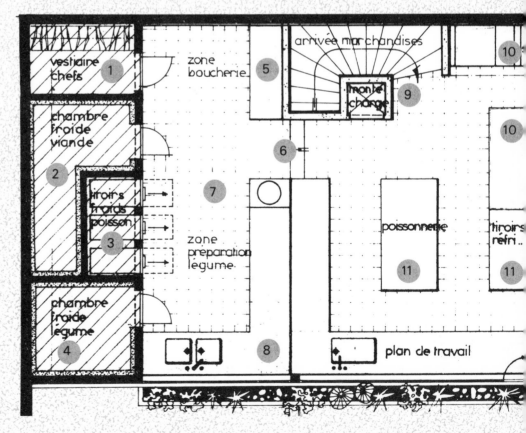

Dishes begin their progress to the dining-room from the *garde-manger* area in the foreground. Jean Troisgros is in the centre of his kitchen, at the *saucier*'s post.

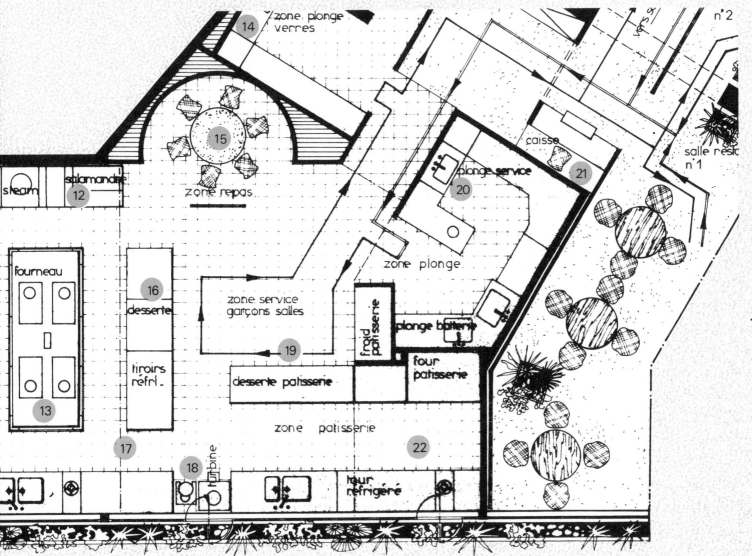

Pâté of vegetables

Warm salad of foie gras and spinach

Scallops in pastry

Salmon in a sorrel sauce

Duck fillets with mushrooms

Rib of beef in a red wine sauce

Grapefruit zests

Terrine de légumes

In separate saucepans of boiling, salted water, cook French beans and peas for about three minutes.

Put a single layer of artichoke hearts (the bases) at the bottom of a saucepan with some butter, cover and cook gently. After seven or eight minutes, cover the artichokes with salted water, cover the pan with baking foil and then put the lid on the pan. Simmer gently for twenty minutes. Let the artichokes cool and scrape them.

Cook carrots in salted water until they are *al dente*.

Chill and dice lean ham and put in a mixer with one egg-white. Season with salt and pepper and beat at high speed, adding lemon juice and ground-nut oil, little by little, until the mixture is a thick paste.

Line a rectangular mould with vine leaves or thinly sliced peeled lemon. Put a layer of the ham stuffing on the bottom, then a layer of carrots, a layer of stuffing, then successive layers of tightly packed vegetables, each separated by a layer of the stuffing.

Cover the terrine with a piece of buttered paper and cook in a *bain-marie* for thirty minutes at a low temperature in the oven. Let the terrine cool and keep it in the refrigerator for at least eight hours.

Cut the terrine into slices and serve with a *sauce froide à la tomate pour Jean Yanne*. To make this sieve the pulp of tomatoes, which have had the pips and the water removed, over a salad bowl, pressing against the tomato skin with the back of a wooden spoon. Refrigerate the *purée*. Just before serving add a spoonful of tomato concentrate and vinegar. When this is well mixed, pour in olive oil, drop by drop, beating constantly to prevent coagulation. Season the sauce with salt, pepper and roughly chopped parsley and tarragon.
Note: When preparing the stuffing, the Troisgros recommend putting the mixing bowl in the refrigerator and chilling the diced ham for at least thirty minutes.

Cut slices of the terrine half an inch thick. They will have the appearance of a mosaic.

Salade nouvelle

Plunge duck *foie gras* in a saucepan of boiling, salted water. When the water comes back to the boil, cook for one minute before removing the pan from the heat. Leave the *foie gras* to cool overnight.

Remove and discard the stalks and central veins from young, tender spinach leaves; wash the leaves in cold water and dry them between two towels.

Mix the yolks of two hard-boiled eggs with mustard, lemon juice, salt and pepper When well mixed, add a wineglass of olive oil, little by little.

Toss the spinach in this dressing and arrange on individual plates.

Take a large frying-pan and heat some ground-nut oil. When it is smoking, put the slices of *foie gras* into the pan and cook for one minute on each side. Remove them from the pan and arrange them in a star shape on the dressed spinach.

Drain the fat from the pan and deglaze what is left with wine vinegar. Moisten each slice of *foie gras* with the back of a spoon dipped in the juices from the frying-pan. Serve immediately as a tepid salad on warmed plates.
Note: So that the final heating of the *foie gras* can be done quickly, the Troisgros suggest using two frying-pans.

Coquilles St Jacques Boulez

Put several scallops in each scallop shell and season with salt and pepper. Lightly moisten with a dribble of white wine.

Take rolled puff pastry and fold over each scallop shell like a lid. Brush with egg-yolk.

Cook the scallops for about twelve minutes in a hot oven.

Meanwhile, make some Nantais butter by mixing butter with some chopped shallot and a little wine vinegar.

When the scallops are cooked, cut a hole in each pastry lid and pour in the Nantais butter; seal the hole.

Serve the scallops on a bed of blanched seaweed.
Note: This dish takes its name from Pierre Boulez, the conductor, who celebrated one of his birthdays at the restaurant.

Escalope de saumon à l'oseille

Lift two fillets off the central bone of a salmon. Split these fillets in two horizontally. Put them between two sheets of oiled paper and with a cutlet bat flatten them carefully to make them of even width.

Tail and wash sorrel, tearing the large leaves into two or three pieces.

Add white wine and a little vermouth and some chopped shallots to a fish *fumet* and reduce until it is a thick liquid. Strain, add *crème fraîche double* and reduce.

Throw into the sauce the well-drained sorrel leaves. Half a minute later, remove from the heat and add small pieces of butter while shaking the pan. Complete the seasoning by adding a twist of lemon, salt and pepper.

Warm a large, non-stick pan or oil and warm a heavy sauté pan. Put in the salmon escalopes, seasoned on the least presentable side, to sauté for no more than half a minute on each side.

Spoon the sauce onto warm plates. Take off the excess fat from the escalopes with a napkin and place them, unseasoned side up, in the sauce.

Sprinkle the escalopes with lightly ground sea-salt, and serve immediately.
Note: Make the sorrel sauce in a china or enamelled pan. A metal pan reacts with the acidity in the sorrel to make the sauce grey and bitter.

Aiguillettes de col-vert aux mousserons des prés

Remove the duck livers and put them through a sieve with some *foie gras;* keep to one side in a cool place.

Roast whole seasoned ducks in a hot oven with ground-nut oil for about twenty minutes. Remove the ducks from the oven and let them stand for an hour. Carve off the wing ends, breasts, the legs and the two *filets mignons* ('oysters') and put to one side.

For the sauce break up the necks, legs

and the carcass with a cleaver and put them into a saucepan. Heat, and when they are cooked golden, pour off the fat and deglaze with brandy. Add red wine and some *demi-glace*, chopped shallots and a *bouquet garni*. Add water to completely cover the bones. Simmer for an hour.

Pass the stock through a sieve. Rinse out the saucepan and return the stock to reduce to an essence. Then pour in *crème fraîche double*; as the sauce comes to the boil, add the pounded duck livers. Taste and adjust the seasoning if necessary.

Cut each skinned duck breast into five *aiguillettes*.

Cook mushrooms in a frying-pan with butter until they are lightly browned; at the last moment, add chopped shallot and parsley.

Put the mushrooms in the middle of a warm serving plate and arrange the *aiguillettes* and *filets mignons* around them.

Put the wing ends on the top of the mushrooms, reheat the dish in the oven for a few moments, then pour sauce all round it. Serve the rest of the sauce hot in sauceboats.

Côte de boeuf au Fleurie

Put a seasoned rib of beef in a tin-lined copper sauté pan in which there is some *beurre noisette*. Let the rib cook for fifteen minutes on each side, basting frequently.

Remove the rib and put it on a plate that will collect the juices. Let it stand for at least twenty minutes in a warm place. Pour the cooking juices from the sauté pan into a frying-pan. Keep both pans for later.

Put sliced bone marrow in a small saucepan and cover with cold salted water. Slowly bring to the boil and when boiling remove from the heat.

Deglaze the sauté pan with red wine (Fleurie) and *glace de viande*. Reduce the liquid by half. Remove the pan from the heat and whisk in small pieces of butter. When the liaison is complete, correct the seasoning and strain.

Reheat the beef in the frying-pan with the original fat before placing the rib on a warm serving plate.

Pour the juices that have run off the meat while cooling into the *sauce au Fleurie*.

Cover the beef with the sauce and place the drained, dried bone marrow on top.

Carve the meat in front of your guests.
Note: The Troisgros recommend serving this dish with *gratin de pommes de terre à la Forezienne*, which is substantially the same as a *gratin Dauphinois* or a *gratin Savoyard* (see Bise's recipe) without the cheese.

The marrow bone should be soaked in cold water for twelve hours before preparation to whiten the marrow.

Pamélas

Cut the base and top off half-a-dozen large grapefruits. Stand them upright and, turning them with a spiral motion, cut each one diagonally into four quarters so that a third of the flesh is left on the skin.

Cut each quarter into four strips of equal length. This should give you ninety-six sticks. Cover these zests with cold water and bring them slowly to the boil. Boil gently for five minutes and strain. Perform this operation four times. Once again, return the pan to the heat, this time without water but with 600 grams of caster or finely granulated sugar. Cook for about an hour over a very low flame, stirring often with a wooden spoon. Spread the zests on a grill so that excess syrup runs away.

When they are cold, roll them one by one in sugar.
Note: All the chefs serve wonderful sweet delicacies with coffee; this is one of the easier to make.

The ever-economical Troisgros suggest that you keep the flesh, left sugared overnight in the refrigerator, to brighten up the breakfast table.

OILS IN THE KITCHEN

As the crown of olives was the highest distinction given to a citizen of Ancient Greece, so olive oil, with its crowning taste, is put only with dishes with the character to carry it.

In the Troisgros kitchen, the *huile d'olive* comes from Provence, where a tree will yield about fifty kilos of olives. The unripened fruit is washed and cleaned and left to mature, thereby losing its bitterness, before being pressed (as in the oilerie, right).

The first (cold) pressing produces 'virgin' oil (so-called because the Greeks allowed only virgin men and women to take part in the culture of the tree and a vow of chastity was demanded from those who gathered the harvest); it has a rich texture and colour and a distinctive taste. The second pressing is made from heated olives, has a less fruity taste and is cheaper.

In cuisine the choice of oils is crucial: the right oil enhances the taste and character of other ingredients; the wrong one will impair their taste, colour and texture. The Troisgros use *huile de noix* (walnut oil) in their *salade de faisanes* and *salade riche*—and in an orange zest sauce, *sauce costelloise*. This is a strong-flavoured oil, cold-pressed and very expensive.

For cooking, *huile d'arachide* (ground-

nut) gives the tasteless, odourless characteristics the Troisgros require, particularly when they are preparing lightly-flavoured ingredients. It is used in sautéing, often as an addition to butter. The oil serves to raise the temperature at which butter burns and discolours other ingredients.

Other refined oils include *huile de colza* (rapeseed), which is often mixed with soya oil, and used to make commercial mayonnaise and salad cream. Cottonseed, mustard, palm, coconut, safflower and sunflower all produce oils—for other cuisines at other levels.

VERGE: WILD AND INFINITE SKILL

Roger Vergé's menu, probably the most expensive of all, has a certain exuberance and wildness of style, though as a rule he controls it with infinite skill. The limitations of *haute cuisine* mean little to Vergé—no other three-star chef would make buckwheat *blinis* to go with Beluga caviar, for instance.

Far more than his neighbour, Louis Outhier, he has accepted the challenge of his region and bases several dishes on Provençal recipes. The *gâteau de lapin dans sa gelée au Chablis* is authentically rural, down to the odd bone which may stick in your throat. The catch of the Mediterranean fishermen (with whom Vergé likes to mix) appears in his *terrine de rascasse* and *biscuit de loup*. Believing in strong tastes, he uses all the herbs of the mountains with a free hand.

Vergé reveals his original touch in his unexpected juxtapositions: pickled *griotte* cherries with the *dodine de caneton* (duckling) *au foie gras;* a sauce of sweet wine with his *fricassée de homard;* grapes in the pepper sauce served with the *filet de Charolais* (for this dish, he keeps the name *à la Mathurini* —from the French equivalent of Popeye— because he used to serve it with spinach).

Vergé's travels in Africa and the Caribbean have given him an enviable freedom to experiment and improvise with unusual ingredients and thereby to discover new and original combinations.

His desserts, however, are strictly French (except for the lime sorbet); they reveal more of his skill, as opposed to his flights of fancy, than do his main dishes.

SUPREME FRESHNESS

A good salad is essentially a showcase for the freshest of produce; no wonder the chefs, with their devotion to purity of ingredients, give as careful attention to their salads as to their most exalted creations.

To the basic formula for a salad as given by Alexandre Dumas (in his *Grand Dictionnaire de Cuisine*) as 'vegetables to which are added aromatic herbs and seasonings,' the chefs will add spectacular flavours: Vergé has salads with crayfish tails or sliced truffles.

Plain salads (*salades simples*) are of one main vegetable, either raw or cooked, usually

---

Notre Carte

LES FILETS DE CANARD DES LANDES EN JAMBON, AVEC LE BOUQUET DE SALADE	50.00
LE CAVIAR BELUGA D'IRAN, AVEC LES BLINIS les 100 gr	280.00
LE SAUMON FUME DANOIS	90.00
LE JAMBON DE PARME	50.00
LE PATE DE SOLE EN CROUTE, AVEC LA SAUCE GRELETTE	52.00
LE GATEAU DE LAPIN DANS SA GELEE AU CHABLIS	40.00
LE FOIE GRAS FRAIS DE CANARD DES LANDES FAIT A LA MAISON	55.00
LE FOIE GRAS FRAIS D'OIE DES LANDES FAIT A LA MAISON	68.00
LA DODINE DE CANETON AU FOIE GRAS AVEC LES GRIOTTES EN AIGRE-DOUX	50.00
LA GERBE D'ASPERGES VERTES DU VAUCLUSE, SAUCE MOUSSELINE	48.00
LA SALADE DE TRUFFES FRAICHES DE GRILLON	100.00
LE BOUQUET DE SALADE DE QUEUES D'ECREVISSES	68.00

LE BLANC DE TURBOTIN A LA FONDUE D'OSEILLE	60.00
LES FILETS DE SOLE DE LIGNE AUX PETITS NAVETS NOUVEAUX, AVEC LE BEURRE D'HERBES	66.00
LES COQUILLES ST JACQUES FRAICHES A LA JULIENNE DE LEGUMES	68.00
LA LANGOUSTE ROYALE GRILLEE AU BEURRE DE BASILIC	130.00
LE BISCUIT DE LOUP AUX POINTES D'ASPERGES AVEC LA SAUCE MOUSSELINE	64.00
LA FRICASSEE DE HOMARD A LA CREME DE SAUTERNES	130.00

LA FRICASSEE DE POULET DE L'ALLIER AU VINAIGRE DE VIN	50.00
LE FILET DE CHAROLAIS AU POIVRE, A LA MATHURINI	70.00
LE CARRE D'AGNEAU DE SISTERON ROTI AVEC LE CONFIT DE LEGUMES NICOIS	65.00
LA FRICASSEE DE ROGNONS ET DE RIS DE VEAU A LA CREME DE MOUTARDE	68.00
LE FOIE GRAS D'OIE AU VINAIGRE DE JEREZ, AVEC LES HARICOTS VERTS FINS A L'ECHALOTTE	72.00
LE PIGEONNEAU DE BRESSE ROTI AVEC LA COMPOTE DE PETITS LEGUMES	62.00

LES FROMAGES DE LA FERME SAVOYARDE	25.00
LES FAISSELLES DE FROMAGE BLANC A LA CREME	20.00

Tous nos plats sont servis accompagnés de légumes.

Les prix indiqués sont calculés par personne.
Service 15% en sus.

Roger Vergé aujourd'hui vous suggère...

son menu

LA TERRINE DE RASCASSE AU CITRON AVEC LES CONCOMBRES A LA CREME

***

LE GRATIN DE QUEUES D'ECREVISSES AUX EPINARDS, SAUCE CHAMPAGNE

***

LE GRANITE DE PAMPLEMOUSSE AU VERMOUTH

***

LES AIGUILLETTES DE SELLE D'AGNEAU DE SISTERON AVEC LA SAUCE ESTRAGON ET LA GARNITURE BONNE BOUCHE

***

LES DESSERTS ET LES GOURMANDISES DU MOULIN

PRIX: 180 FRANCS + SERVICE 15%

28 Mars 197

Roger Vergé

AVEC CE MENU NOUS VOUS CONSEILLONS

VIN BLANC	MEURSAULT LES CHEVALIERES 1974	90.00
	BARON DE L POUILLY FUME LA DOUCETTE	85.00
VIN ROUGE	CHATEAU BRANAIRE DUCRU 1969	100.00
	BEAUNE TOUSSAINT 1973	80.00
CHAMPAGNE	RESERVE DU MOULIN BRUT 1971	78.00

Les prix indiqués sont calculés par personne.
Service 15% en sus.

L'origine de nos produits est respectée, nous les choisissons toujours avec soin, dans la meilleure qualité.
Fruits et légumes sont en partie de culture naturelle dite biologique.
Nous préférons manquer momentanément d'un produit à notre carte, plutôt que de choisir une qualité inférieure qui risquerait de vous déplaire. Merci de votre aimable compréhension.

Vins   : 1/1 à partir de   Frs. - 1/2 à partir de   Frs.
Infusion :   Frs. - Café :   Frs. - Eau Minérale :   Frs.

served with a main course. They are usually dressed—at the last moment—in a vinaigrette of oil, mustard, wine vinegar, salt and pepper. Favoured herbs are parsley, tarragon, chervil and chives. Salad dressings were unknown in Britain and the United States until introduced by French refugees from the Revolution. *Salades composées* of various vegetables have meat, poultry, fish or crustaceans added to turn a mixed salad into a total course.

Dumas' six basic salad vegetables are sorrel, lettuce, chard, orach, spinach and purslane, but the list can be extended almost infinitely. Lamb's lettuce or corn salad (*mâche*) appears in many salads; one may also come across dandelion, which, without scruple, is given its proper Gallic appellation of *pissenlit*. (Both go well with a dressing of bacon fat poured over the seasoned salad, followed by a tablespoon of warm vinegar.)

The great chefs often include warm ingredients in their salads: Chapel for instance, combines tepid *foie de canard* with artichokes. Outhier's tepid salads include his famous *salade Oasis*. The Troisgros' *salade nouvelle* is served with warm slices of *foie gras*.

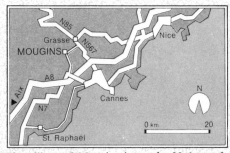

The village of Mougins is on the N567 road, seven kilometres north of Cannes and eleven kilometres south of the perfume centre of Grasse.

Nos Desserts

LE FEUILLETE LEGER AUX PRUNEAUX AVEC LA CREME A L'ARMAGNAC	32.00
LE CAFE GLACE A LA CREME ET AU VIEUX RHUM	32.00
LE GATEAU PARADIS AU CHOCOLAT ET A L'ORANGE	32.00
LA TIMBALE DE MOUSSE DE CHOCOLAT AMER	32.00
LE BISCUIT FRAIS AUX AMANDES DE FRAMBOISE, AVEC SON COULIS	32.00
LE VACHERIN GLACE AU MIEL DES ALPES AVEC LA FONDUE D'ABRICOT	32.00
LA CHARLOTTE ROYALE AU SIROP DE FRAISE	32.00
LA PECHE BLANCHE GLACEE AVEC LE SABAYON AU CHAMPAGNE	32.00
LES GLACES VANILLE, CHOCOLAT, MIEL	30.00
LES SORBETS : CITRON VERT ORANGE, FRAMBOISE	30.00
LES FRAISES DE JARDIN	32.00
LES FRAISES DES BOIS	34.00

Tous nos desserts sont servis
avec les Petits Fours faits à
la Maison

Service 15 % en sus

LE MOULIN DE MOUGINS
ROGER VERGÉ

EDITIONS 06 : Le Cannet. Photo Touillon

229

THE CHEESE TRADITION

In eulogising cheese, poets and gourmets praise the subtle co-operation of many factors—the seasons, the grass, the cow or goat, the farmer, the cheesemonger. Like wine, cheese is a living thing, needing time and careful tending to achieve its potential. Looking after cheeses in the crucial period between youth and maturity is the task of the *affineur*. For most of the three-star chefs, there is no-one more skilled at this than Édouard Ceneri, *Maître Fromager Affineur* and proprietor of Le Ferme Savoyarde in Cannes.

The shop, in the rue Meynadier, is rich in sweet, subtle and pungent scents—the intermingling of more than two hundred kinds of cheese. '*Il faut toujours garder une*

place pour le fromage,' says the sign hanging from the wooden-beamed ceiling.

'Cheese is traditional and one should be wary of new cheeses,' says Ceneri. However, he does from time to time experiment with what he calls *fromages de fantaisie*. Such a cheese is his *brie de Meaux de truffes*; a Brie enveloping a cream cheese speckled with truffles. Ceneri also mixes peppers and herbs into some cheeses, but these he regards not as new cheeses, but as variations on a traditional theme.

As an *affineur*, Ceneri buys cheeses fresh from the farms. For example, goats' cheeses from Charente are delivered every Thursday, from spring to autumn, to his cellars, two hundred metres from the shop. They are kept at a constant temperature of 7°–10°C (45°–50°F) with a humidity of 85 per cent and take about two weeks to reach perfection. They are considered just right when they are completely covered by a white bloom. While this is developing, the cheeses are turned three or four times a week, as all soft cheeses should be.

The nearest approximation to these conditions in the home is a cool store or, preferably, a cool, damp wine-cellar. Soft cheeses should be kept on straw, to absorb the moisture and prevent them cracking. A straw is put through the middle of some kinds of goats' cheese and only taken out just before serving.

As cheeses are difficult to keep, they should ideally be eaten on the day of ripening. Left-over cheese should be wrapped in baking foil and put in a cool spot, rather than in the refrigerator. There is no virtue in a runny cheese. This only shows that it has not been dried enough in the making and may be fermenting again.

'One should remember,' Ceneri pleads, 'that cheeses are organic and must be allowed to *live*.'

Petite nage de queues d'écrevisses au beurre blanc

In a covered pan, cook thinly chopped carrot rings, white of leek, shallots and onion very gently with butter and four soupspoons of water. After twenty minutes pour in half a bottle of dry white wine, add a *bouquet garni* and simmer for fifteen minutes. The vegetables should be slightly crunchy.

Drop live prepared crayfish in a pot of boiling, salted water for four minutes. Remove, drain, and allow to cool. Remove the tail meat and keep one head to decorate each serving.

Make a *beurre blanc* by putting in a pan some finely chopped shallot, six soupspoons of dry white wine and three of vinegar. Reduce to two soupspoons of liquid. Take the pan off the heat, and add butter, little by little, whisking vigorously all the time to obtain a light, foamy liaison.

Bring the vegetable *nage* to the boil and add the crayfish tails and the *beurre blanc* and chopped tarragon, parsley and chervil. Adjust the seasoning and pour into individual bowls.

Place a crayfish head upright in each bowl and serve.
Note: It may seem extraordinary that vegetables can be cooked for so long and stay crunchy, but this is what Vergé does. He also says that to keep the *beurre blanc* warm, put its saucepan into a bigger one lined with newspaper and leave it on the edge of the heat.

Crème au lait d'amandes

Put the white of leek, cut into fine rings, in a large saucepan with a soupspoon of water and one of butter and cook for five minutes on a gentle heat.

Pour in a litre of water and bring to the boil, adding chicken stock cubes, ten grams of washed round-grain rice and 100 grams of ground, sweet almonds. Cook in a covered pan on a low heat for twenty-five minutes.

Beat thirty centilitres of *crème fleurette* together with a couple of egg-yolks.

Put the rice and almond mixture in a mixer and pour in the cream. Whisk thoroughly, put it back into the saucepan over a low heat till it shows the first sign of boiling. Add salt and sieve. Serve hot in cups.

Blanc de Saint-Pierre à la crème de petits légumes

Skin a John Dory and cut it into finger-sized fillets.

Cut a peeled carrot, leek and celery into a large julienne, and cook rapidly in a soupspoon of butter, a half cupful of water with a pinch of salt until *al dente*, and all liquid has boiled away. Keep warm.

Boil a large, peeled, diced potato in lightly salted water.

Cover the bottom of a saucepan with a layer of *crème fleurette*, add salt and the fillets of John Dory. Bring the liquid to the boil and simmer for no more than two minutes.

Remove the fish and strain the cooking juices into the bowl of a mixer. Place the fish on the vegetable *julienne*, still in its pan.

Beat half the cooked potato with the fish juices in the mixer until the liquid has taken on the consistency of a lightly thickened sauce. Add more potato if necessary. Add a small piece of butter, salt and pepper to taste. Pour the sauce over the fish, bring to the boil. Sprinkle with chopped chives and serve in wide soup bowls.

Note: Vergé suggests using the carrot as the basis to judge the cooking of the julienne. Vergé might substitute French beans for the potato to thicken the sauce.

Canard comme au Moulin

Singe and clean a duck, leaving in the heart, lungs and liver. Truss it, having cut off the feet, wings and neck. Salt and pepper the bird inside and out and put inside four juniper berries and a sprig of thyme.

Chop the wings and neck into small pieces and put them together with the duck in a roasting dish with a pat of butter (the dish should be not much larger than the duck itself). In a medium oven, roast it eight minutes on each side and ten minutes on its back. Take the duck from the oven and let it rest for ten minutes.

Discard the fat from the dish and pour in a quarter-litre of heavy red wine. Boil the liquid so that it takes up the flavour from the bottom of the pan. Add the thyme and juniper berries taken from the duck and put this juice to one side. Take off the legs and remove the skin from all other parts of the bird. Cut five long thin strips from each side of the central bone.

Remove the liver, heart and lungs from the carcass and break it up. Put the carcass bones, except for the triangular bone found where the neck starts, in some heated butter and brown them. Add roughly chopped shallots and a little tomato concentrate. Allow to cook for a couple of minutes, and then flame them with a little cognac. Pour in the contents of the roasting pan. Reduce the liquid. When reduced, add hot water and a chicken *bouillon* cube and boil the liquid for about twenty minutes.

Chop up the hearts, lungs and a quarter of the liver and, at the last moment, add this to the reduced and sieved sauce. Boil and pass once more through the sieve. Put in no more than one turn of freshly milled pepper. Keep the sauce warm in a *bain-marie*.

Salt the legs with sea-salt and grill them for about fifteen minutes.

Pour the sauce onto a serving plate and slide the *aiguillettes* into it. Reheat briefly and serve. On a second plate, serve the grilled legs with a salad made from curly endive, and a dressing of walnut oil and wine vinegar.

Filets mignons de veau citron

Pare julienne strips of lemon peel from half a lemon and put them in a saucepan of cold water. Bring to the boil and drain. Refresh under cold water. Put in a saucepan with a soupspoon of water and a touch of sugar. Lift from the heat when the water has evaporated and the julienne is a brilliant yellow.

Salt and pepper both sides of the veal fillets and colour them on both sides in a pan of heated butter. Remove the veal and set on a warm plate.

Tip out the cooking butter, pour in four soupspoons of dry white wine and reduce by two-thirds over a low flame. Mix in butter to make an emulsion and then add a teaspoon of chopped parsley. Adjust seasoning with salt and pepper.

Pour into the sauce the juices which have run from the fillets and then cover the fillets in the sauce.

On each fillet place a peeled slice of lemon with no rind or pith and add a pinch of the lemon julienne.

Serve with a risotto or little vegetables cooked in butter.

Mousse au chocolat amer

Gently heat in a *bain-marie* 125 grams of broken, bitter chocolate with two tablespoons of very strong, hot coffee and fifteen grams of cocoa powder (without added sugar). Stir well to form a smooth paste and remove the pan from the heat.

Clean the inside of another bowl by rubbing it with lemon and rinse well with water. Dry the bowl and break in eight egg-whites, add a pinch of salt and beat until they start to stiffen. Incorporate sixty grams of sugar and continue beating until the egg-whites are firm.

Whisk about a quarter of the egg-whites into the lukewarm chocolate and fold in the rest with a spatula.

Put the mousse in a bowl in the refrigerator for at least an hour and serve chilled.

Note: It is easier to break chocolate when it is cold.

Rubbing with lemon juice is the best way of removing grease from copper pans.

Menu

Petite nage de queues d'écrevisses au beurre blanc

Crème au lait d'amandes

Blanc de Saint-Pierre à la crème de petits legumes

Canard comme au Moulin

Filets mignons de veau au citron

Mousse au chocolat amer

Crayfish soup

Almond cream

John Dory with young vegetables

Duck with juniper and thyme

Veal fillets with lemon

Bitter chocolate mousse

INDEX

A

affineur 230
Aga Khan 39, 118, 145
Agaricus bisporus 189
Agaricus campestris 189
Agronomic Research, French
 National Institute for 217
aiguillette 178
Aix-les-Bains 58
alcools blancs 208
Almanach des Gourmands 16, 22
Alix, Kléber 92
allemande, sauce 20,29
almond milk 11, 13
alouette (lark) 219
Alsace 208-9
Amandier de Mougins 171
amuse-gueule 9, 84, 120, 124, 194,
 198
à l'anglais 15
Annecy, Lake 57, 58, 61, 62, 67,
 84, 191
aperitifs 82, 84, 223
Apicius 73
apple-corer *(vide-pommes)* 221
arachide, huile d' (ground-nut oil)
 227
Arbre Vert 104, 108, 114
Archestrate 22
armagnac 96, 99, 200, 205, 208,
 220
Art Culinaire, L' 28
Art du Cuisinier, L' 24
Asnières 92
Auberge de l'Ill 8, 56, 104-15, 207,
 209
Auberge du Père Bise 8, 56-67,
 190, 191
Audiger *(La Maison Réglée)* 14
Audouze, Jean 85
Avignon 11

B

Baccarat, glassmaker 77
Bailly, *pâtissier* 20
Bajulaz, Edmond 65
bande à Bocuse 171, 172, 195, 196
Banville, Theodore de 26
Bar, Duchesse de 13
bar (sea bass) 213
Barbotan 99

Barrier, Charles
Born Cinq Mars La Pile, April 30,
1916. Central Hotel, Tours,
1928-9; Family Hotel, Langeais,
1929-31; Restaurant du Nègre,
Tours, 1931-3. Restaurant Barrier
opened April 8, 1944. *Meilleur
Ouvrier de France*, 1958. Michelin
stars: first, 1955; second, 1958;
third, 1968.

Barrier, Charles 9, 10, 29, 44-55,
 165, 186-9
Barrier, François 49, 50, 54
Barrier, Madame 54

Barrier restaurant 44-55, 187
Barry, Sir Charles 26
Barthélémy hotels 94
baudroie (angler-fish) 213
Beaulieu 217
Beauvilliers 16, 21
 L'Art du Cuisinier 24
 Grande Taverne de Londres 22
beccafico (fig-pecker) 207, 219
béchamel, sauce 14, 20
Belfort 116, 118
Belley 16
Bering, Michel 166
Bernachon, Jean-Jacques and
 Françoise 78
Biglie 32
Bignon 26
Bise, Charline 62, 64

Bise, François
Born Talloires, January 19, 1928.
La Pyramide, Vienne, 1946-7;
Lucas-Carton and Larue, Paris,
1950; L'Auberge du Père Bise,
Talloires, 1951. Took over
L'Auberge du Père Bise, 1968.
Michelin stars: (achieved by his
parents) first, 1947; second, 1949;
third, 1951.

Bise, François 8, 10, 34, 56-67,
 190-3
Bise, Georges 61
Bise, Grandpère 58, 61
Bise, Marguerite (Mère) 58, 61-67
Bise, Marius (Père) 58, 61-67
Bise, René 62
Bise, Sophie 67
Bize-Leroy, Madame Lalou 196
blackberries *(mures des forêts)* 200
Blanc, Honoré 15
boar, wild *(marcassin; sanglier;
 solitaire)* 207
Bocuse, Georges 68
Bocuse, Madame 71, 77

Bocuse, Paul
Born Collonges-au-Mont-d'Or,
February 11, 1926. Restaurant de
la Soierie, Lyon, 1940-3;
Restaurant La Bressane, Lyon,
1946-7; La Mère Brazier, Lyon,
1947-9; La Pyramide, Vienne,
1949-52; Lucas-Carton, Paris,
1952-3; La Pyramide, Vienne,
1953-6; Restaurant La Gérentière,
Mégève, 1956-8. Took over the
family restaurant, 1959. *Meilleur
Ouvrier de France*, 1961. *Chevalier
de la Légion d'Honneur*, 1975.
Michelin stars: first, 1961;
second, 1962; third, 1965.

Bocuse, Paul 8-9, 31, 34, 39, 47,
 56-8, 64, 67, 68-79, 88, 95, 98,
 115, 126, 130, 149, 153, 156,
 163, 168, 171, 172, 186,
 194-197, 203, 206, 214, 215
Boeuf à la Mode 22
Bongéant 31
Bougival 92
Boulanger 22
Boxberger, René 148, 150

Braly, Patrice 166
brandy 179, 188, 192, 193, 208-9,
 222, 227
bream, gilt-head 213
Bresse chickens 62, 83, 89, 134,
 148, 180, 194, 198
Briand, M. *(Dictionnaire des
 Aliments)* 14, 102
brigades 67, 98, 124, 131
Brillat-Savarin, Jean 16, 18-20,
 145, 207, 213, 219
 Physiologie du Goût 16, 207
brioche 109, 178, 209, 210, 220
Brittany, fish from 83, 86, 106, 134
Brunoy 31

C

Cabro d'Or 145, 146, 148, 150
Café Anglais 22
calvados 211
Cambacérès, Jean-Jacques Régis
 de 21
Camélia 92
Carême, Marie-Antoine 11, 16, 18,
 20-3, 29, 46, 150
casserole 202
cassis 223
cavage 217
caviste 182
Ceneri, Édouard 230
cèpe (Boletus edulis) 189
Cézanne, Paul 61
Challans ducks 134, 148
Chalon 154
Chalosse beef 98
champagne framboise 223
champagnes 109, 138, 145, 148,
 170
chanterelle (Cantharellus cibarius)
 189

Chapel, Alain
Born Lyon, December 30, 1937.
Chez Juliette, Lyon 1952-5.
Worked at La Pyramide from
1955. Chez La Mère Charles,
Mionnay, 1967; became *chef-
patron*, 1970. *Meilleur Ouvrier de
France*, 1972.
Michelin stars: first (achieved by
his father) 1958; second, 1969;
third, 1973.

Chapel, Alain 9, 17, 40, 43, 56, 61,
 64, 67, 68, 80-91, 142, 149, 153,
 156, 163, 177, 178, 196, 198,
 199, 213, 219, 222
Chapel, Roger and Eva 91
charcutiers 73
Chariel, Jean-André 142
Charles V 11

Charollais cattle 156, 160
Château Batailley 182
Château Lafite-Rothschild 182
Chauvon, Pierre 38
cheese: 230; *fromage blanc* 96;
 goat 89
chefs
 common characteristics 107
 dispersal, after Revolution 16,
 22
 dress 8, 28
 foundation of profession 116
 privileges 160
 status 7, 11, 28, 31, 45, 171
 unionization 171
 women 14, 126, 159
 working conditions 20-1, 28
chefs-patron
 Chapel on 90
 Outhier on 123
 provincial phenomenon 22
cherry brandy *(kirsch)* 208
Chevet, Germain 16
chevreuil (deer, roe) 207
chickens
 Bresse 62, 83, 89, 134, 148, 180,
 194, 198
 preparation 75
Chinon 187
Churchill, Sir Winston 43
Clerico family 92
Club des Optimistes, Roanne 160
crabs 87,
Cocteau, Jean 38
coffee
 Brillat-Savarin on 18
 Rumford on 21
cognac 184, 208
Colette 38
Collonges-au-Mont-d'Or 68, 195
Colmar 104, 110, 114
colza, huile de (rapeseed oil) 227
Commentry 165
Condé, Prince de 13
Condrieu 182
consommé 178, 186, 188, 197, 216
cookery books 16
 bourgeois 13-14
 Carême and 20
 early 11-12
 Escoffier 29
 La Varenne 13
 Marin 14
 Menon 14
 popular 25
 Soyer 26
coquille Saint-Jacques (scallop) 64,
 65, 102, 190, 205, 212, 213, 226
cordon bleu 15
Cormier, Hubert 224
corncrake 207
corn-salad (lamb's lettuce; *mâche)*
 132, 168
Costelle, Madame 46
Côte Rôtie 182
couperet de cuisine (meat cleaver)
 221
courses and service 24
courtly love 140
croissants 66
Croque-en-bouche (Deschamps)
 91
Cuisine Artistique, La 19
Cuisine Classique, La 28

INDEX

INDEX OF DISHES

THE RECIPES, IN ENGLISH

BIBLIOGRAPHY

The authors are listed alphabetically within each century. When an author is listed under his *nom-de-plume*, his real name appears in brackets.

PRE-EIGHTEENTH CENTURY

Apicius, Coelius *De Re Coquinaria*
Latin Manuscript, *c* 1420
Audiger *La Maison Réglée*
Nicolas le Gras, Paris, 1692
La Varenne, François Pierre de *Le Cuisinier François* Pierre David, Paris, 1651
La Varenne, François Pierre de
Le Pâtissier François Jean Gaillard, Paris, 1653
L.S.R. *L'Art de Bien Traiter, ouvrage nouveau, curieux et fort galant*
Jean Du Puis, Paris, 1674
Massialot, François *Le Cuisinier Roial et Bourgeois* Charles de Sercy, Paris, 1691
Nostredame, Michel de *Les Prophéties de Michel Nostradamus* Rigaud, Lyon, 1555
Platina, Johannes-Baptista (Bartolomeo de Sacchi) *De Honesta Voluptate* Lorenzo de Aquila and Sibyllinus Umber, Venice, 1475
Scappi, M. Bartolomeo *Cuoco Secreto di Papa Pio Quinto* Michele Tramezino, Venice, *c* 1570
Taillevent (Guillaume Tirel) *Le Viandier* France, compiled 1375, first printed *c* 1490
(Author unknown) *A Booke of Cookerie* (otherwise called *The Good Huswifes Handmaid for the Kitchin*) E. Allde, London, 1597
(Author unknown) *The Good Hous-Wives Treasurie* E. Allde, London, 1588

EIGHTEENTH CENTURY

Briand, M. *Dictionnaire des Aliments*
Gissey, Paris, 1750
La Chapelle, Vincent *The Modern Cook*
London, 1733
Marin, François *Les Dons de Comus*
Prault fils, Paris, 1739
Menon *Nouveau Traité de la Cuisine*
Michel-Étienne David, Paris, 1739
Menon *La Cuisinière Bourgeoise*
Guillyn, Paris, 1746
Menon *Les Soupers de la Cour*
Guillyn, Paris, 1755
Pegge, Samuel (ed) *The Forme of Cury*
J. Nicholls, London, 1780 (first compiled in 1390 by the Master-Cooks of King Richard II)

NINETEENTH CENTURY

Audot, Louis-Eustache *La Cuisinière de la Campagne et de la Ville* Audot, Paris, 1818
Beauvilliers, A.B. *L'Art du Cuisinier*
Pilet, Paris, 1814
Brillat-Savarin, Jean Anthelme *Physiologie du Goût* A. Sautelet et Cie, Paris, 1826
Carême, Marie-Antoine *Le Pâtissier Royal*
J.G. Dentu, Paris, 1815
Carême, Marie-Antoine *Le Maître d'Hôtel Français* Firmin-Didot, Paris, 1822
Carême, Marie-Antoine *L'Art de la Cuisine Française au Dix-Neuvième Siècle* Paris, 1833
Doran, Dr *Table Traits* Bentley, London, 1854
Dumas, Alexandre *Grand Dictionnaire de Cuisine* Alphonse Lamerre, Paris, 1873
Francatelli, Charles Elmé *A Plain Cookery Book for the Working Classes* London, 1862
Francatelli, Charles Elmé
The Cook's Guide London, 1862
Garlin, Gustave *Le Cuisinier Moderne*
Garnier, Paris, 1887
Gogué, Antoine *Les Secrets de la Cuisine Française* Hachette, Paris, 1856
Gouffé, Jules *Le Livre de Cuisine*
Hachette, Paris, 1867
Gouffé, Jules *Le Livre de Pâtisserie*
Hachette, Paris, 1873
Kettner, Auguste *Kettner's Book of the Table* Dulan, London, 1877
La Reynière, Grimod de (Alexandre-Balthazar-Laurent) *Almanach des Gourmands* Maradan, Paris, 1803-12
La Reynière, Grimod de (Alexandre-Balthazar-Laurent) *Manuel des Amphytryons* Maradan, Paris, 1808
Monselet, Charles *Le Triple Almanach Gourmand* Librairie du Petit Journal, Paris, 1866
Monselet, Charles *Gastronomie*
Charpentier, Paris, 1874
Nicolardot, Louis *Histoire de la Table*
E. Dentu, Paris, 1868
Soyer, Alexis *The Gastronomic Regenerator*
Simpkin, Marshall & Co, London, 1846
Soyer, Alexis *Soyer's Charitable Cookery*
Simpkin, Marshall & Co, London, 1848
Soyer, Alexis *The Modern Housewife*
Simpkin, Marshall & Co, London, 1849
Soyer, Alexis *The Pantropheon*
Simpkin, Marshall & Co, London, 1853
Soyer, Alexis *A Shilling Cookery for the People*
G. Routledge & Co, London, 1855
Soyer, Alexis *Soyer's Culinary Campaign*
G. Routledge & Co, London, 1857
Soyer, Alexis *Instructions for Military Hospital Cooks* London, 1860
Stomach (S. Whiting) *Memoirs of a Stomach*
W.E. Painter, London, 1853
Ude, Louis Eustache *The French Cook*
Cox & Baylis, London, 1813
Urbain-Dubois, Félix (with Émile Bernard) *La Cuisine Classique* Paris, 1856
Urbain-Dubois, Félix *La Cuisine Artistique*
Dentu, Paris, 1872-74
Urbain-Dubois, Félix *Nouvelle Cusine Bourgeoise* Dentu, Paris, 1878
Viard, A. *Le Cuisinier Impérial* Paris, Barba, 1806; in later editions, published as follows:
Cuisinier Royal 1817, *Cuisinier National* 1852, *Cuisinier Impérial* 1854, *Cuisinier National* 1875
Walker, Thomas *Aristology*
G. Bell & Sons, London, 1881

TWENTIETH CENTURY

Arbellot, Simon *Curnonsky* Paris, 1965
Aron, Jean-Paul *The Art of Eating in France*
Peter Owen, London, 1975
Aresty, Esther B. *The Delectable Past*
Simon & Schuster, New York, 1964
Benoit, Félix (with Henry Clos-Jouve)
La Cuisine Lyonnaise Solar, France, 1972
Cobban, Alfred *A History of Modern France* (3 vols) Jonathan Cape, London, 1962
Curnonsky (Maurice Edmund Sailland)
Le Trésor Gastronomique de France
Librairie Delagrave, Paris, 1933
Curnonsky (with Gaston Derys)
Gaietés et Curiosités Gastronomiques
Librairie Delagrave, Paris, 1933
Dumaine, Alexandre *Ma Cuisine*
Éditions de la Pensée Moderne, Paris, 1972
Ellwanger, George Herman *The Pleasures of the Table* Doubleday Page & Co, New York, 1902
Escoffier, A. *Le Guide Culinaire* Paris, 1903 (to be published in 1979 in an entirely new English translation by William Heinemann Ltd)
Escoffier, A. *Ma Cuisine*
Flammarion et Cie, Paris, 1934
Hallgarten, S.F. *Alsace and its Wine Gardens*
André Deutsch, London, 1957
Herbodeau, E.A. (with P. Thalamas)
Georges Auguste Escoffier Practical Press Ltd, London, 1955
Kingsford, P.W. (with E.B. Page)
The Master Chefs Edward Arnold, London, 1971
Montagné, Prosper *Larousse Gastronomique*
Librairie Larousse, Paris, 1938
Nignon, Édouard *Les Plaisirs de la Table*
Paris, 1926
Nignon, Édouard *Éloges de la Cuisine Française* Paris, 1933
Oliver, Raymond *The French at Table*
The International Wine and Food Society, London, 1965
Rabaudy, Nicolas de *Guide des Meilleurs Restaurants de France* Éditions Jean-Claude Lattès, Paris, 1976
Ray, Cyril (ed) *The Gourmet's Companion*
Eyre & Spottiswoode, London, 1963
Simon, André-Louis *A Concise Encyclopaedia of Gastronomy* The Wine and Food Society, London, 1939
Simon, André-Louis *Bibliotheca Gastronomica* The Wine and Food Society, London, 1953
Zeldin, Theodore *Ambition, Love and Politics* (vol i) Oxford University Press, 1973

The chefs' own books include:
Bocuse, Paul *La Cuisine du Marché*
Flammarion et Cie, Paris, 1976
Guérard, Michel *La Grande Cuisine Minceur*
Éditions Robert Laffont, Paris, 1976
Guérard, Michel *La Cuisine Gourmande*
Éditions Robert Laffont, Paris, 1978
Point, Fernand *Ma Gastronomie*
Flammarion et Cie, Paris, 1969
Troisgros, Jean and Pierre *Cuisiniers à Roanne* Éditions Robert Laffont, Paris, 1977

ACKNOWLEDGEMENTS

The Publishers received invaluable assistance from many individuals and organizations, in particular:
Hubert Cormier, architect of the new kitchen at Les Frères Troisgros
Justin and Melanie de Blank
Crispin Dunn-Meynell, The International Wine and Food Society, London
Ann Edwards
Lionel Grigson
Poulka Hall, Principal of *La Petite Cuisine*, London
Richard Hargreaves, Savoy Hotel, London
Maria Hely-Hutchinson
L'Institut Français du Royaume-Uni, London
Caroline Landeau
Emile Lefebure, Westminster College (Hotel School), London
London Library
Catherine Manac'h, Food from France, London
Suzie Manby
Yves Martial, Cultural Attaché, French Embassy, London
Michelin Tyre Company
Musée de l'Art Culinaire, Villeneuve Loubet, France
Michael Pickup
Janet Sacks
Stephen Smallwood
John St John, William Heinemann Ltd, London

Anthony Blake wishes to thank:
Jane Barnett
John Gollop, who made the prints of the black and white photographs
Pierre Lemonnier, Impact-FCB, Paris
Jean Macandier, Mumm Champagne
Michael Rand, *The Sunday Times* Colour Magazine, London
Odile Volpe, stylist

Quentin Crewe wishes to thank:
Sam Chesterton
Cosmo Fry
Bernard Gaume, *chef-des-cuisines*, The Carlton Tower Hotel, London
Jane Grigson
David Levin, Capital Hotel, London
Piers Russell-Cobb
Richard Shepherd, *chef-de-cuisine*, Langan's Brasserie, London

Picture Credits
Bettmann Archive 27 top left; Giraudon 25 top; Mansell Collection 12, 14, 23 below left, 27 top right; Mary Evans Picture Library 19 right, 24 left; Michelin Tyre Company 17 © *d'après Guide France du Pneu Michelin;* Radio Times Hulton Picture Library 23 top left, 23 below right, 27 below right; Roger-Viollet 18 top, 22, 23 top right, 24 right; Royal Institution of Great Britain 21; Snark 19 left, 25 below.

Ian Garrard, James Robins and Michael Woods did the line drawings in The Chefs at Work.

Production consultant: Ray Smith
Origination: Gilchrist Brothers, Ltd, Leeds
Typesetting: Art Reprographic (London) Ltd
Printing and binding: Heraclio Fournier SA, Vitoria, Spain